THE
FINGER
OF GOD

THE FINGER OF GOD

FROM THE LINEAGE OF DAVID TO THE
PRESIDENCY OF THE UNITED STATES

JESSE L. JACKSON JR.

FOREWORD BY DR. JAMES A. FORBES JR.
AFTERWORD BY DR. CORNEL WEST

ARCHWAY
PUBLISHING

Archway Publishing books may be ordered through booksellers or by contacting:

Archway Publishing
1663 Liberty Drive
Bloomington, IN 47403
www.archwaypublishing.com
844-669-3957

Interior Image Credit: Smithsonian Institution, and Istock Chris Gorgio

Scripture taken from the King James Version of the Bible.

ISBN: 978-1-6657-1527-0 (sc)
ISBN: 978-1-6657-1525-6 (hc)
ISBN: 978-1-6657-1526-3 (e)

Library of Congress Control Number: 2021923240

Print information available on the last page.

Archway Publishing rev. date: 04/29/2022

To the God of Abraham, whose face we cannot behold and whose finger we can only discern.

And the King shall answer and say unto them, Verily I say unto you, Inasmuch as ye have done it unto one of the least of these my brethren, ye have done it unto me.[1]

Now unto him that is able to keep you from falling, and to present you faultless before the presence of his glory with exceeding joy.[2]

The Finger of God

CONTENTS

ACKNOWLEDGMENTS ix
FOREWORD xiii
PRELUDE TO THE INTRODUCTION xix
INTRODUCTION xxv

PART I
THE FINGER OF GOD 1

1   MY EXPERIMENT … MY DISCOVERY 3
2   TOOLS FOR THE EXPERIMENT 13
3   THE LINEAGE OF ABRAHAM AND DAVID 19
4   THE DECLARATION OF INDEPENDENCE, THE
     CONSTITUTION, AND GOD 35
5   IN THE BEGINNING 45
6   A SECT OF ONE 49
7   THE FOUNDERS AND SLAVERY 53
8   THE GREAT SEAL 55
9   THE FOUNDING FATHERS 65
10 THE LORD'S PRAYER 73
11 THE CONSTRUCTS OF THE CONSTITUTION 87
12 THE LINEAGE OF DAVID 91
13 A SINGLE IDEA 99

PART II
MY JOURNEY 117

14 COURT 119
15 ALL WERE CREATED EQUAL 123

16 THE METAMORPHOSIS OF "FELLA"   127
17 MY CONSTITUTION   133
18 MY YEARS IN CONGRESS   139
19 MY CAMPAIGN FUNDS   145
20 SHAME, BLAME, AND GUILT   147
21 MY PREAMBLE   153
22 A NEW EARTH   159
23 SOLITARY CONFINEMENT   163

PART III
HUMAN RIGHTS AND GOD THROUGH US   185

24 FORGIVENESS   187
25 A BRIEF HISTORY OF LAWS   193
26 A MATURE FAITH   209

AFTERWORD   221
NOTES   225
REFERENCES   231
ENDNOTES   243

ACKNOWLEDGMENTS

Abrahaman Muhammad was the first person in prison to embrace me and share with me that I had fallen further than anyone in the prison from my previous station in life. Early one morning, the spirit arose within him, and he leaned over the side of the bunk and said, "They locked up the wrong one this time, didn't they?"

"I'm not sure, but I think so."

He asked permission to chronicle my journey in pencil, and he produced several dozen images that I cherish. My father, recognizing my melancholy spirit after prison, encouraged me to attend homecoming at NC A&T State University in 2016; he told me that my classmates would lift my spirits.

While there, I connected with my classmate, friend, and now agent April Smith, who has guided me and this project through every draft and through four years of mountaintops and valleys on this journey, for which I am eternally grateful. She enlisted the help of her sister, Nicole Jones, to produce *Loving You, Thinking of You, Don't Forget to Pray*, a book of letters my mother wrote me every day for the thirty months I was incarcerated. These letters and my mother's spirit were a sustaining force.

Upon my release from prison, I shared with my mother that I had found the finger of God in the Constitution and that I believed it had the power to lift our nation above the current morass of American political life. My mother responded, "Everyone in prison finds God. I don't believe you found anything unless you go to meet with Dr. Cornel West and convince him you found something." She said she would believe it if he said so. My first trip after prison was to New York to meet with Dr. West, but his schedule never presented us the opportunity for me to fully share the nature of my discovery.

A few years later, I was in Raleigh, North Carolina, when my father called and said that he was under the weather with the flu and that he could not serve as keynote speaker for Shaw University's MLK celebration. He asked me to surrogate for him, and I did.

In the audience was Dr. James A. Forbes Jr., the Senior Minister Emeritus of Riverside Church in New York. After the speech, I pursued him for almost a year to share my discovery. I'm so grateful that he took me under his wing and broadened my understanding of providence, spirit, and the need to respiritualize the nation.

Frank E. Watkins was also at my presentation. He worked with my father for more than five decades, and he dedicated seventeen years to my service in Congress. After April Smith and Dr. Forbes worked with me for nearly a year, we circled back to Dr. West, for it was my belief that this work could not be presented to the public unless he wrapped his mind around its premise. Simplifying the concept to a single idea, I turned to my college professor Dr. Dong Kuen Jeong, who attended my undergraduate ceremonies and my graduation from law school at the University of Illinois in Champaign years later. I am grateful for the time he spent with me on this work.

I express my gratitude to Alanna Ford, Jackie Pickett, Tami White, and Regina Jackson for the moral support and encouragement they have provided me over many years and continue to provide me.

I thank Dr. Elizabeth Hersch, Dr. Nassir Ghaemi, and Dr. Ndidi Onyejiaka, my physicians who guided me through a very personal journey that included deep, personal valleys and high mountaintops. The journey included a postgraduate level understanding of the psychology of transformative leadership.

Over the course of the journey, I received encouraging words from Rev. Al Sharpton, Dr. Eddie Glaude, Rev. Dr. William

Barber II, and Dr. Alexis Felder. While I was incarcerated, Dr. Felder provided me with books and research material that allowed me to function at a graduate student's level, and I am eternally grateful for that support.

I thank the late Rev. Clay Evans, who was fascinated by my work and discovery, and the late Rev. Samuel McKinney, who prayed the first prayer on the day I was elected to Congress ordaining my work in the institution. Rhoda McKinney has been a source of inspiration for which I am grateful.

I thank Dr. Alfred Seawright for his input and valuable support for this project along with Keela Seawright. I thank my siblings—Santita, Jonathan, Yusef, Jackie, and Ashley—who pulled for me when I could not pull for myself. And I thank my children, Jessica Jackson and Jesse L. Jackson III, who in their formative years saw their parents incarcerated. I hope that this work replaces any clouds of shame that may have hovered over those years. It is my prayer that they too understand providence and develop the knowing that without this journey, the nation would be in greater peril.

I thank the people of the Second Congressional District of Illinois, who granted me eight terms, seventeen years of my life, the highest opportunity to serve them. I thank the people of Chicago, and the State of Illinois, who to this day walk up to me on the streets and say, "Welcome home."

I thank the men and women in Washington, DC, Edward Kofi Asante, Veronica Pugh, Ted and H at the O Street Mansion, the Capitol police who over the years continue to embrace me wherever I go.

I thank Judge Amy Berman Jackson, who shared with me from the bench that she still had great expectations for me. And I thank US Attorney Michael Atkinson, who prosecuted me and shared with me that he had never met a defendant like me, and Warden Dennis W. Stamper, who allowed me time to focus on the needed transformation that only prison could provide.

FOREWORD

Dr. James A. Forbes Jr.

In 2007, I retired from Riverside Church in New York City after serving as senior minister for eighteen years. Shortly thereafter, I started the Healing of the Nations Foundation. The name of the organization was inspired by Revelation 22:2: "On either side of the river, was there the tree of life, which bare twelve manner of fruits, and yielded her fruit every month: and the leaves of the tree were for the healing of the nations."

The theological understanding that buttressed the spirit of our work was the assurance that divine providence was invested in the health and well-being of all creation. Concern for personal health and wellness was usually thought to relate to God's care for individuals, but largely overlooked was the health of society at large.

Exodus 15:26 highlights God's commitment to the health of the people with these words. He said,

> If thou wilt diligently hearken to the voice of the Lord thy God, and wilt do that which is right in his sight, and wilt give ear to his commandments, and keep all his statutes, I will put none of these diseases upon thee, which I have brought upon the Egyptians: for I am the Lord that healeth thee.

Ezekiel 47:12 introduces the idea of the leaves as being for healing physical ailments. These verses serve as powerful images of God's care for our health and well-being as individuals. It may come as a surprise that God has no less interest in the body politic than in our individual health. The case may be made that the biblical perspective places even greater emphasis on the corporate personality than on individual well-being.

"What kind of people are you?" is as significant as the question "What kind of person are you?" With both these concerns in mind, our foundation was required to promote the divine scope of concern—the health of each individual as well as the collective well-being of the whole creation. To the individual, God says, "Be whole," and "Be well," and God reminds all realms of creation, "You are one family called to be the beloved community. You are a universe. I am at work to call you into the loving relationality of one healthy family. Just as I feel the pain of the infirmities of each of you, fragmentation, alienation, and separation between you is a cause of divine displeasure and unrest. I will not cease my divine urging until the unity of my love tethers you to me and to each other."

To the United States, God's message is more likely to be, "I had great plans for what you might become. Though you were conceived with imperfections, I blessed you with a dream of what a truly democratic society would look like. Beyond your broad diversity, I moved your Founders to affirm the equality of all and to embrace the dream of liberty and justice for all. I planted the seeds of possibility that in time could become a light on the hill and a beacon to the nations around the world.

"I even planted ideals within your Constitution and Bill of Rights upon which you could evolve and be corrected and transformed into a more perfect union. Even though I knew you would be confronted by principalities and powers representing dominating and oppressive instincts and impulses, I blessed you with a blueprint for being a more perfect union on the way to becoming the beloved community of equality, power, and justice."

The spirit of the divine mandate for social, economic, and political equity is more clearly reflected in the jubilee motif of the Torah and the Gospels. Sabbath laws and regulations for years of release and jubilee legislation leave no doubt that justice and righteousness are binding expectations of the God of creation. Without liberty and justice for all, creation is a flawed vessel that in the words of Jeremiah 18:4 would need to be reworked into another vessel as seemed good to the Creator. From time to time, some version of this mandate is sent to the nation. Do we believe it is a message we must take seriously? Are we free to ignore it with impunity? Are there signs that our society may be experiencing warnings that will determine how America's story will end?

A press conference and book launching of *A More Perfect Union: Advancing New American Rights* by Jesse L. Jackson Jr. and Frank E. Watkins was planned for the end of the week of September 11, 2001, in the largest Borders Book Store in New York, which was in the World Trade Center. For a number of years during his tenure as a congressman representing the Second District of Illinois, Jesse Jr. had been paying attention to the glaring imperfections in our society and proposing ways to enable us to live up to our ideals. His book contained serious criticisms and proposed paths toward a more perfect union. Of course, the launching was postponed due to the attacks on and subsequent destruction of the Twin Towers.

In the spirit of God's care for the health of our nation, Jesse Jr. described the national malaise—the perpetual flaws plaguing our nation's future and calling us back to the faith of our Founding Fathers. He sought to show the depth of moral and spiritual disease reflecting the source of racism in shaping every aspect of our national life. He yielded his service to the great spirit still pleading with us to rise to the occasion and embrace principles and actions that would help us recapture hidden clues to the spiritual renewal of this nation.

In 2020, the presidential election in the midst of the COVID-19 pandemic and the George Floyd and Breonna Taylor movement forced us to acknowledge how close we had come to being a totalitarian nation. Perhaps we now know the profound relevance of what a more perfect union would look like and why we desperately need to revise and recover some hidden and largely overlooked clues as to what God has been trying to say to us.

In our gratitude and humility, we may be able to discern why all citizens should be made aware of what was close to being taken away from them and why we needed a rededication to what democracy means and what it demands of us.

After the World Trade Center attack, the national administration swiftly began to mobilize for war and seemed not prepared to be engaged in self-critical analysis of our national policies. I remember being interviewed by someone who claimed to be a reporter for a major newspaper. He asked me how we pastors were responding to the attacks. I told him our first task was to provide pastoral care to those who lost loved ones in the tragic events and then we would have to take time to examine our policies to see if there were reasons based on those policies our adversaries hated us so much that they would assault us with such savagery. Following that conversation revealing my willingness to encourage self-criticality, I received cancellations of four invitations to speak at memorial events; the powers that be could not risk public speakers who were not dead set to go to war. Perhaps the nation was not ready to hear what Jesse Jr. was asking them to consider at that time.

Before Jesse Jr.'s book could awaken our nation to its nearly forfeited legacy, an unfortunate occurrence took place. Jesse Jr. was charged with misuse of campaign funds. He surrendered to authorities and was incarcerated for a brief time. During his imprisonment, he had an episode in solitary confinement. What happened there became an event of radical revelation and renewed his calling to bring the nation some forgotten or overlooked insights found in our Constitution that if taken seriously could profoundly change the country's direction and finally make it a more perfect union.

In *The Finger of God*, the author addresses two major issues that cry out for attention. The first has to do with the spiritual state of the nation. Are we still a religiously inclined society? What is the general disposition of our fellow citizens to the importance of God? This matter was spoken to in a very direct way in Joel Kovel's *History and Spirit* (1991). In it, he made the case that we have become a despiritualized society. When a society loses its vital connection to its source of values, meaning, purpose, mission, responsibility, accountability, environmental hospitality, and fundamental aspects of personal, psychic, emotional, natural, and divine relationality, that is despiritualization. In such a society, the categories of spirit, God, or sacred things are kicked to the curb and material matters take center stage. This does not mean that religious practices are eliminated or that claims of faith disappear but rather that values and convictions do not rely on a sustained reference to the ultimate transcendent reality.

Leaders of the major religious traditions teach that the loss of the spiritual dimension diminishes the quality of human life and results in profound social dysfunctionality. Jackson sees in our culture evidence of such a loss. The Founders believed that trust in divine providence was essential to a strong republic. Jackson urges us to recover that shared faith dimension as we seek the renewal of our democratic heritage.

A second key issue he deals with in his work is the reprieve and pardon of offenders of the law. During the administration of recent national leadership, respect has been eroded in regard to the importance of the integrity that should be at work in cases of presidential pardon and clemency. What has been used to protect and reward supporters is more deeply rooted in divine judgment and mercy. Just as we all are subject to mistakes, transgressions, and violations, it is the will of God that provisions be made for justice that is restorative. No one should be forced to live under permanent condemnation or stigmatization. Felonization as a lifelong designation as criminal is contrary to the spirit of restoration that is codified in jubilee legislation and regulations in regard to the year of release. While incarcerated, Jesse Jackson

Jr. was inspired anew to reveal a constitutional basis and process for honoring God's passion to set captives free from bondage as well as the chains of shame, blame, and guilt.

This book is not intended simply to propose liberty and justice for all. It goes to great lengths to show how far racism has steered us away from that goal. It sets forth concrete steps we must take to start the trek toward a more perfect union. Some may be disinclined to accept wisdom that was revealed in the depth of solitary confinement. But don't forget the Birmingham jail, Robben Island, or the Isle of Patmos. Don't overlook John Lewis, Angela Davis, Viktor Frankl, or John Bunyan, who spoke prophetic words while imprisoned. What is contained in these pages may show us the chains that still bind us. I hope we will also find paths this nation must take while so many of us are screaming, "We Can't Breathe!"

PRELUDE TO THE INTRODUCTION

I always consider the settlement of America with reverence and wonder as the opening of a grand scene and design in Providence for the illumination of the ignorant, and the emancipation of the slavish part of mankind all over the world.[3]

—John Adams

I will insist that the Hebrews have done more to civilize men than any other nation. If I were an atheist, and believed in blind eternal fate, I should still believe that fate had ordained the Jews to be the most essential instrument for civilizing the nations. If I were an atheist of the other sect, who believed or pretend to believe that all is ordered by chance, I should believe that chance had ordered the Jews to preserve and propagate to all mankind the doctrine of a supreme, intelligent, wise, almighty sovereign of the universe, which I believe to be the great essential principle of all morality, and consequently of all civilization.[4]

—John Adams to F. A. Vanderkemp, 16 February 1809

LET ME OFFER an early disclaimer. I know exactly who the Founders were. I know exactly the crimes against humanity that they were responsible for and those they inherited and were not responsible for. I do not spend time extolling the virtues of Jefferson, Adams, Franklin, or Madison. Nothing in this work or in my experiment (my life's work) can change the fact or alter the history of the debasement of humanity that preceded the Declaration of Independence (1776), the Constitution (1787), and the Bill of Rights (1791) they were a part of and the obvious fact that the major accomplishment of the Founders' theories about self-government did not apply to African Americans and Native Americans, women, and specifically Black women in their thinking.

Still, there exists in their theological imagination infinite hope for their experiment. This work seeks to identify the evidence that shows and suggests that some of them were aware of a grand architectural experiment and design for the nation and its future.

Every cracked, broken, and imperfect vessel can be used to bring forward hope. I am a personal witness to this fact of human existence. As human beings, we cannot afford to abandon a single person because that person, that stranger on life's Jericho Road, is our test. It is not just what we do for the many but what we do for the one, the lost sheep, the stranger on the road to Jericho, the untouchable, the least of these. This is the test. If we dismiss the one, the work for the many is judged by the act of dismissing the one. This burden is particularly difficult for Black people in that they have endured the long, dark night of a journey with destiny. We,

> Sing a song full of the faith that the dark past has taught us, full of the faith the present has brought us. We have come over a way that with tears has been watered, We have come, treading our path through the blood of the slaughtered,[5]

but it is always that slow third verse that most go silent and three-quarters of the crowd fail to sing,

> Lest our feet stray from the places, our God, where we met Thee. Lest our hearts, drunk with the wine of the world, we forget Thee.[6]

For the great journey that is before us, we are going to need providence and to pray that providence makes room in our hearts for whom Lyndon Baines Johnson called the "lowest"[7] among us. We must defend ourselves, but we must not destroy them in the process. So, we have to think. We have to find creative ways to disarm the lowest, miseducated, cracked vessels in our time and space.

Christianity is a thinking person's religion. It is not as simple as just going to church and following ecclesiastical authority. Every step on the journey from life at home, to a trip to the grocery store, to a ride on the elevator, to adherence to traffic laws and the just laws that govern our society are all part of a national good-neighbor policy.

Martin Luther King Jr. said about this journey, "We must accept finite disappointment, but never lose infinite hope. There is some good in the worst of us, and some evil in the best of us."[8] I find that these character traits King acknowledged existed among certain Founders who were instrumental in directing the future of the republic. This work therefore explores the theology of certain of the architects who gave thought to a glorious future for their theological experiment in spite of themselves. It is no different from any prayer we have prayed with hopes of a change in our lives and in our circumstance or any New Year's resolution we make no matter how well intentioned only to find ourselves a year later still struggling with the previous year's resolutions.

From our system established by the architects has emerged an archetype that is often imitated through the idea of an adherence to what is called the original intent of the Founders' thinking, ideas, and direction for this nation. The original intent of the architects can never truly and accurately be ascertained because we were not there and did not set this nation in motion. Either way, by the courts and Congress, the presidency, and the states, legislatures, and governors—all who stand in the long line of succession since the inauguration of our system—we are told to believe in the original intent of the deeply flawed Founders and asked to live it or be outside the law.

My discovery is the original intent in their theological

experiment. We as a nation should discard the centuries-old mythology of the purveyors of the social order and make room in our thinking for a new enlightenment. Their theological imagination will lay the foundation for every one of us as Dr. Eddie Glaude, the James S. McDonnell Distinguished University Professor of African American Studies at Princeton University, asked us to question how we can begin again. As Thomas Paine recognized in *Common Sense*, "We have it in our power to start the whole world over again."[9]

Thousands of years after Moses led the children of Israel out of Egypt, the lessons of slavery and human debasement were seemingly ignored by the Founders. On one hand, these learned and enlightened men seemed to have learned nothing from the scriptural accounts of slavery and human debasement, but on the other hand, their theological experiment in self-government is equally astounding and unlike anything that has ever been attempted in history at the moment of inception. My discovery suggests that we have not given them credit for what they had planned for our nation's future, which they would not live to see. My discovery of the finger of God and the coupling with the amendment process has provided us with the ability to change America. But here is the catch—It can be done only with the help of a firm reliance on divine providence and a rededication of our nation to the same.

With all of their brilliance, these were deeply flawed men, but aren't we all? Haven't we all fallen short of the glory of God? We all hope for transformation and that our shortcomings public or private are not the final statement of our contribution and self-worth.

Nothing about this work should be read to conclude or suggest or ignore the facts of who the Founders were or the roles they played in their time to maintain or justify the debasement of humanity. I believe that many earned their way to heaven and that many did not. Heaven bound or not, the afterlife seems to be the place in which they, like each of us, will get an opportunity to plead their cases to the divine governor for their behavior on earth including the issues that unapologetically maintained their status quo. With that said, they left us something we can build on. The baby does not need to be thrown out with the bathwater, for in their theological imagination as within ours exists the grandest of all ideas known and unknown to man.

Once we get finished complaining and regurgitating our litany of complaints about America—and I have plenty—we will have to figure out how to make this thing work for everyone. We will have to imagine a better world. And while it is not the focus of this work, it would not hurt to imagine a world without America. In my mind, that is unimaginable.

I hope this work will lift all our thinking above the current morass that is America. My father said, "We must turn to each other and not on each other"[10] to the promise of America, to the possibility of America, and leave the foundation for one of humanity's greatest hours.

—Inmate 32451-016

INTRODUCTION

And the Word was made flesh, and dwelt among us, and we beheld his glory, the glory as of the only begotten of the Father, full of grace and truth. (John 1:14)[11]

I T WAS COLD that night in federal prison when I was unceremoniously arrested for the second time and thrown into solitary confinement, the Special Housing Unit, better known by those who have experienced it as the SHU, at Butner Federal Prison in Butner, North Carolina. I had been helping men who could not read or write fill out pardon applications, a process that at our nation's founding, the Founders could not have imagined as part of their constitutional process; if they had, they certainly would have included such a process in the Constitution and in their deliberations, and if they deemed it necessary, they would have explicitly stated that.

On my first night in solitary, the arresting officers could not give me a reason I was being arrested. It was on the third day, Monday, in the morning that the captain told me that I was being charged with organizing in prison.

I told the captain that the prison chaplain had given me permission to help these men and use the chapel for that purpose, but the chaplain who had authorized my activity had been moved to some other location in the Federal Bureau of Prisons and the current chaplain had not authorized me to do so. Never had I been told that I needed additional permission from the new ecclesiastical authority.

I remember how cold it was. The SHU seemed to be made of

steel and concrete. The toilet, the showers, the mattressless bunk, and even the peephole in the iron-reinforced door were cold, and I was shivering. I had exchanged my camp uniform (a button-up shirt, pants, and standard-issue boots) for an orange jumpsuit, which was like overalls. To stay warm that night, I shriveled my head into my jumpsuit and relied on my breath to warm my body.

By the next morning, the anger had set in because I had in my opinion been denied my due process rights to hear the charges against me and to defend my actions in the camp.

However, that Saturday night, a warmth descended on me that defied explanation. The ambient temperature had not changed; it was still very cold, but I was no longer angry. I said, "And he shall, and he shall, and he shall grant reprieves and pardons." Article II, Section 2, Clause 1 reads, "And he shall have Power to grant reprieves and pardons" is the language of Article II, Section 2, Clause 1 of our Constitution, and I could not stop saying it. I said, "Who in the hell begins a sentence with the word *and*?" I knew that I needed to get out of the mental and spiritual hell I had put myself in.

In that cell, I knew that the Spirit had descended on me and that I would be granted an opportunity to share with the nation the only way out of the hell I was in and consequently a way out of the hell the nation was in.

My mind and the energy that flowed through me transformed my cold cell into a steam room of thought, reflection, and activity. I was directed to the first book I had read and completed; it had been given to me decades earlier by my younger brother, Jonathan Luther Jackson. "And," I said, "he shall grant reprieves and pardons." I remembered the first chapter of *Strength to Love*[12] by Martin Luther King Jr., and after I was released from solitary confinement, I couldn't wait for a friend on the outside to send me a copy of that book.

In chapter 1, Dr. King titled that sermon "A Tough Mind and a Tender Heart" and relied on Matthew 10:16: "Be Ye therefore wise as serpents and harmless as doves."[13] King began,

A French Philosopher said, "No man is strong unless he bears within his character antithesis strongly marked. The strong man holds in a living blend strongly marked opposites. Not ordinarily do men achieve this balance of opposites. The idealists are not usually realistic, and the realists are not usually idealistic. The Militant are not generally known to be passive, nor the passive to be militant. Seldom are the humble self-assertive, or the self-assertive humble. But life at its best is a creative synthesis of opposites in fruitful harmony. The philosopher Hegel said, 'that truth is found neither in the thesis nor the antithesis, but in an emergent synthesis which reconciles the two.'"[14]

King wrote,

Jesus recognized the need for blending opposites. He knew that his disciples would face a difficult and hostile world, where they would confront the recalcitrance of political officials and the intransigence of the protectors of the old order. He knew that they would meet cold and arrogant men whose hearts had been hardened by the long winter of traditionalism. So he said to them, "Behold, I send you forth as sheep in the midst of wolves." And he gave them a formula for action, "Be ye therefore wise as serpents, and harmless as doves." It is pretty difficult to imagine a single person having, simultaneously, the characteristics of the serpent and the dove, but this is what Jesus expects.[15]

King concluded,

We must combine the toughness of the serpent and the softness of the dove, a tough mind and a tender heart.[16]

I had found it. The circumstances and the pain of the hour in my life had exposed me to an interpretation buried deep in the logos of our Constitution placed there by the architects to be revealed at our nation's most desperate hour; it was a character trait not just for an individual but for the entire government. The Founders had placed the supreme character traits in history in the Constitution, but they had obscured it.[17] I had found Madison's hidden "Finger of the Almighty Hand."[18] I had found Alexander Hamilton's "Finger of God."[19] I understood for the first time why Franklin's prayer at the opening of the Constitutional Convention on June 27, 1787, was so poignant and among the greatest contributions to rhetoric in English; his words captured the spirit of the occasion.

> Sir, that we have not hitherto once thought of humbly applying to the Father of lights to illuminate our understandings? In the beginning of the Contest with G. Britain, when we were sensible of danger we had daily prayer in this room for the divine protection. Our prayers, Sir, were heard, and they were graciously answered. All of us who were engaged in the struggle must have observed frequent instances of a Superintending providence in our favor. To that kind providence we owe this happy opportunity of consulting in peace on the means of establishing our future national felicity. And have we now forgotten that powerful friend? I have lived, Sir, a long time, and the longer I live, the more convincing proofs I see of this truth— that God governs in the affairs of men. And if a sparrow cannot fall to the ground without his

notice, is it probable that an empire can rise without his aid? We have been assured, Sir, in the sacred writings, that "except the Lord build the House they labour in vain that build it."[20]

By the end of the convention, the devout Franklin had moved beyond his admonishment of the conveners to the idea that something special had been accomplished at the convention.

Outside Independence Hall when the Constitutional Convention of 1787 ended, Mrs. Powel of Philadelphia asked Franklin, "Well, Doctor, what have we got, a republic or a monarchy?" With no hesitation whatsoever, Franklin responded, "A republic, if you can keep it."[21]

I had found the religion[22] of the Founders. And within its words were the supreme character traits and the supreme character test and vetting process for the nation's leader and the form of government the American people should have. It was hidden in plain sight in the Constitution. For on the other side of the word *and* was "the President shall be Commander in Chief of the Army and Navy of the United States, and of the Militia of the several States." The architects had combined the character traits of a serpent and a dove, an army commander and one who granted reprieves and pardons. To paraphrase King, "It is hard to imagine a single individual having both the character traits of a tough military commander and chief *and* the softness of a merciful and forgiving dove, but this is what I believe Jesus and the Founding Fathers expected."(emphasis added)

It is even more difficult for an insecure people who have been hardened by fear over many generations, whose ancestors in their first generation fought the Revolutionary War, whose ancestors died in the Civil War, whose great-grandparents fought in World War I, whose grandparents fought in World War II, whose parents fought in Korea and Vietnam, and whose current family members continue to fight a global war on terror. Fear had become a part of our national psychology; therefore, it is impossible to imagine that they were once a fearless people who could combine these character traits and emerge as a "City on a Hill."[23]

The power to pardon in Article II, Section 2, Clause 1 had been extracted by the Founders from a theological system that included Jesus. Early Americans had the power to forgive others, but the architects also gave the people the power to forgive entire regions, an entire country, and even foreign adversaries. At the inception of the experiment, the architects imagined unlimited terms for such an empathetic leader supported by election of the people. However, this idea has been lost to time, and now, he or she may be blessed only with one or two four-year terms.

It was placed in the Constitution four years before the Bill of Rights (1791) added the First Amendment that protected congregationalism and denominationalism and the Tenth Amendment (states' rights) and therefore constituted the original intent of the architects. It was in the Constitution six years before the founding of the Democratic-Republican Party of 1793 (that party later organized itself into the Democratic Party of Andrew Jackson in 1828, a proslavery party), and it was in the Constitution sixty-seven years before the founding of the Republican Party in Ripon, Wisconsin, in 1854. (That party organized itself as an antislavery party under the leadership of Abraham Lincoln.)

The Founders had protected the religion of a man from the sect of one, meaning the highest form of religion for the architects was not congregationalism, denominationalism, or groupthink; it was the personal relationship a believer had with God. This person in the sect of one descends from the linear theological system, a person who believed in transferring people's guilt to himself and offering them a do-over, a "new life *in* earth."[24] America is a theological system, and no one is outside the grace of almighty God in this belief system.

Providence had given me a new task. I had to imagine the person, the avatar, the disciple, the leader with such an enormous responsibility whose skeleton so to speak had been placed in the Constitution but whose country's educational system had not prepared the nation for his or her arrival or with the tools necessary to judge its leaders by this standard and subsequently vote them into office. Therefore, I extracted the structure of the language from the Constitution and began an experiment with commander of the army and repriever pardoner® not as two separate responsibilities but as a single character trait, the spirit and energy of an individual.

Providence has assigned me to create the curriculum necessary to train a person, a series of people, who would have the potential to fill up that skeleton with "arteries, with veins, with nerves, muscles, and flesh."[25] From these words of spirit and action—reprieves and pardons—I extracted the person, the one who would be the future redeemer of the nation, a repriever pardoner.[26] And because we have not seen this person as a Democrat or a Republican, a liberal or a conservative, in our history, we must imagine and educate people on the necessary character traits our presidents must have. The African American Vitruvian[27] is neither Jew nor Gentile, Democrat nor Republican, liberal nor conservative; he or she just is. Adams stated the problem succinctly.

> There is nothing I dread so much as the division of the republic into two great parties, each arranged under its leader, and concerting measures in opposition to each other. This, in my humble apprehension, is to be dreaded as the greatest political evil under our constitution.[28]

Initially, it was hard for me to accept that the divine religion of the linear theological system of Abraham and its function at the hour of our nation's founding were not meant for me to discover or for Black people. However, when I read *Canaan Land* by Albert J. Raboteau, the words of David Walker spoke to me: "If ever the world becomes Christianized ... it will be through the means, under God of the *Blacks*, who are now held in wretchedness, and degradation by the white *Christians* of the world."[29] Maria Stewart explained it this way.

> America, foul and indelible is thy stain! Dark and dismal is the cloud that hangs over thee, for thy cruel wrongs and injuries to the fallen sons of Africa. The blood of her murdered ones cries to heaven for vengeance against Thee ... You may kill, tyrannize, and oppress as much as you choose, until our cry shall come up from the throne of God; for I am firmly persuaded, that he will not suffer you to quell the crowd, fearless and undaunted spirits of the Africans forever; for in his own time, he is able to plead our cause against you, and to pour out upon you the ten plagues of Egypt.[30]

The Founders provided a skeleton for a future Anglo American to discover. Over time, I came to accept that the burden of conceptualization would ultimately have to be carried out and completed initially by a Black man, Black people, in a lineage of persons in America because our recurring experience is like the experience of Jesus on the cross.

The DNA of White Christianity, evangelicalism, and piety have certain corrupting factors[31] that run contrary to the authentic teachings and precepts of Jesus.[32] Dr. James A. Forbes Jr. reminded me, "White supremacy is not just a social arrangement: it is a race-based faith."[33]

34

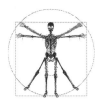   

Why an African American Vitruvian? Because Black Americans are the most forgiving people on earth. The very forgiveness that Black Americans often complain about is the grace that God has bestowed on them and only them. We can and must defend ourselves, but the destruction of our frenemy has never been and will never be part of our DNA.

Why an African American Vitruvian? Because White American Christianity forgives and pardons only itself. This is true from the genocide of Native Americans to the enslavement of African Americans from the Civil War to the present. No immigrant or ethnic group will forgive the least of these en masse because it will never be politic for them to do so. Many are too busy joining, appeasing, and attempting to be part of the majority culture. The politic sees the existence of African American and brown bodies and life as outside the grace of God and unworthy of forgiveness on earth as it is in heaven. But African Americans have and consistently forgiven all.

Why an African American Vitruvian? Because Jesus came to liberate the least of these, and as long as the so-called master race and those who practice any form of supremacy every Sunday morning consider themselves as the least of these and therefore victims of exploitation, progress for the poor, the disenfranchised, and those of all races who yearn to be free will be stifled and their condition justified in the name of the Creator and the Savior.

Why an African American Vitruvian? Because the nation's immigrant narrative has never been taught that rights in America have been earned over time, not granted. In every generation, the nation's newest immigrants inherit American history including the addition of the 13th, 14th, and 15th Amendments. They were not struggles they or their ancestors participated in but were struggles they are beneficiaries of. Therefore, the enduring legacies of these struggles escape their knowledge, interest, and memory. I am super-sensitive and skeptical of Constantine and the Roman Empire's oppressive, colonizing, and coopting midnight conversion to the leadership of the human liberation movement begun around the Sea of Galilee in the province of Judea it once colonized during Jesus's time. That is the context of his ministry. Such co-option would have little if any moral authority.

I am very skeptical of Democrats and Republicans, liberals and conservatives, on economic and social issues emerging after 235 years as leaders of this progressive movement after having shown little if any moral authority. They are welcome to join, but this movement is not looking for their leadership. This movement belongs to the poor, the least of these, in every succeeding American generation.

We must recapture the revolutionary spirit of love, mercy, justice, nonviolence, and forgiveness of a Palestinian Jew whose ministry transformed history. The African American community has inherited the forgiveness gene, the DNA of the linear theological system that began with Abraham and ended with Jesus. This is God's gift to the American descendants of slavery; it is not different from the Israelite descendants of Egyptian slavery and captivity—the same God. A redeemer of all people is promised to us. Unconditional forgiveness is the most powerful and yet the most unexplored power on earth. I liken it to a single grain of sand on a beach. It is the least used power in the Constitution and yet is the Constitution's source of power.

The Vitruvian comes from the lineage of Abraham, not from any system that came into existence in reaction to White Christianity or its culture. The modern Christian mind is divided by race and caste and is intellectually dichotomized by notions of church and state and even the more dubious idea that one's religion is not manifested in one's politics or the way one nonviolently practices Christianity. Nothing could be further from the truth. The profundity of this differentiating and splitting can never be understated. It has given birth to its own form of "tyranny over the mind of man."[35] The intellectual schism is so deep that even the first African American president would not forgive the American people let alone his own. Therefore, on earth as it is in heaven is a cruel hoax perpetrated on all people without this corrective. I do not believe the Lord's Prayer is wrong or in error. I believe America, as blessed as it is, is presently operating outside the grace of God.

36

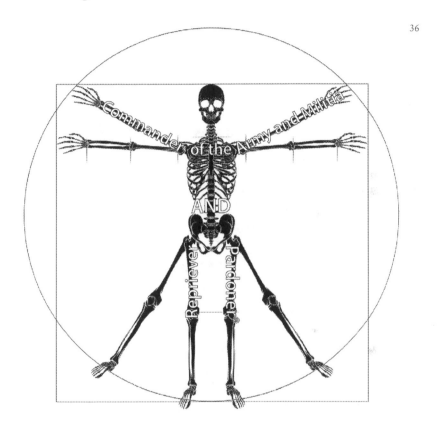

Ultimately, we must imagine from raw material this person, and he or she must have the nerves and flesh to put on this suit so that "these words can be made flesh and dwell amongst us."[37] It's a simple system, and the sect of one is a simple religion.

> Master, which is the great commandment in the law? Jesus said unto him, Thou shalt love the Lord thy God with all thy heart, and with all thy

soul, and with all thy mind. This is the first and great commandment. And the second is like unto it, Thou shalt love thy neighbour as thyself. On these two commandments hang all the law and the prophets.[38]

In its simplicity, its complexity is astounding. The articulation of the absence of a national educational system to support the idea is my devotion, my ministry, and my last will and testament. All Americans have within them the opportunity to be this person, but it would require the most comprehensive reform of our nation's value system through education, an overhaul beyond states' rights and localism to a genuine global quest for knowledge, information, and wisdom, and the broadest appreciation of math, science, languages, and history. It will require an appreciation and serious study of all faiths and nonfaiths, the welcoming of all points of view, and the cross-fertilization of these points of view in all disciplines to teach and educate a comprehensive, whole person. It would be an educational system unlike anything we have seen in our country.

Our present system is designed to support a caste-based system where everyone's lot in life is predetermined—to get a job and work for the prevailing economy. Rarely does the nation's educational system teach self-reliance. Ultimately, we all must be freed from the shackles of this "tyranny over the mind of man."[39]

My discovery impacts the lives of 68 million federal and state offenders.[40] When these offenders and their families understand and embrace what the Founders bequeathed to them, and when they recognize that they are still children of God and that their errors are not outside God's grace, they will gain the power to usher in a new interpretation of Article II, Section 2, Clause 1 of our Constitution and start their lives over and be empowered to start the entire world over.[41]

The experiment predates the Declaration of Independence. I cannot narrow down when it began, but it continued long after the Declaration of July 4, 1776, the appointment of the Great Seal committee, the first draft of the Constitution in August 1787, the signatory process of the Constitution in September 1787, and certainly before the Bill of Rights in 1791. All along the way, the Founders left breadcrumbs for social scientists of the future to follow and for archeologists and historians to discover and exhume for the day the nation would have to resurrect its spirit and move the nation past the errors of its ways to a new future.

The correspondence between Adams and Jefferson, the second and third presidents of the United States (December 1787—October 1813), point to an extraordinary theological experiment that had taken place in the faith of the architects of our republic. It was a theological experiment involving the resurrection of the human spirit. On October 12, 1813, Jefferson responded to a request by Adams to return a copy of a letter and a "syllabus" that Jefferson had provided the late Benjamin Rush by which the principles of Jesus could be placed in a narrative that could be followed by a pious and reflective believer in Jesus. The resulting octavo was titled by Jefferson *The Life and Morals of Jesus of Nazareth, Extracted Textually from the Gospels in Greek, Latin, French and English*.[42] It would later be called the Jefferson Bible. The translations of the Greek, Latin, and French to English mattered. Accurate translations and the words that conveyed the spirit of the life of Jesus mattered to Jefferson, who understood their power. Jefferson knew something else—That on September 17, 1787, the architects had already provided "the skeleton."[43]

Jefferson responded to Adams,

> I now send you according to your request, a copy of the syllabus. To fill up this "skeleton" with arteries, with veins, with nerves, muscles, and flesh, is really beyond my time and information. Whoever would undertake it would find great aid

in Enfields judicious abridgement of Brucker's History of Philosophy.[44]

To compare the morals of the Old with the New Testament would require an attentive study of the former, a search through all the books for its precepts, and through all its history for its practices and the principle they proved.[45] Jefferson accomplished this by synthesizing the Gospels into a single account and carefully removing the miraculous things and wonders that only Jesus could have done from the workings that true believers and followers could actually accomplish.

Jefferson removed the evidence-based narratives, words, precepts, teachings, parables, lessons, and stories that man could actually emulate, duplicate, and even imitate to be like Jesus. Jefferson must have understood as Ralph Waldo Emerson surmised, "The foundations of a person are not in matter but in spirit"[46] with a similar conclusion reached by Joseph Priestly in *Disquisitions Relating to Matter and Spirit* (1777).[47] Jesus's words captured his spirit and would need to become flesh to dwell among us in the present.

Jefferson also recognized that Jesus's ministry had been cut short by his crucifixion. From the earliest accounts of the Gospels in Greek to Latin, French, and ultimately English, the preservation of Jesus's spirit can be felt in the construction of the language that represented his most unique and authentic teachings. The experiment was about Jesus, the person and his character, not the ecclesiastical and church-based constructions or the millions of sermons delivered over time dealing with the Christ figure we have come to know as Christians. The only way we have come to know him is through his authentic words and spirit with nothing lost in translation. Words and their spirit capture divine truth, the foundation of human liberty.

The first time Jefferson undertook to create his own version of scripture had been in 1804. His intention, he wrote, was "the result of a life of enquiry and reflection, and very different from that anti-Christian system, imputed to me by those who know nothing of my opinions."[48] Correspondence indicates that he assembled forty-six pages of New Testament passages in *The Philosophy of Jesus of Nazareth*, but that has been lost. It focused on Christ's moral teachings organized by topic. The 1820 volume contained Jesus's teachings and the events of his life.

The Smithsonian acquired the surviving custom Bible in 1895 when the institution's chief librarian, Cyrus Adler, purchased it from Jefferson's great-granddaughter, Carolina Randolph. Originally, Jefferson had bequeathed the book to his daughter Martha. The acquisition revealed the existence of the Jefferson Bible to the public. In 1904, by act of Congress, his version of scripture regarded by many as a newly discovered national treasure was printed. Until the 1950s, when the supply of 9,000 copies ran out, each new senator received a facsimile Jefferson Bible.[49]

Two thousand years of ecclesiastical corruption, dicta, and dogma had been separated from what was actually accomplishable by his followers. Jefferson accomplished that by capturing the words that painted a picture of Jesus's spirit. For Jefferson, words and the spirit mattered.

Words matter in the conveyance of spirit. John 1:1–17 canvassed history and proclaimed that no other human had had a more perfect say/do ratio than Jesus. A perfect say/do ratio is a one-to-one ratio between word, thought, and deed. Without words, the indescribable is not describable. We use words to shape a mental picture of Spirit. But the idea of a word is already self-limiting when we speak of the spirit because the Spirit defies definitions made up of words. This is also true of the biblical chroniclers, and it was particularly true of our Founders. Above all else, they understood the impact of words and their ability to convey an indescribable Spirit. Words can attempt to define the Spirit but cannot limit the Spirit because words paint a picture of only what the mind can grasp. Without words to convey meaning, we would not be able to describe what we see and feel in the realm of Spirit. There are many times when we cannot find the words to describe Spirit, so we smile, cry, laugh, embrace, and offer symbols and gestures that convey gentle meaning.

Sometimes, words escape us, and other times, we need courage to express care and concern with words. Words matter. John 1:1 makes this point clear; without the word, we cannot adequately convey spirit because our minds cannot completely grasp it. We need a mental image of spirit to begin to comprehend it. Among the words that contain life are *respiration* (divinity), *aspiration* (will), *perspiration* (work), *inspiration* (love of neighbor), and *expiration* (death), and they have at their roots the Latin word *spiritus*.

The modern English word *spirit* comes from the Latin *spiritus* but also "spirit, soul, courage, vigor," ultimately from the Indo-European (s)peis. It is distinguished from Latin *anima*—soul—which also derives from an Indo-European root meaning "to breathe." From our first to our last breaths, there is spirit. In each word we utter and each action we take is a spirit that defines who we are, and our actions can define history.

The most ancient civilizations painted pictures on cave walls to convey meaning. The ancient Egyptians used hieroglyphics to immortalize their civilization and to convey meaning and purpose. The ancient Greeks developed a language that conveyed meaning, purpose, and spirit. Is it possible to enter the Louvre in Paris and not be overwhelmed by the conveyance of spirit in the form of the Renaissance and its masters who expressed eternal spirit in their work? Their works make us ask, "What were and are they trying to say? What was on their minds?" We use lots of factors to try to determine what they were thinking. Were they in love when they created their works? Had they experienced tragedy? Was there inspiration from a mountaintop of hope or a valley of despair? Indeed, the words *inspiration, aspiration,* and *respiration* have breath and spirit as their foundations.

It is impossible for a person of pious reflection to tour the Vatican and not be overwhelmed by the thinking, the commitment, and the seriousness with which Michelangelo took his faith and conveyed his spirit. The spirit is conveyed in his work. Michelangelo said, "I saw the angel in the marble and carved it until I set him free."[50] "I created a vision of David in my mind and simply carved away everything that was not David."[51]

The phenomenon of the spirit is conveyed in words, in art, in marble. Today, Confederate statues and monuments—indeed all statues and monuments—are meant to convey spirit however one might align oneself along a domestic political spectrum. There is a reason Christians erect the monument of the cross. We erect monuments to men and women who have served our nation, not corrupt, villainous, and brutal dictators and figures. Some spirits we want to move forward, and some we wish never to see again.

Even biblical fundamentalists and literalists journey to the Bible for the words of inspiration and can quote scripture with the best of them often failing however to convey spirit, meaning, and context.

The Declaration of Independence and the Constitution are just words if the words do not contain spirit. What picture did the Founders paint with the words of these documents? As architects of our republic, what was the grand design in the schematics, the drawings, the plans that they drew with words? As Founders, what was the foundation? As sculptors of a new nation that could possibly play a unique role in history, what modeling clay did they discard while creating the new republic? Why did they do so?

The Founders believed that theological education was the highest form of liberal arts education because words carried meaning and the possibility of divine spirit. Between birth—respiration—to one's last breath—expiration—was an opportunity to build on the foundation of the supreme character of the greatest teacher and philosopher. "Our constitution was made only for a moral and religious people. It is wholly inadequate to the government of any other,"[52] Adams said.

A person of pious reflection who receives the blessing of

providence and education, who understands the skeleton in the Constitution, who is willing to provide the "arteries, the veins, the nerves, muscles, and flesh" and function in the spirit of David and Jesus should be the leader of the nation. It is my sincerest hope that before the American experiment gives in to tyranny, totalitarianism, or fascism that America gives consideration to this work. It is not just the path of a single leader; it is the path of a nation and its people who have been taught it, believe it, and are willing to vote for it.

PART I
THE FINGER OF GOD

1

MY EXPERIMENT ...
MY DISCOVERY

It is impossible for the man of pious reflection not to perceive in it [the Constitution] a finger of that Almighty hand which has been so frequently and signally extended to our relief in the critical stages of the revolution.[53]

—James Madison

For my part, I sincerely esteem the Constitution, a system which without the finger of God, never could have been suggested and agreed upon by such a diversity of interests.[54]

—Alexander Hamilton

America is destined to be peopled by one nation, speaking one language, professing one general system of religious and political principles, and accustomed to one general tenor of social usages and customs.[55]

—John Adams

The Ten Commandments and the Sermon on the Mount contain my religion.[56]

—John Adams

The doctrines of Jesus are simple and tend all to the happiness of man, that there is only one God and God is perfect that God and man are one. That to love God with all your heart, and your neighbor as yourself, is the sum of religion. These are the great points on which I endeavor to reform and live my life.[57]

—Thomas Jefferson

Whilst we assert for ourselves a freedom to embrace, to profess, and to observe, the Religion which we believe to be of divine origin, we cannot deny an equal freedom to those whose minds have not yet yielded to the evidence which has convinced us. If this freedom be abused, it is an offense against God, not against man: To God, therefore, not to man, must an account of it be rendered.[58]

—James Madison

In the beginning God created the heaven and the earth. And the earth was without form, and void; and darkness was upon the face of the deep. And the Spirit of God moved upon the face of the waters. And God said, Let there be light: and there was light. And God saw the light, that it was good: and God divided the light from the darkness. And God called the light Day, and the Darkness he called Night. and the evening and the morning were the first day.[59]

IN THE BEGINNING, before my awareness, I contemplated the structure, order, and process of reviewing, expressing, implementing, and teaching history, law, and theology. My journey through life was one of observation, absorption, intrinsic learning, understanding, seeking of knowledge, trial and error, and mistakes—plenty of mistakes. It was only after I lay in a cold, dark cell in solitary confinement that I came into the light of myself. God said in Genesis, "Let there be light," and with the power of God's spoken words, there was enlightenment.

I had pondered the language of Article II, Section 2, Clause 1 for weeks as I sought to help men who could not read or write and had a limited understanding of the law come to terms with the ideas that they could be forgiven and that their actions were not outside God's grace. I repeated the language, and then like Michelangelo, I saw the angel in the marble of the Constitution, the hard words that governed our lives and society, and "I began carving until I set him free."[60] I asked my "cellee," Abrahaman Muhammad, to capture the three nights I spent in solitary and the moment of enlightenment. He drew the following images.

61

"And he shall grant reprieves and pardons." My mind was awakened to my voice hovering over this thought, this statement. I said, "Who in the hell starts a sentence with the word *and*?" When a work is considered, there is first thought and consideration before action. This is the process by which thought becomes tangible; it is the process of creation, innovation, and moving from curiosity to proof. *And* is the synergy or synthesis, the ebb and flow that creates a balance between idea and implementation. It requires more than one action.

I used all my inquiry, research, education, experience, and exposure to enter what is now required as a result of all my efforts during the first half of my life's journey. Now after awakening to *and*, I present the extraordinary enlightenment of the Great Seal committee.[62] Adams, Franklin, and Jefferson were appointed to it immediately after the adoption of the Declaration of Independence on July 4, 1776, and evidence supports Hamilton's and Madison's knowledge of a theological experiment with infinity.

Evidence supports the idea that an experiment was planted and hidden in the Constitution for a time when consideration of a new life for individuals and our nation would not be a dream but a requirement, new life "on earth as it is in heaven."[63] My discovery requires consideration of a person, an avatar, who can honor the love of one God and the love of neighbor because the law of the prophets hang on these two commandments.[64] The Founders were in agreement with the finger of God when they completed the Constitution. In fact, according to Hamilton, it was the only thing the Founders agreed on.

My work in the laboratory of my life started when I was a young adult; however, after pondering the structure and impact that wording could have on our country and its citizens and the enlightenment that the wording of our Constitution would have on our world and what it actually reveals as the key to heaven on earth,[65] I went to work for the first time in full awareness of my mission and purpose to produce the work I call the discovery.

My experiment started long ago with my moving through my inquisitive thoughts, my quest for continuous learning, my eagerness to rise to the level of the bar set high by my father, and to the next generation of lofty goals started by the pioneers of the civil rights movement I had always been surrounded by. I was driven by a mission, a purpose, and ultimately the pursuit of a God-given assignment to free 68 million debt-paid felons from shame, blame, and guilt. I am now steeped in that purpose and moved by my assignment of presenting the discovery I found through research and experimentation. While in solitary confinement, I scribbled these notes.

66

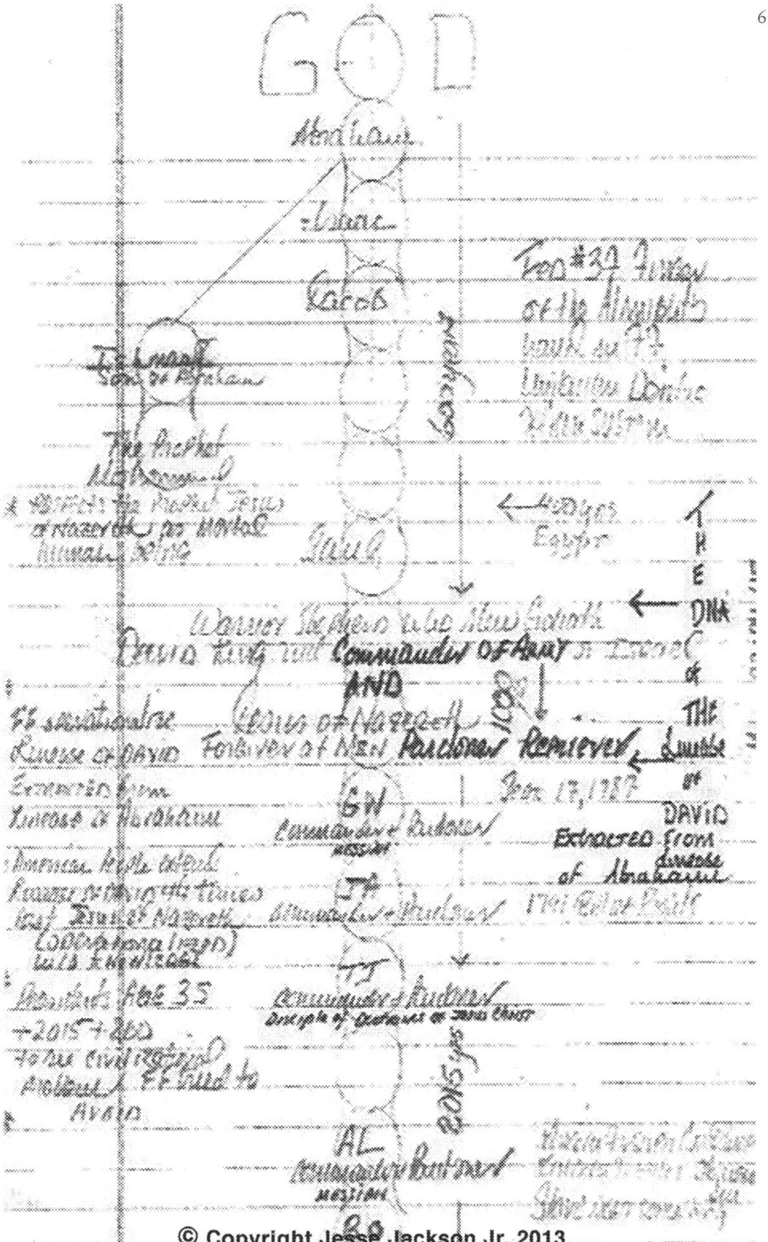

Upon exiting solitary confinement, I was determined to document the intent of the Founders and an original interpretation of the Constitution inclusive of all the people of what was created, structured, planted, and hidden in our Constitution 234 years ago for the present. I had to consider the purpose that Adams, Franklin, Hamilton, Jefferson, Madison, Thomson, and Rush must have had to be committed to the meaning of the two great commandments.

The power of their ultimate creation of a document that would have more impact today than it did when they created it could have come only from a place greater than self. These Founders knew that after birthing a nation and creating the documents to govern it, they had to consider what would be required to take corrective action as growth, development, and maturity would bring new concerns. These Founders wanted their new nation to be one of Abraham's "many nations."[67]

At the time the Constitution was written, felons and their subsequent lifelong felonizations were not the issue of the day. In 2021, 68 million debt-paid felons and their burden of shame, blame, and guilt they bring to their families and nation create a national security concern. They create a community and family concern. They create a concern for generations to come. Our country is experiencing labor pains for a corrective that recognizes some of the growth, innovation, and corrective actions based on race, sex, and class that need to be remediated. The national spirit energy of law-based, structured inequality in wealth requires a new understanding of what it means to pursue life, liberty, and happiness in this man-made but God-ordained system. I say God-ordained because America is an extension and manifestation of the faith of the architects of our republic.

The office of the president was conceived as a position in which an elected person would function with unlimited moral power and authority based on divine and universal truths but limited constitutional authority. The president was to be a moral, not just a military, leader. The primary concern of the architects was "We the People" in Article I. The person elected by the people to the presidency was a secondary, Article II, concern. However, the vetting process for this individual was a stringent character test.

Today, the presidency is evolving into an unlimited constitutional authority with little to no moral authority or power to lead the people. If a former president can be impeached and cause concern for the nation as he considered pardoning himself at the end of his term, if presidents influenced by the poultry industry can continue the annual mockery and abomination of pardoning turkeys as each president has done at Thanksgiving since Abraham Lincoln,[68] there is no limit to the crimes that can be committed by an unaccountable sovereign. The Founders in their theological experiments in 1776 and in the Constitution of 1787 had "a firm reliance on the protection of Divine Providence,"[69] not the poultry industry, when then they presented the Constitution to the people for ratification.

The laboratory is a collection of my research, writings, and documentation of our country's history, the passing of laws, the transition of political parties, and the undeniable black line that precedes the inception of our country and its evolution that impacts federal and state law today.

In my laboratory, I awake to a knock at midnight. I work best after midnight writing the events of the past and present, and my discovery will show my natural inclination to journal the path to our future by recording the past and present.

My discovery and the teaching system I have developed will ensure that the America we love will endure. I began my experiment in my laboratory in 1996 and published it in 2001 while in Congress with hopes of mapping out a strategic plan for my work as a congressman. I wanted to position my agenda on the pulse of the country and its history and of course on my constituents in the Second District of Illinois. I created hundreds of timelines that allowed me to connect points in time of the nation's behavior, an often repetitive behavior because of the nation's race habit.

When I began to study the work, I was able to identify and capture gaps in the history of our liberty system and to develop an understanding of the corrective actions for the betterment of all citizens. One of my accomplishments was recognizing how the Civil War became revisionist history that excluded slavery as a reason for its cause. I documented this understanding in my book *A More Perfect Union*,[70] volume II of this two-part series. My efforts to correct revisionist history allowed me to push for changes in the law with the National Park Service and add new landmarks to highlight the missing history.

I offered the Rosa Parks legislation[71] to place her statue in Statuary Hall and then name the Capitol's visitors' center Emancipation Hall[72] in a bipartisan effort with Congressman Zach Wamp of Tennessee. We wanted to broaden the story of all our heroes and she-roes that must be reflected in our nation's capital. With a more complete story of everyone's contribution to our nation, we can develop a mutual appreciation and understanding of each other as neighbors and all our contributions.

Knowing this linear history, I thought that if the American people knew the driving force behind American politics, many statues of our history would come to be held in disdain and contempt because of their historically fascist and racist contexts and that citizens would call for their removal or simply rally and tear them down.[73]

These two examples I presented as insight into how my work in the laboratory enabled me to push an agenda that opened America to the acceptance and belief that all people must be represented and protected by our laws including our laws that preserve history. I work today to introduce the greatest education of the guiding principle our country was founded on. Only by the revelation of what our Constitution holds can we remove our caste-based system and free our citizens and ourselves because all of us are steeped as a result of our history in SBG—shame, blame, and guilt. We can restore our collective mental health and start the search for life, liberty, and the pursuit of happiness based on truth for all.

The laboratory provides the solitude, the tools, and the structure I need to explore ideas, conduct research, and express my findings through my observations and assessments. My experiment came together as I validated what I had awakened to while in solitary confinement. I hovered over the thought and then started to follow the path of books, letters, and experiments by certain of our Founders and to organize their understanding that I gathered in my timelines.

The Founders' theology and prayers were very instructive. They elevated their highest and solemn petitions for the intervention of divine providence in our lives. Prayers are part of an infinity process. This process assured me that my discovery was documented for future generations beyond what the Founders would have been able to attest to.

The Founders knew for sure that a new country would implement laws, legislation, and cultural biases and establish norms with separate and unequal accountabilities among the people of our country. They knew that as we matured, corrective action would need to be given full consideration to avoid the nation's destruction. The people would need the antidote the Founders had as part of their intuition and foresight to write and confirm as a part of our Constitution. Our state of affairs 234 years after the commencement of the experiment requires us to give serious consideration to what I am presenting.

2

TOOLS FOR THE EXPERIMENT

I HAVE LEARNED A lot from business, economics, law, and theology; those fields of study gave me an understanding of what I was journeying through due to my birthright. As the son of Rev. Jesse Jackson, I was exposed to all these areas. Venturing into a formal understanding of each path allowed me to map out my path while not really understanding that this was my personal journey.

My tenure in Congress was well mapped out because I decided to help ensure that all laws would give every citizen equal rights under our Constitution. My goal was to seek and pass on in the form of constitutional amendments support for an image of America for all people that was *de facto*, not just *de jure*.

My timelines enabled me to walk right into the next chapter of my purpose with full understanding of how all facets of business, history, law, and theology could work together to build a nation or work separately to tear it down. I created a picture of our country's strengths and weaknesses and its original sin of slavery that still affects every major decision in the laws that govern us.

A color line in my timelines enters before the Declaration of Independence (1776), the Constitution (1787), and the Bill of Rights (1791), and it moves our nation—all of us—to seek redemption through forgiveness. Our country was built literally and figuratively on the backs of the individuals brought to a new world in 1619 in bondage. All Americans live to experience redemption. Our Founders created our Constitution with an understanding that as the country was being formed, mistakes would be made, and slavery, an affront to almighty God, was a serious stain on the nation at its inception and would ultimately have to be ended by civil war.

It would be redeemed and reconciled by civil disobedience and civil rights, by an appeal to conscience and radical empathy, or by rebelling against tyrants with violent force. The last I find unacceptable. My timelines worked as tools to map out my experiment, and they ultimately enabled me to discover the key to our enlightenment.

Research is a tool that requires continuous documenting, discovering, questioning, reading, and validation. I compiled a list of works that will help us walk through each point on the timelines while providing proof that I did not create what I was exposing. I dug deep into our history to unlock what was hidden in our founding documents. I believe there is no greater excavation. It is with this new understanding of what was hidden in plain view in our Constitution that the amendments of our country can be reviewed, renewed, reestablished, and expanded into law and expose the key to the closed door and secret meetings at the Constitutional Convention and the secret to heaven on earth. In essence, we would maintain our status as the beacon on the hill[74] not in the future or in a place in the clouds but in the present and right here on earth as it is in heaven.[75]

Humility

This tool enables me to own what my enlightenment exposed me to and to walk in ownership of my purpose without wondering what anyone would think about me. I do not worry that some will say, "Jesse Jackson Jr. has lost his mind." If that happens, I will consider myself no less fortunate than John the Baptist was. I do not worry that some will say, "You want me to believe you found something no one else has discovered in 234 years?"[76] To that, I say that I walk knowing not all will believe me but that all should research for themselves what I expose as the work of our Founders, who believed in the one true God with all their hearts, souls, and minds.

The Founders knew that "a man of pious reflection"[77] would lead the men and women of the nation to the same understanding in the future. I am but the messenger of what was written before I was born.

I do not worry because humility enables me to restore the love of God and neighbor to their rightful place for a country founded on those two great commandments. Humility enables me to walk in deism, theism, and universalism as a disciple of the doctrines of Jesus. I walk honoring the one true God of Abraham, Ishmael, Isaac, Jacob, David, and Jesus, for they were all in their deism, theism, and universalism and had to accept humbling assignments.

This work is my assignment for this life. Humility allows me to present my findings in their entirety with the hope that excellence will be part of building a new nation.

Before the Constitutional Convention, there was chattel slavery, a form of slavery that had to be overcome by the constitutional process. Before the founding documents declared America as a country free of British rule, there was slavery. At the time of our commitment to building a nation based on freedom and the pursuit of life, liberty, and happiness, our ancestors here were using the labor of a people to construct it. As the Puritans sought to build a new life in a new land, they savagely stripped a people of their human rights to build it. It is with this in mind that I present a continuous black line in our history.

In his book *American Gospel*,[78] Jon Meacham quoted William Bradford as follows when referring to the American founding generation.

> They fell upon their knees and blessed the God of
> Heaven who had brought them over the vast and
> furious ocean, and delivered them from all the
> perils and miseries thereof.[79]

Bradford and his company saw the hand of God in their journey.[80] That was the beginning of the experiment we call America.
We have continued to believe that America is an incomplete
experiment. We are still seeking to balance, we are still seeking
recovery from past failed experiments, and we are still trying to
ensure that the experiment we call America will exist forever.
Our goal is to ensure that each generation is closer to experiencing the heaven on earth we all dream is possible.

My discovery is one rooted in the fact positioned in our
Constitution. In the laboratory, I am still spending hours researching and uncovering conversations, actions, and measure-
ments taken by the Founders to protect America long after they
were gone. I believe that they were committed to God and worked
to place God in our governing documents to secure the rights of
the people.

The Founders continued to validate their knowing long after
the Constitutional Convention was over. They could not have
known that some of the laws would take away some people's
God-given, inalienable rights. Could they have known that the
recovery from slavery would require a way to forgive prior generations for their participation in such an inhumane misuse of their
brother, the slave, as labor for their gain? Could the Founders
have envisioned a time when we would have to recognize the
character of a president as being decent or indecent? If the president is decent, the president can sustain our country. However, if
the president is indecent, the potential for the president to expose
our country to great peril is a great concern.

Today in America, we face unequal health care and education,
gender discrimination, massive wealth inequality, a pandemic of
biblical proportions, police brutality, and authoritarianism. All

these issues were addressed in secret by the Founders for a time when the experiment of starting a country needed to be reevaluated and the hypothesis changed to include a corrective for the miscalculations of our past. Though the experiments of the past may have been stopped, the damage they created was never corrected and restoration was never implemented for those who suffered. What I have found allows me to provide the antidote for the restorations of old and to complete the experiment for the current events of today taking America into the future.

3

THE LINEAGE OF ABRAHAM AND DAVID

Here is my Creed. I believe in one God, creator of the Universe. That he governs it by his Providence. That he ought to be worshiped. That the most acceptable service we render him is doing good to his other children. That the soul of Man is immortal, and will be treated with justice in another life respecting its conduct in this.[81]

—Benjamin Franklin

I acknowledge myself a unitarian—Believing that the Father alone, is the supreme God, and that Jesus Christ derived his Being, and all his powers and honors from the Father ... There is not any reasoning which can convince me, contrary to my senses, that three is one, and one three.[82]

—Abigail Adams

The doctrines of Jesus are simple and tend all to the happiness of man, that there is only one God and God is perfect. That God and man are one. That to love God with all your heart, and your neighbor as yourself, is the sum of religion. These are the great points on which I endeavor to reform and live my life.[83]

—Thomas Jefferson

MATTHEW 1:1–17 GIVES us the lineage of the God of Abraham; it is a linear blood and spirit line from Abraham to Jesus, forty-two generations. The Founders believed that this lineage had not been tampered with by ecclesiastical authorities for their selfish ends. This is the source of their understanding of history, and they believed in the linear theological system of Abraham.[84]

The Founders' theology was central to their new country on September 17, 1787. In the Old Testament, David was a poor shepherd who defeated Goliath and was elevated to command the army before he became king. There were fourteen generations from Abraham to David and twenty-eight from David to Jesus[85] as mentioned in Matthew 1:1–17.

Jesus came on the scene as the son of Joseph and Mary. Jesus's ministry centered around love, forgiveness, compassion, and mercy for the poor and downtrodden. He is considered the greatest of the greatest empaths ever. Among the greatest stories and moral lessons in the New Testament are those of Jesus asking a repentant and redeemed thief, murderer, and prostitute to transfer their guilt public and private to him to release their psychological and emotional burdens. In consideration for the transfer of guilt, he offered them forgiveness and the promise of a new redeemed life "on earth as it is in heaven."[86]

The power of forgiveness and new life that flowed from the lineage of Abraham allowed the people Jesus touched to gain psychological freedom and to break the crippling cycle of personal and colonially imposed shame, blame, and guilt. Jesus recognized that guilt could be externally and internally imposed and that once the guilt was removed, rebirth and human liberty became possible. Jesus offered complete mercy and forgiveness— reprieves and pardons—by extending the promise of a new life to the sinners of his day and those who lived outside the laws moral and civil—today's felons. He offered them an opportunity to change their lives and behavior and "to go and sin no more."[87] Jesus drew his moral authority from the lineage of the God of

Abraham with no splitting and differentiating in his system of understanding.

Splitting and Differentiating

Joel Kovel offered in his book *History and Spirit: An Inquiry into the Philosophy of Liberation*[88] profound insight on the question of splitting and differentiating.

> Splitting refers to a kind of "being" in which the Other is not recognized as having any common "being" with the self. By the same kind of reasoning we might say that a society or person which was not split from nature, but rather differentiated (so that the Other was recognized as sharing "being" with the self) would exist more integrally in itself and experience a richer and more benign otherness. The notions of splitting and differentiation pertain to a full state of "being," and are to play a major role in our understanding of spirituality. And indeed splitting is the basis for western civilizations estrangement from nature and attitude of domination toward nature, exemplified in the philosophy of Descartes.[89]

Kovel argued,

> The quintessence of a differentiated spirituality of nature, is that it unites the Spirit power of holiness with an otherness in which every part of the universe is recognized in the self, and every part of the self exists in the universe as a whole.[90]

> The identity between women and nature is an archaic symbolic foundation of society first mediated

through the mysteries of birth and mothering, the association became both reinforced and degraded in the emergence of modernity. The degradation was manifested as a splitting in which women were to accept dumbness and passivity projected into nature, hence, to alienate their own specifically human powers, while men were to arrogate to themselves the function of reason and self-autonomy. Acceptance of the degraded form of identity, and the alienated Otherness this imposes, has played a major role in the domination of women. At the same time, Recognition of the strength inherent to nature-as-Other has provided a launching point for major feminist movements these have reestablished a differentiated spirituality which develops a sense of the interconnectedness of things within the context of contemporary struggles for emancipation and saving the earth it is no accident, then, that women have assumed leadership in the anti-militarist, anti-nuclear, and ecological movements.[91]

Wherever there is domination there is going to be splitting,

Let us say, then, that if spirituality is the passing beyond the self, madness is a kind of coming apart of the self in the process, because of the violent nature of spirit-being and its relation To the self. That's not all spirituality need engage madness. On the other hand, madness can still remain spiritual, but it also can become real emotional illness. This happens if the state of being loses connection to the whole i.e. becomes split, in which case it becomes asocial, uncreative, or frankly destructive.[92]

In *Tragic Soul Life: W.E.B. DuBois and the Moral Crisis Facing American Democracy*, author Terrence L. Johnson shared his thoughts on DuBois and the possibilities of differentiating.

> If we relinquish the fear, however, the future holds unlimited possibilities. Human flourishing will sit as a central concern within the cultivation of democratic principles. Of primary importance might be what DuBois called in a 1944 essay "the right of variation; the richness of a culture that lies in differentiation. In the activities of such a world, men are not compelled to be white in order to be free ... the hope of civilization lies not in exclusion, but in inclusion of all human elements" to create human flourishing. As long as we marginalized the tragic sense of life from public deliberations, we will always imagine a flawed version of freedom and justice in which white supremacy and the strongman ideology reigns supreme. This is not a call to attack white men or censor Anglo-American beliefs or traditions. Instead, what DuBois called "the right of variation" calls for an inclusion of competing ideas in an attempt to give birth to a "truer"—more comprehensive—democracy.[93]

In short, splitting and differentiating is like "speaking with a fork tongue."[94] It separates mind, body, and spirit from everything else when the mind, body, and spirit should function in unity. The idea of splitting is also the equivalent of the government offering the Native Americans a treaty that it does not enforce and allows to drift from its agreed-upon intent.

American history has struggled to overcome this splitting and differentiating no different from the way women have been degraded through time; the idea that all men were created equal did not extend to them or Black people. To despiritualize a society is to engage in splitting and differentiating to the point that words and actions, thoughts and deeds are not believable. Those who achieve a perfect say/do ratio are lights in a world that splits and differentiates. In a room, a mind, a country, or a jail cell engulfed in darkness, one candle, one enlightenment, one illuminated pathway has the power to challenge that darkness.

As a result of this splitting and differentiating, Americans cannot see the religion of the Founders, the finger of God.

This then is the religion of the Founders.

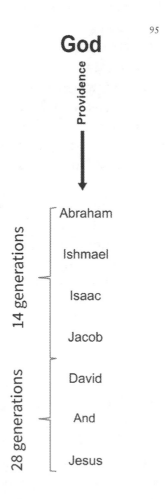

The Founders believed that this ancient religion had been corrupted by ecclesiastical authorities for seventeen hundred and seventy-six years (1776) at the hour of the writing of the Declaration of Independence. From the Declaration of Independence to the writing of the Constitution in 1787, they set out to establish a new country on the basis of this religious system, and their experiment did something fairly remarkable; they extracted the function of the lineage of David *f(lod)* and wrote Article II, Section 2, Clause 1 of our Constitution.

96

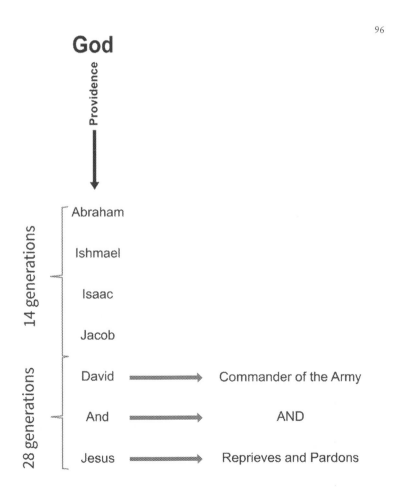

The lineage of Abraham and David was examined, researched, debated, and constructed, and ultimately, the governing function of the lineage was extracted by function from the linear theological system and presented itself in our Constitution as Article II, Section 2, Clause 1. This is the finger of God extracted by function from the linear theological system of Matthew 1:1–17 that combined the character traits of a commander of an army and a granter of love, mercy, and a new life as a repriever pardoner.[97] The Founders extracted the primary function of forty-two generations of theological development and placed the aspirational government function of that development—twenty-eight generations—in a people's constitution. They vested that moral power in a single person we the people would elect.

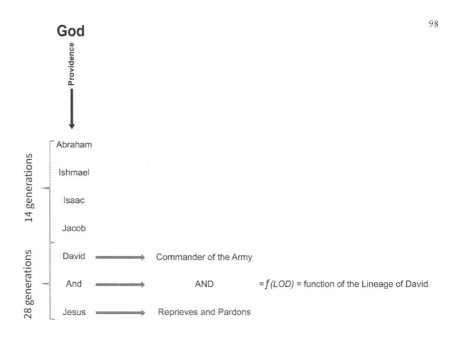

It was placed in our Constitution as a function of the lineage to be protected and available to the people for all time thus, as Madison said, "making a man of pious reflection"[99] and character with the aid of the providence of God, the guiding light and force for America, a "City on a Hill."[100] This is what I believe Adams meant when he said, "Our Constitution was made only for a moral and religious people. It is wholly inadequate to the government of any other."[101] How could informed voters of the future elect someone to the highest office in the land without a fundamental understanding of this primary tenant? The future success of America is not in the Constitution; it is in a moral people who will vote for someone in every generation to function for all in the lineage of David *f(lod)*, which is a function of the only known theological idea in the Constitution. If the people are unaware of their obligation under the lineage of Abraham, *(x)* becomes the unknown Democrat or Republican. Ignorance of the *f(x)* will lead the American people to vote for any old Democrat or Republican out of habit.

The people may also vote wittingly or unwittingly for tyranny. The future success of America is the construction of this wording that honors the two great commandments of Jesus, "Honor thy God with all thy heart, all thy soul, and all thy mind, and a second commandment, like unto it, love thy neighbor as thyself."[102] The Founders made the great commandments the center of the United States government by operation and function for a person in a sect of one.

My recognition of this unique lineage is where my work begins; the linear system is the system of Moses, more specifically the God of Moses, who heard the "cry of the people of Israel and saw their affliction."[103] Generations of Americans have had to ignore this point to justify slavery, racism, sexism, and casteism not in the name of the God of Moses but tragically in the name of Jesus. As a result of this blindness, the finger of God remains invisible to them though it is written in plain sight and available for all to see. America is an incomplete and troubled experiment without this understanding.

My work in the laboratory produced the functional extract of the lineage of David, the key to moving the American experiment forward. As Thomas Paine said, "We have it in our power to begin the world over again!"[104]

At the conclusion of their theological experiment, the architects had to determine the appropriate constitutional constraints on this universal moral power and make it accountable to the people as a function of the theological development of the Abrahamic system and hence a function of the lineage of David, a gift from infinity.

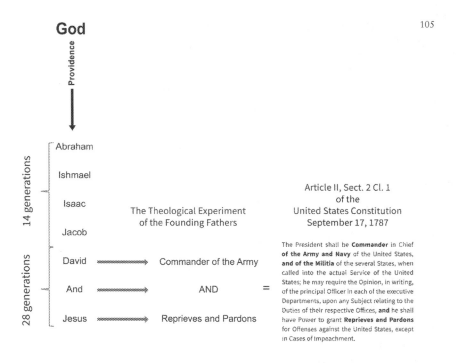

The words *commander of the army* represent the aspirational hopes of a religious people in the Old Testament for a military commander, and the words *reprieves* and *pardons* represent the hopes of a people for a redeemer who forgives and grants mercy and new life on earth. These two concepts are verbs of action with the commandment "the President Shall" leaving the occupant of Article II, Section 2, Clause 1 no choice in the performance of the duty for everyone covered by the Constitution.

These two concepts come together only in the lineage of David extracted by function from the aspirational hopes of an ancient and primitive religious people who believed in the Septuagint and the hopes of a religious people who believed in the return of a great redeemer. "Our Constitution was made only for a moral and religious people. It is wholly inadequate to the government of any other"[106] said Adams, our second president, signer of the Declaration of Independence and member of the First Great Seal Committee.

Madison wrote,

> It is impossible for the man of pious reflection not to perceive in it [the Constitution] a finger of that Almighty hand which has been so frequently and signally extended to our relief in the critical stages of the revolution.[107]

Hamilton said,

> For my part, I sincerely esteem the Constitution, a system which without the finger of God, never could have been suggested and agreed upon by such a diversity of interests.[108]

Charles Thomson, the secretary of the Constitutional Convention, left the convention and spent the next nineteen years translating the Septuagint and the Gospels into English. Jefferson, while not in attendance at the convention, synthesized the four gospels written in Greek, Latin, French, and English into a single extract leaving little room for a contradictory interpretation of their intentions to capture words and spirit.[109]

The leader the Founders were looking for in the future wasn't called Democrat, Republican, liberal, or conservative. In 1787, they were looking for a leader who would be a protector of the people, a reconciler, a granter of mercy and forgiveness, a person who understood love and wanted the best for all people. When properly educated and placed in the Founders' system, the great empath who carried the divine, providential spirit energy in his DNA would look like this, and the American people would be the beneficiary of his love, justice, and mercy.

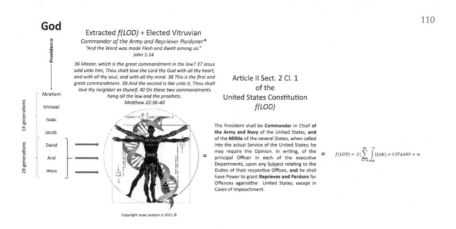

110

Along the great American journey, we ended up with this.

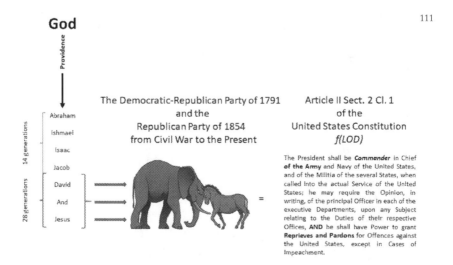

111

In 1785, Madison wrote,

> Whilst we assert for ourselves a freedom to em-
> brace, to profess and observe the religion which
> we believe to be of divine origin, we cannot deny
> equal freedom (1st Amendment 1791) to those
> whose minds have not yet yielded to the evidence
> which has convinced us. If this freedom is abused,
> it is an offense against God, not against man. To
> God, therefore not to man, must an account of it
> be rendered.[112]

Jefferson, Madison's close friend, later called himself "a disciple of the doctrines of Jesus of Nazareth."[113] He declared that
he was not a Calvinist but that he believed he was of "a Sect all
by himself."[114] In an 1822 letter to Waterhouse, Jefferson wrote,

> I rejoice that in the blessed country of free inquiry
> and belief has surrendered its conscience to neither
> Kings nor Priests the genuine dicta of only 1 God
> is reviving and I trust that there is not a young
> man now living in the United States who will not
> die a Unitarian.[115]

Referencing the lineage of the prophets from Matthew 1:1–
17, each prophet was a sect of one. My research suggests that on
September 17, 1787, the Founders began the public religion of the
United States extracted by function from the linear theological
system. They combined the character traits of David and Jesus, a
serpent and a dove who believed in one God, and put them in the
Constitution to perform in our system of checks and balances.

To give the reader some sense of the length of the experiment,
from the Declaration of Independence in 1776 to the Constitutional
Convention in 1787 and then to the Federalist Papers 1787–89
and the Bill of Rights in 1791 to their post-constitutional letters

and correspondence, the experiment in their faith was nearly five decades long. On February 2, 1816, Adams, in a letter to Jefferson, wrote, "We must come to the principles of Jesus, but when will all nations do as they would be done by? Forgive all injuries, and love their enemies as themselves?"[116]

The Discovery

It is essential to walk through the documentation, research, and timeline of our Founders as well as other great scientists of the period and into the future the Founders would not have contemplated. However, I hope this journey will allow you to understand why this discovery is significant to our human liberty system. I did my best to reconstruct what I believe is the original intent of the Founders to protect America during a time they would not live to see. From the Declaration of Independence in 1776 to September 1787, the Founders had eleven years to produce a draft of the Constitution and the language for the function of the lineage of David in the sect of one. Their thinking centered around our God-given liberty and an infinity of language, words, and spirit to govern America that honored the God of creation.

Napoleon Hill wrote, "Thoughts are things,"[117] "and powerful things at that, when mixed with purpose, persistence and a burning desire to translate into substance."[118] I believe the providence of God was with the architects to ensure an eternal future for a country.

The Founders believed that America was "God's American Israel."[119] They felt that government of, for, and by the people would ensure that America would never slip back into tyranny or despotism. Jefferson was clear: "The God who gave us life gave us liberty at the same time."[120] The New Israel was their opportunity for heaven on earth. Modern Israel was not founded until 1948.[121] Those who believed in a mystical return of the redeemer to Israel that had not been founded yet were not of the religion or of the understanding of the architects of this republic.

Given an opportunity to reach its greatest potential, the American experiment is still the most likely place in the world where we can dare to be a free nation under God. A proper understanding of the language of our Constitution provides a corrective action, an antidote if you will, to what has plagued our nation from the beginning.

We also must accept an America for all people. This requires us to understand the foundation of Christian precepts. These precepts are developed from the linear system of Abraham, Ishmael, Isaac, Jacob, David, and Jesus. We must make very specific distinctions as we work through the layers to affirm what I know to be true.

The America our Founders envisioned was one that gave all citizens equal and high-quality standards of living. This new American Israel would respect individuals' rights to choose their religions, their paths, and their spaces without interference as long as they were within the law agreed upon by all the people and observed by God.

4

THE DECLARATION OF INDEPENDENCE, THE CONSTITUTION, AND GOD

JEFFERSON, THE AUTHOR of the Declaration of Independence, and the signatories specifically placed their belief in nature's God. There are five references to God in the Declaration of Independence: the "laws of nature" and of "Nature's God" entitled the United States to independence. Men were "endowed by their Creator with certain unalienable rights." Congress appealed "to the Supreme Judge of the world for the rectitude of our intentions." The signers, "with a firm reliance on the protection of divine Providence," pledged each other their lives, fortunes, and sacred honor.

Eleven years later, in 1787, the governing document of their new nation, the Constitution, seemingly fell silent on the question of God before the Bill of Rights was added in 1791. The Declaration of Independence has been heralded as one of history's most important aspirational ideals that all men were created equal; it was aspirational in that it was a goal to be achieved. My father said it best: "We don't live under the Declaration of Independence [1776]; it has no force of law. We live under the Constitution [1787], for it is the Supreme law of the land."[122]

It is impossible to imagine that the Founders would ignore the role of God in their national governing document, but this is what history has shown. On August 17, 2017, in a Pew survey, Aleksandra Sandstrom wrote, "God or the divine is referenced in every state constitution."[123] The Constitution never explicitly mentions God or the divine, but the same cannot be said of the states' constitutions. In fact, God or the divine is mentioned at least once in each of the fifty state constitutions and nearly two hundred times overall according to a Pew Research Center analysis.

State constitutions in Mass., N.C. have most references to God or the divine

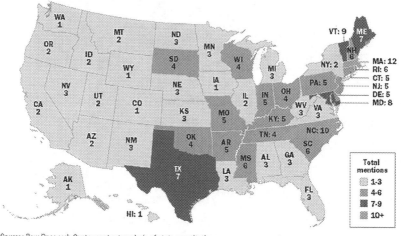

Source: Pew Research Center content analysis of state constitutions.
PEW RESEARCH CENTER

All but four state constitutions—those of Colorado, Iowa, Hawaii, and Washington—use the word *God* at least once. The constitutions in Colorado, Iowa, and Washington refer to a "Supreme Being" or "Supreme Ruler of the Universe," while Hawaii's constitution makes reference to the divine only in its preamble, which states that the people of Hawaii are "grateful for Divine Guidance."

Most state constitutions—thirty-four—refer to God more

than once. Of the 116 times the word appears in state constitutions, eight are in the Massachusetts constitution, and New Hampshire and Vermont constitutions have six references each. Perhaps surprisingly, all three of these states are among the least religious in the country according to a 2016 Pew Research Center analysis.[124]

Nearly all Black Americans believe in God or a higher power regardless of their religious affiliation. But what type of God do they have in mind?

About three-quarters of Black Americans believe in God "as described in the Bible," or if they identify with a non-Christian religion, the holy scripture of that faith according to a recent Pew survey. More than eight in ten say God has the power to control what goes on in the world, and almost seven in ten believe in a God who directly determines all or most of what happens in their lives. Additionally, nearly half of Black Americans believe that God or a higher power talks to them directly according to the survey of 8,660 Black adults conducted November 19, 2019–June 3, 2020.

Almost all Black Americans believe in God or another higher power

% of Black Americans who say they ...

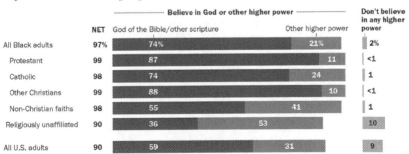

	NET	God of the Bible/other scripture	Other higher power	Don't believe in any higher power
All Black adults	97%	74%	21%	2%
Protestant	99	87	11	<1
Catholic	98	74	24	1
Other Christians	99	88	10	<1
Non-Christian faiths	98	55	41	1
Religiously unaffiliated	90	36	53	10
All U.S. adults	90	59	31	9

Source: Survey conducted Nov. 19, 2019-June 3, 2020, among U.S. adults.
Note: Those who gave unclear responses about the type of God they believe in are included in the NET but not shown. Those who did not answer the questions about belief in God are not shown.
"Faith Among Black Americans"

PEW RESEARCH CENTER

In contrast, overall, Americans are less likely to hold these views. About six in ten adults believe in God as described in the Bible or other holy scripture or that God can control what happens in the world. Fewer than half believe God determines all or most of what happens in their lives or that God talks to them directly.

Eight-in-ten Black adults believe God has power to control what happens in the world

% of Black Americans who say God or a higher power ...

	Has power to control what goes on in world	Judges all people	Determines what happens in their life all/most of the time	Talks to them directly
All Black adults	81%	74%	68%	48%
Protestant	88	82	80	57
Catholic	81	80	65	36
Other Christians	85	76	51	27
Non-Christian faiths	75	70	57	42
Unaffiliated	60	48	39	27
All U.S. adults	62	63	46	30

Source: Survey conducted Nov. 19, 2019-June 3, 2020, among U.S. adults.
"Faith Among Black Americans"

PEW RESEARCH CENTER

When it comes to God's role in the wider world, majorities of Black Americans in all the religious groups analyzed believe that God can and does affect what happens. For example, among Black adults, the view that God has the power to control what goes on in the world is held by 88 percent of Protestants, 81 percent of Catholics, 85 percent of other Christians, 75 percent of non-Christians, and 60 percent of the religiously unaffiliated.

The survey also asked a broad question about belief in God and morality, that is, whether people thought believing in God was necessary "in order to be moral and have good values." More than half of Black Americans said they believed this. As with other questions explored here, Black Protestants (64 percent) were more likely to express this belief than were Black Catholics (44 percent). Overall, Black adults were more likely than adults in the general population (32 percent) to say that a belief in God was necessary for morality.[125]

Black adults more likely than U.S. adults overall to say belief in God is necessary for morality

% of Black Americans who say it is ...

	Necessary to believe in God to be moral	Not necessary
All Black adults	54%	44%
Protestant	64	34
Catholic	44	54
Other Christians	67	30
Non-Christian faiths	37	61
Unaffiliated	28	70
All U.S. adults	32	67

Source: Survey conducted Nov. 19, 2019-June 3, 2020, among U.S. adults.
"Faith Among Black Americans"

PEW RESEARCH CENTER

My research led me to conclude that the Founders planted God's infinite spirit energy through human reliance on providence in the Constitution based on a collective understanding that to build a country with a future, the country would require a possible review or reconstruction based on evolution.

The finger of God is a language construct in the Constitution confirmed by Madison in Federalist Paper 37. It was confirmed by Hamilton, the second of the three authors of the Federalist Papers: "For my part, I sincerely esteem the Constitution, a system which without the Finger of God, never could have been suggested and agreed upon by such a diversity of interests."[126]

The Pew Research Center is partially right and partially wrong. It is right in its confirmation of how they perceive African Americans' "belief in God of the Bible or other holy scripture" but wrong because of its understanding of words and spirit. Madison and Hamilton were at the Constitutional Convention while the Pew Research Center was not, and its researchers failed to recognize that words in the Constitution paint a picture of and contain spirit.

If Pew is wrong on the finger but correct on African Americans, Democrats and Republicans, liberals and conservatives—the historical political categories that White American and White Christians specifically organize themselves politically in since 1791 (Democratic-Republican Party) and Republicans (1854)—are likely wrong as well. Therefore, the responsibility for respiritualizing the nation falls firmly in the hands of Black people, who believe in the power of God to intervene in human affairs as God did in response to the Israelites' captivity in Egypt.

The Founders would give a chosen people and specifically a chosen person all the power they would need four years before the First Amendment was added to authentically function in the ancient religion before congregationalism, denominationalism, and ecclesiastical corruption had occurred, and they had studied over two millennia. The Founders did not place God in the Constitution; they constructed the finger of God as a function of providence in the Constitution. Therefore, the spirit of God is in the Constitution connecting divine providence to the American people and securing their way of life.

Capitalism was the engine that fueled their evolving democratic, love thy neighbor as thy self, social, political, and economic utopia. Commerce, trade, the profit motive, and yes, even slavery were to fuel the utopia, and there was a willingness to pay taxes for their way of life and such a theological system. Make no mistake about it; at its conception, it was a Whites-only system. The signers of the Declaration of Independence, "with a firm reliance on the protection of divine Providence," pledged "each other their lives, fortunes and sacred honor." Today, racism is largely responsible for why our sacred fortunes are no longer pledged to the theological system.

Tax schemes, offshore shelters, foreign investments, and other methods are employed by individuals and corporations to avoid paying taxes to the architects' utopia. The idea of building generational wealth has undermined the Protestant work ethic, and the nation is giving birth to a generation with wealth-entitlement behavior while it complains of a welfare state for the least of these.

The Founders confirmed God's finger in the Constitution as a function of a lineage, a function that is extracted, and by virtue of which it was placed in a document on September 17, 1787; biblical precepts became operational for all in the Constitution.

We indeed have evolved, and the problems of our day certainly require our leadership to rely on the foresight of the Founders to bring forth the truth of our Constitution to reconstruct the country for ensured longevity. The finger of God was written into the Constitution as an extract from the lineage of David, a subset of the lineage of Abraham. This functional extract of the lineage of David, the *f(lod)*, the power of the divine on earth behind the presidency, is unlike anything we have ever seen, experienced, or understood. Thus, the president is the steward of the providence of God for the nation. The functional extract confirms God in the Constitution and a country that is to function under the law of God with democratic constraints placed on the institution of the presidency by the people.

Our president must take an oath to govern by this sovereign power as a public duty. He must honor, respect, and strengthen the rule of law and advocate for the inclusion of the "least of these,"[127] the poor, the despised, and the rejected as their champion, their David, in a world of monumental Goliaths. Those who accept the office of president strip off their personal religion and agree to govern the country under the public religion as the law develops. The essence of a public religion is God. The two great commandments then are the foundation of the public religion: Honor God with all your heart, mind, and soul, and love your neighbor as yourself. These two great commandments ensure that personal gain, agendas, and goals are set aside to ensure a nation of people who have their God-given freedoms and the hope of renewing their lives given a need to be forgiven so they can pay their debts and receive forgiveness to start anew. The Founders surely did not know how the wording would become an antidote in the future; they did not have the foresight to anticipate a time when renewal, rebirth, and reconstruction would stabilize our nation.

It is nearly impossible to reconcile the diametrically opposed concepts of a tough army commander and a lover of humanity, creation, justice, mercy, forgiveness, and hope. But "the truth is found neither in the thesis nor the antithesis, but in the emergent synthesis which reconciles the two," said Hegel.[128] In this case, forty-two generations of moral and ethical precepts have been reduced to eight words—commander of the army and reprieves and pardons—as the central government function. This is the character trait the architects envisioned for our nation's leader; they wanted an individual who would function in the lineage of David for everyone.

Before its combination into a single idea, the language of the finger of God was part of the trail of evidence left by the Founders that the theological experiment was completed before the Constitutional Convention. The future of the United States rests entirely on the ability of the American people to convert two concepts into a single idea. It is not possible to complete such an experiment without research and study. The Fathers couldn't call the Constitutional Convention until the theological experiment was complete. Such language Hamilton suggested "never could have been suggested and agreed upon by such a diversity of interests."[129] Those interests include political as well as theological interests today.

5

IN THE BEGINNING

UPON THEIR ARRIVAL in a new land, the first set-tlers faced a complex task—forming a new world. Can you imagine all they had to take into consideration in their attempts to create a standard for all? Can you imagine the perspective of each individual's take on religion, an infinite God, and the infinite correctness of their individual belief systems over all others and how it would for a time determine if one should live or die? It would determine if the individual would be cast out of the community and or be deemed fit to participate in the evolving, unstructured systems of the land. The opportunity of constructing a government, a rule, a system of law that would allow individuals to read, interpret, and implement how rules were to be followed was vast. In addition to their divisions based on religious beliefs, the thirteen colonies considered themselves separate from the whole; the colonies and religious views would evolve into individual states.

Thirteen of Britain's seventeen mainland North American colonies had won independence having united in the face of a common threat to their political institutions, traditions, and liberties. They had created a joint military command, the Continental Army, and a sort of treaty organization, the United States of America, under the Articles of Confederation. These American states was sovereign having agreed to delegate defense, foreign trade, and foreign policy duties only to their shared body, Congress, which had fled from place to place during the conflict. Nobody really knew what this United States was or what it should become or even if it should continue to exist.

The citizens of these new states didn't think of themselves as Americans except in the sense that French, German, and Spanish people might have considered themselves Europeans. If asked what country they were from, the soldiers who occupied Yorktown would have said Massachusetts, Virginia, Pennsylvania, or South Carolina. For years to come, newspaper editors in the former colonies would refer to the new collective not as a nation but as a league or as the American states or as a confederated America being unsure of what it was or how long it might last.[130]

On June 26, 1854, the difficulty of organizing political and religious ideas played out in the famous and notorious caning incident between Senator Charles Sumner of Massachusetts and South Carolina Congressman Andrew Butler. Butler and the South Carolinians attacked the preamble of the Declaration of Independence contending that Jefferson's argument that all men were created equal was "a self-evident lie" and what it really meant was that each state was created equal and so that *ipso facto,* the words actually directed Americans to respect slavery.[131]

The Founders knew that the only way to ensure success of this new endeavor, the American experiment, would require a unifying understanding of what was true among the various groups after their practiced faith by family, tradition, region, and learning had been stripped away. In the case of our nation, the unifying force under intense scrutiny was God, who had unequivocally allowed everything that had breath and in our case humanity to be born free. Freedom was of utmost importance for a people seeking to build a world in which they were free to think, create, grow, and become.

In the American experiment, the settlers' first lesson was to understand that order among individuals did not occur naturally.

To be united, individuals had to find what created bonds. The first tests failed. Each individual attempting to hold the group accountable based on his beliefs created factions and silos and ultimately resulted in excommunication, exile, or death for some who did not accept the religion of the leader of the moment.

It became evident to the settlers that for the American experiment to continue, they had to create a document that ensured that the experiment would be developed. The Founders would have to complete the work of arguing, discussing, researching, analyzing, and revealing what it would take to establish the laws of the new nation.

6

A SECT OF ONE

THE FOUNDERS, SPECIFICALLY Franklin, Adams, Jefferson, Madison, and Hamilton, were all believers in the sect of one. They were pure deists. Ralph Waldo Emerson, the nineteenth-century transcendentalist, poet, philosopher, and essayist, noted that in writing the Constitution, the Fathers "saw God face-to-face; we only see him second hand."[132]

The Founders were forward looking in moving their faith into the dreams of creating a new nation; they were true believers in the sense of Hebrews 11:1: "Now faith is the substance of things hoped for, the evidence of things not seen."[133] The fact that their faith was based on evidence is reassuring. However, facts and evidence for scientists are tested in a lab using a process of trial and error.

Freedom was the burning desire that allowed them to seek the providence of God and to carry forward the writing of the Constitution to protect the people. Their intuition enabled them to set in motion a more perfect union. In seeking freedom from the British king, they had to evaluate their actions against the slaves their ancestors had kidnapped, held in bondage, and forced to build a nation and foster an economy that they reaped the benefits of and at the same time become outraged at a king who levied taxes on their property and prosperity.

The determination to free themselves from such unfair

colonization, which had made them slavish to an unjust king, enraged the settlers and ultimately encouraged their rebellion against the king. But even with this narrative that we have been taught, Madison wrote that the finger of God was "SIGNALLY responsible for the rebellion."[134] He didn't reference the Boston Tea Party, taxes, or the business interests of the colonies because more than a political bond had been broken; a spiritual bond had been broken, and it was "signally responsible for the rebellion." There was great interest among the architects in keeping this spiritual bond broken.

It was only just that the providence of God, which protected them on their journey to the new land, was the same providence that allowed them to suffer the shame, blame, and guilt of profiting from slaves. When fighting for their own freedom, how could they not set their brothers of a different color free? These are the issues the Founders had to discuss, debate, and stand for or against at the birth of a new nation. Each had to seek God for himself and in so doing answer questions reflective of God while moving the country forward.

The Council of Nicaea, which defined Jesus's nature in 325, predated the Declaration of Independence, the Constitution, and American slavery by centuries. Slavery was a fact in the development of every civilization, and the Founders were aware of that. Upon landing in a new world, the settlers disembarked as free men, indentured servants, or chattel slaves. How then could a country fighting to be free contradict itself by asking the God they served to deliver them from a tyrant when they themselves had enslaved fellow members of the human family?

The Founders produced a constitution that honored their fundamental, scientific, and fact-based religious beliefs and operationalized it for posterity while upholding the fundamental tenets of a democratic, representative government. The Founders' experiment in their faith and self-government is counted among the greatest achievements in history. They believed in humanity's capacity to solve all human problems with the providence of God that operates in human affairs through the people. For the Founders, God's providence was not a second or amendable afterthought; providence was the hand that they "frequently signally relied upon in the critical stages of the revolution."[135]

The Founders went to work seeking the answers to a language construction they believed to be from and of God. They set out to build one of Abraham's many nations in the new world, and that led them to understand that the providence of God saved them on the journey and would ultimately lead them to create a new world. In the seed of their journey was planted the understanding of nature's God being with all humanity. Each individual would be birthed into the world free, and each would have to rebel against anything that threatened that freedom. Ultimately, each individual must seek God for himself or herself. The private religions of the individuals, however, would have to rest at their homes while they took the public thread of one God forward to unite a nation.

The seed would bud into an understanding that freedom grew from a very natural and pure existence of being human. How then could they create a country in which their natural gifts could survive by the settlers' private beliefs? How could they all honor their vision of God while being dedicated to the new world they hoped to build?

This balance between their dreams and their religion sparked the embers of the American experiment. It is this foundation that was laid to build the city on the hill[136] that John Winthrop envisioned in 1630, eleven years after slavery had begun in this new world.

7

The Finger of God

THE FOUNDERS AND SLAVERY

I STATED EARLIER THAT there was a continuous black line before the Constitutional Convention, and once the convention concluded, the Constitution included the three-fifths of a person clause for the slave and the debate over small versus large states as well as the compromises the architects had to endure to form a government. I lean closer to Lincoln's understanding of the Founders' slave dilemma.

> In the first place, I insist that the fathers did not make this nation half slave and half free or part slave and part free. I insist they found the institution of slavery existing here. They did not make it so, but they left it so, because they knew of no way to get rid of it at the time.[137]

Not a single architect was alive when slavery began in 1619, more than a century and a half before the Declaration of Independence. The God who led the children of Israel out of Egypt to the Promised Land and provided them the law was the same God who had disdain for American slavery; he is consistent. The Founders placed the finger of God—the God of Abraham, Moses, David, and Jesus—in the Constitution, and as Moses did, we the people can use it to free ourselves from any form of modern slavery.

We will unpack the language of Adams, Franklin, Hamilton, Jefferson, and Madison and explore how they established a Constitution that considered all thoughts, actions, and ideas known and unknown to man. While all did not sign the Constitution, each contributed evidence to their argument for a country that would be uniquely positioned by its governance to honor God and personal freedoms for religion on the basis of equality.

The Founders had a very different understanding of the law; they understood that the whole law came from God and was not to be used for partisan advantage. They knew that the country's values would break down and force a major reevaluation of all institutions, so they prepared the nation for this future by keeping hidden the key for the corrective. The Founders understood human nature and the corruptibility of power.

8

THE GREAT SEAL

PROVERBS 22:28 READS, "Remove not the ancient land-marks, which thy fathers have set."[138] Historic landmarks and symbols are important to human existence. The Great Seals are no less so for national existence.

The First Great Seal Committee included Franklin, Adams, and Jefferson. They were appointed on July 4, 1776, immediately after the Declaration of Independence was signed. There was no space between that and their appointment to this committee; the ink had not dried on their signatures to the Declaration of Independence. They were committed to ensuring that the Great Seal of the United States, the seal of a nation, reflected their values, morals, and beliefs.

They commissioned Pierre Eugene du Simitiere as they had little knowledge of heraldry; du Simitiere could also contribute his American insight as he founded the first history museum in the United States and had experience with the heraldry process as he created the Delaware and New Jersey state seals. This team collaborated on the seal between July 4 and August 13, 1776, and they contributed their perspectives on what the seal should reflect.

Franklin's idea for the Seal was,

> Moses standing on the shore and extending his
> hand over the sea thereby causing the same to

overwhelm Pharaoh who is sitting in an open Chariot, a crown on his head and a sword in his hand. Rays from a pillar of fire in the clouds reaching to Moses, to express that "he acts"[139] by Command of the Deity.

His suggested motto was, "Rebellion to tyrants is obedience to God."[140]

It is possible that they did not want him to draw it or that he had his own vision of what the Seal should encompass. It was Benson J. Lossing in 1856 who created the actual vision articulated by Franklin, and even his drawing omitted the "rays from a pillar of fire in the clouds reaching to Moses"[141] Franklin had specified. Here is Benson Lossing in 1856 giving Franklin's idea artistic content absent the "rays of fire" that were included in Franklin's conception even though du Simitiere in 1776 failed to even consider Franklin's, Adams's, and Jefferson's thoughts.

142

Jefferson's recommendation was that the Seal show

> the children of Israel in the wilderness, led by a
> cloud by day and a pillar of fire by night. While
> Jefferson and Adams were serving their country
> abroad during the Constitutional Convention,
> Jefferson's vision of the Seal contained an unmis-
> takable "infinity symbol" that circled his vision of
> "the children of Israel in the wilderness."[143]

For the reverse side of Jefferson's vision of the Great Seal,
he suggested Hengist and Horsa, the two brothers who were
legendary leaders of the first Anglo-Saxon settlers of Britain.[144]

Finally, Adams described the Seal as

> the painting known as the "Judgement of
> Hercules,"[145] where the young Hercules must
> choose to travel either on the flowery path of
> self-indulgence or ascend the rugged, uphill way
> of duty to others and honor to himself.[146]

Here is an image created of the original intent of Adams for the Seal.

All three men contributed their visions of God in the establishment of the nation. God, character, law, and choices associated with God-given and -ordained human liberty seem to be the overriding themes in their renditions. The providence of God was a united understanding among the committee members and all signers of the Declaration with a conviction to which they all attested.

Pierre du Simitiere was meticulous in his work. He cut out clippings, collected historical documents, and journaled intelligence and all things related to the journey of this new land. According to Adams in a letter to his wife,[147] du Simitiere had a list of every speculation and pamphlet concerning independence and thus had a great understanding of the history and the process of building the country, and he collected information on forms of government.

Adams, however, questioned his ability to capture the spirit of the Seal because the one thing du Simitiere did not have was hands-on experience of the journey; therefore, his research outweighed his experience and his understanding of the struggle. In a letter to his wife, Adams described du Simitiere as a "very curious man."[148] With all of his knowledge and understanding, du Simitiere did not sketch or create the well-expressed visuals articulated by Franklin, Adams, or Jefferson. Here is du Simitiere's vision.

149

Altogether, there were du Simitiere's sketch and three versions of the Seal before the final and fourth Seal was completed and accepted as the Great Seal of the United States. Most of what the first Seal Committee proposed was rejected; all that was retained was the Latin *E Pluribus Unum* motto. While the final design of the fourth committee incorporated elements of the three previous committees, in just six years (1776–1782), it became clear that the idea of God's providence was less pronounced in the final version than in the version offered by Adams, Franklin, and Jefferson in the first Seal Committee of 1776. Below is an image of the fourth and final seal known as the Thomson Seal.

150

Eleven years after the Declaration of Independence spoke of a Creator and the Jefferson Seal carried an infinity symbol at the bottom with "Rebellion to Tyrants is Obedience to God," Franklin in his opening prayer of the Constitutional Convention observed the drift away from the providence of God and reminded the delegates of their amnesia.

In the beginning of the contest with Great Britain, when we were sensible of danger, we had daily prayer in this room for Divine Protection. Our prayers, Sir, were heard and they were graciously answered. All of us who were engaged in the struggle must have observed frequent instances of a superintending providence in our favor. To that kind providence we owe this happy opportunity of consulting in peace on the means of establishing our future national felicity. And have we now forgotten that powerful friend? Or do we imagine that we no longer need His assistance?[151]

In a letter to his daughter Sarah in 1784, Franklin wrote,

I wish the Bald Eagle had not been chosen as the representative of our country; he is a bird of bad character; that does not get his living honestly like those among men who live by sharping and robbing, he is generally poor, and often very lousy. The turkey is a much more respectable bird.[152]

While the Seal changed in representing the Founders' vision of the Seal, they never changed their view of the God of history. Those involved in the First Great Seal Committee carried their point of view through the signing of the Declaration of Independence, the signing of the Constitution, the discussions they continued in letters to each other, and throughout their lives. The understanding of their consistency creates a full story of the Great Seal.

Theologically, there seems to be three phases that the First Great Seal Committee anticipated for their new nation—Franklin's Seal (freedom from Egypt and Pharaonic leadership, the crown), Jefferson's Seal (the wilderness experience), and Adams's Seal (the character of the nation). I believe we have clearly entered the phase of our nation's enduring character, and it charts the perfect course away from the idea of empire and in the direction of God-ordained human rights. The study of the seals is fascinating and is a compelling incentive to participate in America's future.

Evolution of the Great Seals

153

The seal was meant to establish a landmark and remind the nation and most important the future of the Founders' original intent and how we arrived in this place or for that matter any place in history. It was the equivalent of the Founders erecting a statue to the future. Just as a generation of Americans carved Mount Rushmore, Confederate sympathizers placed statues, and still others erect statues and memorials in every corner of our nation, markers have been erected to men and women throughout history. The First Great Seal was the Founders' marker, their original intent.

The evolution of the seal is evidence of the evolution of the nation away from the original intent of the Founders, God's providence, and the abandonment of the human liberty experiment. Today, the Great Seal of the United States and the Great Seal of the President do not reflect the Great Seal offered by Jefferson, Adams, and Franklin at the signing of the Declaration of Independence.

The Founders' experiment in their faith and self-government is counted among the greatest achievements in history. The Founders believed in humanity's capacity to solve all human problems with the providence of God operating in human affairs through the people.

Charles Thomson's Seal that incorporated design elements of all four Great Seal Committees is clear—After six years (1776–1782), God's providence took a back seat to a new nationalism.

I believe that human nature and polemical and partisan interests were understood by the Great Seal Committee as something that man might not be able to reconcile. The corrective for this understanding was the Founders' hiding the finger in the document for those of pious reflection. Their effort was ingenious; they could not determine when it would be discovered, but I believe they understood that the discovery would be a revolution of values of extraordinary and incalculable proportions.

For the Founders, God's providence was not a second or amendable afterthought. His was the hand that they "frequently signally relied upon in the critical stages of the revolution."[154] From the Great Seal Committee to the Constitution, the Founders worked under a unified understanding and agreement that the finger of God would allow the providence of God to be the unifying force of the new country for all time.

9

THE FOUNDING FATHERS

FRANKLIN'S JUNE 28, 1787, opening speech at the Constitutional Convention was a classic.

> I have lived, Sir, a long time and the longer I live, the more convincing proofs I see of this truth … that God governs in the affairs of men. And if a sparrow cannot fall to the ground without his notice, is it probable that an empire can rise without his aid? We have been assured, Sir, in the sacred writings that "except the Lord build they labor in vain that build it." I firmly believe this; and I also believe without his concurring aid we shall succeed in this political building no better than the Builders of Babel: we shall be divided by our little partial local interests; our projects will be confounded, and we ourselves shall become a reproach and a bye word down to future age. And what's worse, mankind may hereafter accept this unfortunate instance, the despair of establishing governments by human wisdom and leaving it to chance, war and conquest.[155]

Once his speech was complete, Franklin made the request

that each session should start with prayer led by clergy. Clearly, Franklin was convinced that nothing could be done by or for humanity without first giving consideration to the providence of God in all human affairs. His great articulation of this fact would indicate that God was his moral compass. However, Franklin did not view slavery in a humane manner; he owned slaves from 1735 until 1781.[156] He advertised his slaves in his newspaper, the *Pennsylvania Gazette*, at the same time he published Quakers' antislavery ads. Franklin viewed humanity based on whether he believed a race of people could be taught.

His friend Samuel Johnson took him to visit one of Dr. Bray's schools for Blacks in 1758, and in 1759, he met Anthony Benezet, who started a school in Philadelphia for Black students. Franklin wrote that African shortcomings and ignorance were not inherent but were due to slavery, negative environments, and a lack of education. He also wrote that he saw no difference in the ability of Black and White children to learn. Benjamin Franklin's litmus test for humanity was to measure intelligence based on one's natural ability to learn. After being introduced to proof that African children could learn, Franklin's initial hypothesis was proven incorrect.

In 1787, he became the president of the Philadelphia Society for the Relief of Negroes Unlawfully Held in Bondage. Addressing the public on November 9, 1789, in Philadelphia, he said, "Slavery is such an atrocious debasement of human nature, that its very extirpation, if not performed with solicitous care, may sometimes open a source of serious evils."[157] With new understanding, Franklin considered the slave to be equal as men being protected by the providence of God.

Adams's response to two abolitionists on January 24, 1801, gives us an indication of his opinion and disposition on slavery. As president at the time, he advised that he had never owned a slave and did not find slavery agreeable. In his writings, he suggested that slavery was declining. However, according to the census of 1800, the number of slaves had grown to almost 900,000.

Adams took the position that slavery should be a winding-down proposition and stated that it had started dissipating on January 8, 1801, when nothing was further from the truth. Adams also compared the White people of Virginia to the slaves and indicated that they were equally if not more oppressed than slaves were.

His writings allow us to see that slavery was a topic of great interest and that he was keenly aware of the delicate balance required to address the issue from a place of humanity; it was a concern requiring dedication to solve with a proper method agreeable to those in bondage as well as all who relied on and profited from their slaves' labors. If slaves had voices and votes at the Constitutional Convention, I am sure they would have been agreeable to ending it immediately.

For Jefferson, race was a far more complicated subject, and his attitude and spirit was far more explosive, intellectually racist, and nasty.

> The first difference which strikes us is that of colour. Whether the black of the negro resides in a reticular membrane between the skin and scarf-skin, or in the scarf-skin itself; whether it proceeds from the colour of the blood, the colour of the bile, or from that of some other section, the difference is fixed in nature, and is as real as if its seat and cause were better known to us. And is this difference of no importance? Is it not the foundation of a greater or less share of beauty in the two races? Are not the fine mixtures of red and white the expressions of every passion by greater or less suffusions of colour in the one, preferable to that eternal monotony, which reigns in the countenances, that immoveable veil of black which covers all the emotions of the other race? Add to these, flowing hair, a more elegant

symmetry of form, their own judgment in favour of the whites, declared by their preference of them, as uniformly as is the preference of the Oranootan for the black women over those of his own species. The circumstances of superior beauty, is thought worthy attention in the propagation of our horses, dogs, and other domestic animals; why not in that of man?

Besides those of colour, figure, and hair, there are other physical distinctions proving a difference of race. They have less hair on the face and body. They secrete less by the kidneys, and more by the glands of the skin, which gives them a very strong and disagreeable odour. This greater degree of transpiration renders them more tolerant of heat, and less so of cold than the whites. Perhaps too a difference of structure in the pulmonary appa- ratus, which a late ingenious experimentalist has discovered to be the principal regulator of animal heat, may have disabled them from extricating, the act of inspiration, so much of that fluid from the outer air, or obliged them in expiration, to part with more of it. They seem to require less sleep. A black after hard labour through the day, will be induced by the slightest amusements to sit up till midnight, or later, though knowing he must be out with the first dawn of the morning. They are at least as brave, and more adventure- some. But this may perhaps proceed from a want of forethought, which prevents their seeing a dan- ger till it be present. When present, they do not go through it with more coolness or steadiness than the whites. They are more ardent after their female: but love seems with them to be more an eager desire, than a tender delicate mixture of sentiment and sensation. Their griefs are transient. Those numberless afflictions, which render it doubtful whether heaven has given life to us in mercy or in wrath, are less felt, and sooner forgotten with them. In general their existence appears to participate more of sensation than reflection. To this must be ascribed their disposition to sleep when abstracted from their diversions, and unemployed in labour. An animal whose body is at rest, and who does not reflect, must be disposed to sleep of course. Comparing them by their faculties of memory, reason, and imagination, it appears to me that in memory they are equal to the whites; in reason much inferior, as I think one could scarcely be found capable of tracing and comprehending the investigations of Euclid; and that in imagination they are dull, tasteless, and anomalous.

It would be unfair to follow them to Africa for this investigation. We will consider them here, on the same stage with the whites, and where the facts are not apocryphal on which a judgment is to be formed. It will be right to make great allowances for the difference of condition, of education, of conversation, of the sphere in which they move. Many millions of them have been brought to, and born in America. Most of them indeed have been confined to tillage, to their own homes, and their own society: yet many have been so situated, that they might have availed themselves to the conversation of their masters; many have been brought up to the handicraft arts, and from that circumstance have always been associated with the whites. Some have been liberally educated, and

all have lived in countries where the arts and sci-
ences are cultivated to a considerable degree, and
have before their eyes samples of the best works
from abroad. The Indians, with no advantages of
this kind, will often carve figures on their pipes
not destitute of design and merit. They will crayon
out an animal, a plant, or a country, so as to prove
the existence of a germ in their minds which only
wants cultivation.

They astonish you with strokes of the most sublime oratory; such as prove their reason and sentiment strong, their imagination glowing and elevated. But never yet could I find that a black
had uttered a thought above the level of plain
narration; never saw even an elementary trait of
painting or sculpture. In music they are more generally gifted than the whites with accurate ears for
tune and time, and they have been found capable
of imagining a small catch. Whether they will
equal to the composition of a more extensive run
of melody, or of complicated harmony, is yet to
be proved. Misery is often the parent of the most
affecting touches in poetry. Among the blacks is
misery enough, God knows, but no poetry. Love
is the peculiar oestrum of the poet. Their love is
ardent, but it kindles the senses only, not the imagination. Religion indeed has produced a Phyllis
Wheatley; but it could not produce a poet. The
compositions published under her name are below
the dignity of criticism.[158]

Countee Cullen, John Coltrane, Thelonious Monk, Etta
James, Billie Holiday, Dorothy West, James Baldwin, Stevie
Wonder, Ray Charles, Duke Ellington, Qunicy Jones, Cab

Calloway, the Nicholas Brothers, the Temptations, Amanda Gorman, Maya Angelou, Gwendolyn Brooks, Sarah Vaughan, Billie Holiday, Toni Morrison, Nikki Giovanni, and Langston Hughes would read Jefferson the proverbial riot act for his language, attitude, disposition, and spirit regarding Black people. Jefferson all but said, "Black lives don't matter." Today, he would definitely be asked to resign from any public or private boards he served.

It is well known that he created children with Sally Hemmings while denigrating her race. He was a cracked vessel moved by the providential spirit to participate in the construction of divine words and spirit, and he clearly understood the infinity language hidden in our Constitution. He was the perfect example of the fact that we all can fall short of the grace of God but even in our faults be used by God to free people. Not one of us should ever be dismissed because of our shortcomings or the errors of our ways.

Franklin was open to the idea of improving the Negro with education. Adams was shifty and undecided and thought certain working-class White people were worse off than Black slaves. Jefferson, a philosophical racist, justified racial behavior and attitudes toward Blacks on a deeply spiritual and intellectual level. On the question of race then, the members of the Great Seal committee were fallible.

Hamilton, Madison, and John Jay authored the Federalist Papers, which originally appeared anonymously in New York newspapers in 1787 and 1788 under the pen name Publius. The Federalist Papers confirm the presence of the finger of the almighty hand.[159] The Federalist Papers were a series of eighty-five essays urging the citizens of New York to ratify the new Constitution. They confirmed that the finger of God, God's providence, was in the Constitution before the Establishment Clause and the Bill of Rights (1791).

As the only member of the First Great Seal Committee in attendance, Franklin, with the aid of Madison, was responsible for ensuring the language was there. Hamilton tinkered with the language in Federalist Paper 74, and he too was at the Convention for he esteemed the Constitution because of the finger of God and the system it represented.[160] The finger of God was the finger of the God of Moses, who was entrusted with the Ten Commandments.

The experiment and my discovery need Jefferson. Jefferson completed *The Life and Morals of Jesus of Nazareth Extracted Textually from the Gospels in Greek, Latin, French, and English* in 1819[161] with a previously lost and unavailable version from 1804. Jefferson was seeking to understand the evidence-based gospel of Jesus because the Bible contained the logos of spirit energy and infinity in English, and the leader of the government the Founders envisioned would be the product of the logos. I understand this very well. I discovered the logos in 2013, and I have been unable to get it out of my mind. I have concluded that I will not be able to fully research its deeper meaning in my life.

10

THE LORD'S PRAYER

AMONG THE FOUR biographers of the life of Jesus of Nazareth, only two offer an account of the Lord's Prayer. Matthew 6:9–13 reads,

> After this manner therefore pray ye: **Our Father** which art in heaven, Hallowed be thy name. Thy kingdom come, thy will be done in earth, as *it is* in heaven. Give us this day our daily bread. And forgive us our debts, as we forgive our debtors. And lead us not into temptation but deliver us from evil: For thine is the kingdom, and the power, and the glory, forever. Amen.[162]

And of the two, only Luke's gospel offers context; 11:1–4 reads,

> And it came to pass, that, as he was praying in a certain place, when he ceased, one of his disciples said unto him, Lord, teach us to pray, as John also taught his disciples. And he said unto them, when ye pray, say, **Our Father** which art in heaven, Hallowed be thy name. Thy kingdom comes. Thy will be done, as in heaven, so in earth. Give us day

by day our daily bread. And forgive us our sins;
for we also forgive every one that is indebted to
us. And lead us not into temptation; but deliver
us from evil.[163]

In Luke, Jesus was praying in a "certain place." When he finished, "he ceased." One of his disciples (there were twelve) asked
him to teach them to pray "as John also taught his disciples." The
most notable distinction between Matthew's and Luke's accounts
is that Matthew recorded that Jesus said and prioritized the "forgiveness of debts and debtors" while Luke's account recalled the
inclusion of "sins and debtors." This is either a huge oversight by
Matthew in that he excluded sins or a huge liberty taken by Luke
in that he included sins. Nevertheless, sin, public and private, was
central to the ministry of Jesus of Nazareth.

But Luke also says, "One of his disciples said to him, Lord,
teach us to pray, as John also taught his disciples." Two of the
biographers, Mark and John, offer no account of the instruction
or the prayer in their gospels; certainly they should have been
included in the "teach us." Again, the account is recorded by two
of the twelve who represented "us."

And even more controversial is the fact that Jesus had the
opportunity to include the Trinity in both accounts of the Lord's
Prayer but did not. "Our Father which art in heaven" does not
read "Our Father, Son, and Holy Spirit or Holy Ghost"; it simply
states, "Our Father," and it comes directly from Jesus's mouth
and not the mouths of future ecclesiastical leadership, who never
met Jesus or lived during his life and times through their dicta
or dogma established by the church. The church in the United
States was protected by the First Amendment in 1791, but the
theology of the Founding Fathers was written in the Constitution
in 1787, the sect of one.

Eighteen centuries later, the architects, in discipleship of
Jesus of Nazareth and primitive first-century Christianity,
looked closely at these two accounts and arrived at different

interpretations of the instruction that Jesus of Nazareth gave to his disciples and with careful thought of *words* and *spirit* offered their personal accounts of the instruction.

Benjamin Franklin

Among the architects, Franklin was the most secular. Franklin, a theist, consistently thought of his religious views in relationship with the general teachings of the life and ministry of Jesus of Nazareth. He believed in providence, the power of prayer, and the final reward. Franklin's interpretation of the Lord's Prayer shows a firm belief in a personal, providential God who is the ground of the moral law and who cares for human beings.

1. Heavenly Father,
2. May all revere thee,
3. And become thy dutiful Children and faithful Subjects.
4. May thy Laws be obeyed on Earth as perfectly as they are in Heaven.
5. Provide for us this day as thou hast hitherto daily done.
6. Forgive us our trespasses and enable us likewise to forgive those that offend us.
7. Keep us out of Temptation and deliver us from Evil.[164]

Charles Thomson

Charles Thomson was the principal and final designer of the Great Seal. He is important to the understanding of the dialogue and concerns that took place during the period when there was no president, only a president of Congress. Thomson was highly esteemed as his job took on the role of the current Department of State, the Secretary of the Senate, and the Clerk of the House of Representatives.

Thomson was so highly respected that the phrase "It's as

true as if Charles Thomson's name were on it," came about. He was considered an authority on the ideas and ideals of America.

After he retired, Thomson spent nearly twenty years comparing the exact words of the evangelists and concluded that they were unified in the understanding of the mission of Jesus and what discipleship meant.

In a letter to Jefferson in 1785, Thomson wrote,

> It grieves me to the soul that there should be such just grounds for your apprehensions respecting the irritation that will be produced in the Southern States by what you have said of slavery. However, I would not have you discouraged. This is a cancer we must get rid of. It is a blot on our character that must be wiped out. If it cannot be done by religion, reason, and philosophy, confident I am that it will be one day by blood.[165]

Here are Thomson's thoughts on harmonization of the Lord's Prayer from *A Synopsis of the Four Evangelists.*

> In this manner, therefore we pray, "Our Father, who art in the heavens! Hallowed be thy name! Thy reign come! Thy will be done on the earth as it is in heaven! Give us to-day our bread-that for subsistence; and forgive us our debts, as we do forgive our debtors. And bring us not to a trial; but deliver us from that which is evil." For, if ye forgive men their offences, your heavenly Father will forgive your offences, neither will your Father forgive your offenses.[166]

Thomas Jefferson

In *The Life and Morals of Jesus of Nazareth, Extracted Textually in the Greek, Latin, French, and English*, Thomas Jefferson[167] offered a version of the Lord's Prayer very different from that in the KJV. Jefferson was not opposed to religion or Christianity, but he was opposed to the corrupting factors of both religion and Christianity. He was a strong believer in a theistic idea of God who governs all things with the aid of providence. Jefferson's version of the Lord's Prayer evidences that belief.

> Our Father which art in heaven; Hallowed be thy name. Thy kingdom come. **Thy will be done in earth, as it is in heaven.** Give us this day our daily bread. **And forgive us our debts, as we forgive our debtors.** And lead us not into temptation; but deliver us from evil: For thine is the kingdom, and the power, and the glory, for ever, Amen.[168]

The Founding Fathers were meticulous in their theological work; they looked, studied, and dissected the gospels for a more accurate and authentic interpretation of the scripture from the earliest English translation including the KJV that directly challenged the orthodoxy of evangelical and conservative literalist interpretation because the idea of a broad inclusive interpretation mattered to the new American Israel. Words and spirit mattered at the nation's founding, and upon my release from prison, I requested a meeting at the Smithsonian Institution with its historians and curators so that I could continue my study of words and spirit in the original Jefferson extracts.

Ben Franklin wrote,

> We have gone back to ancient history for models
> of government and examined the different forms
> of those Republics which, having been formed
> with the seeds of their own dissolution, now no
> longer exist. And we have viewed modern states all
> round Europe but find none of their Constitutions
> suitable to our circumstances.[169]

After great reflection, the people of this new land expressed
their concerns in the fact that they were under the king of the
British and paying taxes but not benefiting from that. Once they
arrived in this new world, the work of how to grow together with
people of different morals, norms, values, and points of view to
create freedom began.

On Monday September 17, 1787, the last day of the

Constitutional Convention, Pennsylvania delegate Franklin, one of the few Americans of the time with international repute, wanted to give a short speech to the convention prior to signing it. Too weak to give the speech himself, he had fellow Pennsylvanian James Wilson do so. The speech is a masterpiece.

> Mr. President I confess that there are several parts of this Constitution which I do not at present approve, but I am not sure I shall never approve them: For having lived long, I have experienced many instances of being obliged by better information, or fuller consideration, to change opinions even on important subjects, which I once thought right, but found to be otherwise. It is therefore that the older I grow, the more apt I am to doubt my own judgment, and to pay more respect to the judgment of others. Most men indeed as well as most sects in Religion, think themselves in possession of all truth, and that wherever others differ from them it is so far error. Steele, a Protestant in a dedication tells the Pope, that the only difference between our Churches in their opinions of the certainty of their doctrines is, the Church of Rome is infallible, and the Church of England is never in the wrong. But though many private persons think almost as highly of their own infallibility as of that of their sect, few express it so naturally as a certain French lady, who in a dispute with her sister, said, "I don't know how it happens, sister but I meet with nobody but myself, that's always in the right—Il n'y a que moi qui a toujours raison." In these sentiments, Sir, I agree to this Constitution with all its faults, if they are such; because I think a general Government necessary for us, and there is no form of Government

but what may be a blessing to the people if well administered, and believe farther that this is likely to be well administered for a course of years, and can only end in Despotism, as other forms have done before it, when the people shall become so corrupted as to need despotic Government, being incapable of any other. I doubt too whether any other Convention we can obtain, may be able to make a better Constitution. For when you assemble a number of men to have the advantage of their joint wisdom, you inevitably assemble with those men, all their prejudices, their passions, their errors of opinion, their local interests, and their selfish views. From such an assembly can a perfect production be expected? It therefore astonishes me, Sir, to find this system approaching so near to perfection as it does; and I think it will astonish our enemies, who are waiting with confidence to hear that our councils are confounded like those of the Builders of Babel; and that our States are on the point of separation, only to meet hereafter for the purpose of cutting one another's throats. Thus I consent, Sir, to this Constitution because I expect no better, and because I am not sure, that it is not the best. The opinions I have had of its errors, I sacrifice to the public good. I have never whispered a syllable of them abroad. Within these walls they were born, and here they shall die. If every one of us in returning to our Constituents were to report the objections he has had to it, and endeavor to gain partizans in support of them, we might prevent its being generally received, and thereby lose all the salutary effects & great advantages resulting naturally in our favor among foreign Nations as well as among ourselves, from our real or apparent unanimity. Much of the strength & efficiency of any Government in procuring and securing happiness to the people, depends, on opinion, on the general opinion of the goodness of the Government, as well as of the wisdom and integrity of its Governors. I hope therefore that for our own sakes as a part of the people, and for the sake of posterity, we shall act heartily and unanimously in recommending this Constitution (if approved by Congress & confirmed by the Conventions) wherever our influence may extend, and turn our future thoughts & endeavors to the means of having it well administered. On the whole, Sir, I cannot help expressing a wish that every member of the Convention who may still have objections to it, would with me, on this occasion doubt a little of his own infallibility, and to make manifest our unanimity, put his name to this instrument.[170]

11

THE CONSTRUCTS OF
THE CONSTITUTION

WHAT I PRESENT to you is the Founders' theological experiment in self-government, a Constitution for the United States. I propose my constitutional interpretation based on a life spent researching the Founders. They intended to extend forgiveness on earth as it was in heaven and protect God-given human liberty for all time.

The first draft of the Constitution was introduced on August 6, 1787. Article X, Section 2 reads in pertinent part,

> [The president] shall have power to grant reprieves and pardons: but his pardon shall not be pleadable in bar of an impeachment. He shall be Commander in Chief of the Army and Navy of the United States, and of the militia of the several States.[171]

For the final act, forty-three days later on September 17, 1787, the two complete thoughts of August 6, 1787, were inverted and combined in a single thought with the word *and* revealing a theological construct; the function of the lineage of David as articulated and documented in the Constitution. The finger of God was placed in chronological order. First, there was the commander, and then there was the pardoner, David and Jesus, by function. Look closely at the constitutional function that came first, before the inversion—reprieves and pardons.

The final draft states,

> He shall be Commander in Chief of the Army and Navy of the United States, and of the militia of the several states,

and

> He shall have power to grant reprieves and pardons: but his pardon shall not be pleadable in bar of an impeachment.[172]

The Extraction of ƒ(lod)   [173]

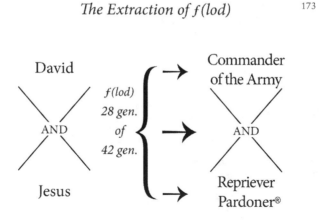

The functional extract envisions a single person who would perform the function of David and Jesus and be part of the evolution of the linear system. The inversion and conjunction allowed the chronological ordering of the language that properly began with David in the sect of one, the commander of the army, and it ended with the function of the repriever pardoner, Jesus. The DNA of the Abrahamic system was extracted by function for a single person to perform, and it extended the grace of God to the people in the Constitution; it represented the continuous, infinite possibility for the American experiment to continue and evolve through the generations of the person the people elected as president. If the people elected this person, he then carried the function of the providence of God forward for every American, for we are all children of the Most High, therefore confirming under the right leadership heaven on earth as a real possibility in our system.

His mandatory function under our Constitution was to command an army—"He shall"—and grant reprieves and pardons—"He shall." The unfortunate practice has shown a far greater desire on the part of presidents to command the army including all the pomp and circumstance that accompanies the most powerful military leader in the world. But on the question of the function of reprieves and pardons, there is a great historical reluctance. So I extracted the person from the function so we could add nerves, flesh, and a spine to the spirit of the function.

174

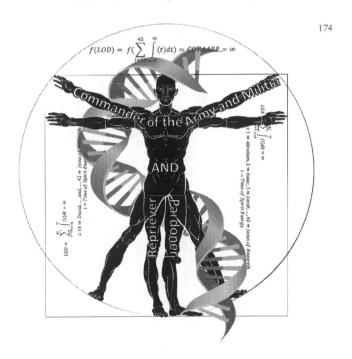

In Summary

The extraction of the person, the avatar, the flesh, nerves, arteries, sinew, and spine from the lineage of David, commander of an army and repriever pardoner®,[175] is part of the evolution of the linear theological system of God in the sect of one, the Abrahamic religion of one. The Founders extended the grace of God to the people through an elected human being who synthesized the spirit energy of that system in his person. The function belongs in the Constitution because it applies to everybody in the life, liberty, and happiness system. Any other interpretation doesn't belong.

For the Founders, this construction was the key to the longevity of our nation. They expected the government to function at the highest level of faith and truth. As long as there were believers, there would be a government of, for, and by the people. When the Founders placed the functional extract in the Constitution, they gave our nation a clean slate unencumbered by European monarchical and ecclesiastical history, and they made their new country one of Abraham's many nations, God's covenant with Abraham. The Founders also extended the lineage of David on earth through Jesus by election. This act made the power of the lineage available to all Americans in all generations. This is why Jefferson called himself a disciple of the doctrines of Jesus from a sect of one.

12

The Finger of God

THE LINEAGE OF DAVID

THE FOUNDERS PUT the lineage of David, the shepherd boy, the king and commander of the army of Israel, and Jesus, the repriever pardoner, in the Constitution. The finger of God was operationalized by this language and by election by all the people of someone under God's watchful eye. It is a language created for a person in the sect of one, the religion of one, and each president is a successor. Each president must remove his personal suit and don the suit of the person who guides the country understanding these two great commandments.

> Honor God with all of your heart, soul and mind, and love thy neighbor as thyself, understanding that all laws were built on the Prophets. (Matthew 1:1–25, 22:35–40; Mark 12:28–34)

The Finger of the Almighty Hand

The abandoned constitutional experiment, the extracted lineage of David from the lineage of Abraham, was operationalized in the Constitution on September 17, 1787. The lineage of David was the governing lineage from the lineage of Abraham, from King David to the King of Kings, Jesus.

The Bible chronicles Jesus as the end of this lineage. The

debt-paid but unforgiven felon needs to be restored and renewed in the life, liberty, and happiness system by the character traits of this leader. The Founders designated all offenders for forgiveness, and Federalist Paper 74, written by Hamilton, suggested that state felons were available for this power too. Hamilton argued that forgiveness should be distributed by a single hand, and since the lineage of Abraham and David was put in the Constitution (1787) before the Bill of Rights (1791), state offenders are within its scope as well. Our divine grant of life and liberty is not divided between state and federal rights.

The construction of the language of the finger of God before its inversion and combination into a single idea is evidence that the theological experiment was completed before the Constitutional Convention. The future of the United States rests entirely upon the ability of the American people to invert and then convert two concepts into a single idea.

Article II, Section 2, Clause 1

> The President shall be Commander in Chief of the Army and Navy of the United States, and of the Militia of the several States, when called into the actual Service of the United States; he may require the Opinion, in writing, of the principal Officer in each of the Executive Departments, upon any subject relating to the duties of their respective offices, AND he shall have power to grant Reprieves and Pardons for offenses against the United States, except in cases of impeachment.

Once the Constitution was ratified, Hamilton, in Federalist Paper 74, said that certain language in the construction of the finger was redundant, but even with the redundancy, it is clear that the language impacted all affairs of state; no cabinet appointees can ignore the fact that they are in the service of the president and must implement policies that impact the least of these as their primary function; they have to report to the individual who is elected and is operating in the function of the theological lineage. This was so obvious to Hamilton that he wrote,

> [The president] may require the opinion, in writing, of the principal officer in each of the executive departments, upon any subject relating to the duties of their respective offices. This I consider as a mere redundancy in the plan, as the RIGHT for which it provides would result in itself from the office.[176]

What right exists in Article II, Section 2, Clause 1 as presently practiced? Hamilton was referring to the rights inherent in all humanity and every American from the lineage of Abraham. With the strike in the language, the function of the finger of God becomes more apparent.

> The President shall be Commander in Chief of the Army and Navy of the United States, and of the militia of the several States, when called into the actual Service of the United States, and he shall have Power to Grant Reprieves and Pardons for offenses against the United States except in cases of impeachment.[177]

Hamilton said that the interests at the convention were so diverse that there never could have been agreement on the Constitution itself without the finger of God. I believe Hamilton in Federalist Paper 74 was telling us, the future, that he understood what we have done and that he was part of obscuring the truth until a future time.

With Hamilton's stricken language, the finger of God in the

sect of one is revealed. Furthermore, Hamilton's big reveal in Federalist Paper 74 and the punctuation confirm the theological idea as a single thought, not two distinguishable jobs.

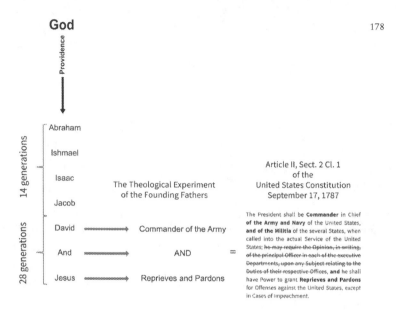

178

"He shall be Commander of the Army and the Navy of the United States, and the militia of several states," *and* "He shall have power to grant reprieves and pardons, but his pardon shall not be pleadable in bar of an impeachment." The structure of this language is not two job responsibilities; it is a single theological idea that vests in a single person in every generation!

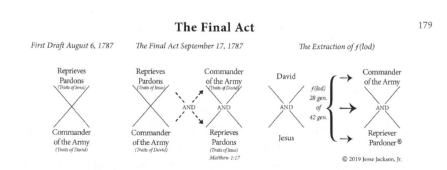

The Final Act

179

Forty-three days after the first draft of the Constitution had been constructed, the two complete thoughts of August 6, 1787, were combined into a single theological construct with the word *and* revealing the Abrahamic DNA in the Constitution. Madison confirmed this in Federalist Paper 37 without identifying its location. This was the final act, the finger of God in our Constitution intended to ensure forgiveness of a people in a country founded with the providence of God that would endure its shortcomings. The final act placed the supreme and divine character trait of forty-two generations of theological development in the Constitution and vested it in a single office and person.

Two hundred years later, Tom Hughes, the president of the Alliance for Religious Freedom, wrote about the significance of Washington's inauguration in 1789 two years after the Constitutional Convention and two years before the Bill of Rights was added.

> On April 30th, 1789, America had a constitution and a newly formed government. On that day, the government, the House, and the Senate gathered for the Inauguration of our first president, George Washington. In his Inauguration Address, Washington gave a prophetic warning: "We ought to be no less persuaded that the propitious smiles of heaven can never be expected on a nation that disregards the eternal rules of order and the right which heaven itself has ordained." Washington's warning was, if we would begin to depart from God, He would remove His blessings, His prosperity and His protection from our nation.

After Washington's address, the government, the House, the Senate, and America's first president traveled on foot to Saint Paul's Chapel. No one knows exactly what was said inside but we do know the entire government was on their knees praying and consecrating this nation to God. In the chapel there is also a plaque above Washington's pew with the words "Almighty God, we make our earnest prayer that you will keep the United States in Holy protection." Saint Paul's Chapel is located at the corner of Ground Zero and is the spiritual birthplace of America.

America's first Presidential Inauguration—that of President George Washington—incorporated seven specific religious activities, including [1] the use of the Bible to administer the oath;[2] affirming the religious nature of the oath by adding the prayer "So help me God!" to the oath;[3] inaugural prayers offered by the president;[4] religious content in the inaugural address;[5] civil leaders calling the people to prayer or acknowledgement of God;[6] inaugural worship services attended

en masse by Congress as an official part of congressional activities;[7] and clergy-led inaugural
prayers.[8][180]

Tom Hughes wrote that "the entire government was on their
knees praying and consecrating this nation to God." Was it
the three-tiered branches of government that dropped "the entire government to their knees"? Was it the idea of the balance
of powers? Was it the as yet established arcane rules of the
Senate? The prayers and consecration of the government had a
far higher purpose on August 30, 1789. It is the same warning
issued by Franklin delivered in Philadelphia at the opening of the
Constitutional Convention: "And have we now forgotten that
powerful friend?"[181]

In the Great Seals, we see the nation and the body politic grad-
ually moving from Jefferson's, Franklin's, and Adams's accounts
of the spirituality that drove the revolution and their revolutionary ideals deeply rooted in biblical stories to the present seal.
Time, history, bias, contemporary memory, racism, prejudice,
and the incrementalism and inefficiencies of the two-party system
are among the factors that have despiritualized the nation. The
government was dedicated to the one true God before the congregationalism and denominationalism of the First Amendment
in 1791. The trappings of the contemporary presidency—from
Air Force One to a limousine called the Beast, from the nuclear
football to a navy and satellites that circumnavigate the world,
to a nuclear arsenal capable of destroying creation 10,000 or
more times over, to superhighways and infrastructure, to tech-
nological achievement, to control of global financial systems and
the grotesque skewing of the world's financial resources in the
hands and under the control of the few—were not available to
Washington. Some of this would have been unimaginable to him
including the idea of blowing up and polluting God's creation
meant for all God's children. Nevertheless, the entire government fell on its knees in St. Paul's Chapel in New York because

its members had been given stewardship over the most powerful force and theological idea on earth—the function of the lineage of David. Returning the nation to its spiritual core will require our understanding of a single idea.

13

A SINGLE IDEA

Verily, verily, I say unto you, He that believeth on me, the works that I do shall he do also; and greater works than these shall he do; because I go unto my Father.[182]

—John 14:12

I am a historian, I am not a believer, but I must confess as a historian that the penniless preacher from Nazareth is irrevocably the very center of history. Jesus Christ is easily the most dominant figure in all of history.[183]

—H. G. Wells

The highest, the transcendent glory of the American Revolution was this—it connected, in one indissoluble bond, the principles of civil government with the precepts of Christianity.[184]

—John Quincy Adams

EVEN THE SINCEREST liberal and conservative intellectual and constitutional scholars, historians, and public servants have based their lives' work and scholarship on intellectual, spiritual, and theological racism because they do not see or understand the *function*. America is unique in overcoming this problem. We truly shall overcome.

The reform I advocate for is simple. We are all God's children, and we are all covered by the lineage of David. The function of the lineage of David was placed in the Constitution by the Founders to be protected and preserved as a gift from almighty God by the architects of our republic to ensure that God-ordained human freedom, liberty, happiness, and emancipation would endure for all time. Therefore, the first right we have as Americans is not in the First Amendment. In the new Israel, unconditional forgiveness, the grace of God, is the first American birthright. The first right we have is to be covered and forgiven by the lineage of Abraham by way of the lineage of David. This function cannot be performed unless the president does his or her job without regard for the influence of politics or the political ramifications for his or her reelection.

We have the God-given right to start our lives over again in the life, liberty, and the pursuit of happiness system; people sacrificed their lives to make that possible. I advocate for the end of the death penalty and the end of federal and state felonization by a single hand in our democracy.[185]

With this right comes a domestic and global obligation. We do not have the right to exclude Muslims, to persecute Jews, Christians, atheists, or agnostics, to ignore the poor domestically and internationally, to ignore our neighbor, to declare one race superior to others, or to discriminate on the basis of race, gender, or sexual orientation. We live in a human liberty system, not a corporate liberty system run by lobbyists and corporate interests on Wall Street, money changers who must be directed out of the temple of our democracy, the people's government.[186]

It took forty-two generations beginning with the sacrifice of Abraham and Isaac to the crucifixion and resurrection of Jesus to develop this language. The presidency has unlimited moral power from the lineage of Abraham and limited constitutional power. The presidents owe an account of their behavior toward the poor and the least among us to the people of the United States. This is what Madison meant when he said,

Whilst we assert for ourselves a freedom to profess, and to observe the religion which we believe
to be of divine origin, we cannot deny an equal
freedom to those whose minds have not yielded
to the evidence which has convinced us. If this
freedom be abused, it is an offense against God,
not against man: To God, therefore, not to man,
must an account of it be rendered.[187]

The Architects and the influence of Architecture

It's hard to imagine given some of the Founders interest in architecture, specifically Franklin, Jefferson, and Madison that
they would not have read, *De architectura: The Ten Books on
Architecture*, published in antiquity, a treatise on architecture
written by architect and a Roman military engineer Marcus
Vitruvius Pollio. It is the only treatise to survive from antiquity
and it is considered the most important book on architectural
theory in the renaissance. *The Four Books of Architecture* published in 1570 by Andrea Palladio must have made their reading
list as well. During this period the Learned man and architecture
were considered synonymous.

In reading the Preface, Chapter 1, and Chapter 2 of *Vitruvius,
De achitectura: The Ten Books on Architecture* it is clear that the
Learned man must understand the perfection of architecture and
symmetry from points of skill and scholarship. Vitruvius writes,

1. The architect should be equipped with knowledge of many branches of study and varied kinds
of learning, for it is by his judgement that all
work done by the other arts is put to test. This
knowledge is the child of practice and theory.
Practice is the continuous and regular exercise of
employment where manual work is done with any

necessary material according to the design of a drawing. Theory, on the other hand, is the ability to demonstrate and explain the productions of dexterity on the principles of proportion.

2. It follows, therefore, that architects who have aimed at acquiring manual skill without scholarship have never been able to reach a position of authority to correspond to their pains, while those who relied only upon theories and scholarship were obviously hunting the shadow, not the substance. But those who have a thorough knowledge of both, like men armed at all points, have the sooner attained their object and carried authority with them.

3. In all matters, but particularly in architecture, there are these two points:—the thing signified, and that which gives it its significance. That which is signified is the subject of which we may be speaking; and that which gives significance is a demonstration on scientific principles. It appears, then, that one who professes himself an architect should be well versed in both directions. He ought, therefore, to be both naturally gifted and amenable to instruction. Neither natural ability without instruction nor instruction without natural ability can make the perfect artist. Let him be educated, skilful with the pencil, instructed in geometry, know much history, have followed the philosophers with attention, understand music, have some knowledge of medicine, know the opinions of the jurists, and be acquainted with astronomy and the theory of the heavens.[188]

These points would create the ideal man and they called him Vitruvius. Leonardo da Vinci would be inspired by Vitruvius when he drew the Vitruvian man who was perfect in his symmetry (all dimensions of his life). Martin Luther King Jr. referred to this person as having three Dimensions of a Complete life in a sermon titled the same. Chris Gorgio used graphic design technology to create a Vitruvian figure modeled after the written work of Marcus Vitruvius Pollio in Book III, Chapter I: On Symmetry: In Temples And In the Human Body, and after the artwork of Leonardo Da Vinci in 1490. In 1521, Cesare Cesariano translated the De architectura into Italian and came up with yet another vision of the Vitruvian. I combined the language construction of the architects with the Vitruvian symbol of form and flesh to give spirit to the idea of the ideal American President, the person of God, free of historical political parties and financial influences that have overtaken and corrupted the original intent of the Architects of the Republic.

 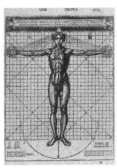 

In Federalist #37 Madison is clear that the Finger of God is "signally responsible for the rebellion" therefore, to use an architectural term, the $f(lod)$ is the foundation, the cornerstone of the Constitution and therefore the cornerstone of America.

If the *f(lod)* is "signally responsible for the rebellion," then it is
the theological underpinnings of King George and British and
European theology, at the time of the nation's founding, that ultimately was the turning point in ending the colonial relationship,
not a Tea Party in Boston over taxes.

But signally important for this work is that the Architects
are not just builders of buildings. The architects of our republic
turned their attention to the education of an ideal person modeled on architecture and theology, with this theological being as
the cornerstone of the function of the Constitution.

The bottom line is the Founders are builders, the architects
of our republic.

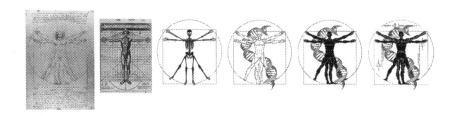

There are many images inspired by Marcus Vitruvius Pollio,
in the graphic above the first image was draw by Leonardo Da
Vinci in 1492, the second image was drawn by Cesare Cesariano
in 1521, the 3rd through the 6th images are images created by
Chris Gorgio. I believe the participants in the construction of the
Declaration of Independence and the Constitution understood
the applications of Marcus Vitruvius Pollio's construction of man
and participated in the creation of the architectural skeleton of
leadership based on the principles of Vitruvius Architecture. The
3rd image represents the Vitruvian skeletal image that I believe
Thomas Jefferson in a letter to John Adams on October 12, 1813
was referring to in his syllabus. The 4th image represents the vast
majority of occupants of the White House who did not see the
f(lod) and treated it as two job responsibilities. Since the inception of the nation and the architect's theological experiment, the

5th image represents the only African American president, and the final image is a figure in American and human history that we have not seen yet. Whether or not the American people will ever see this empathic figure is in direct correlation to the masses of the American people receiving an education of equal high quality that is commensurate and consistent with the experiment. The theology of the true believer in the one true God of human history is simple, "Love of one God and Neighbor as oneself." And this life, in our system, as it has evolved, is a direct challenge to States Rights on all matters of God ordained human rights that have resulted in the balkanization of the American people by race, by state, by culture, by caste, and by religious sects.

Fleshing Out the Skeleton

Finally, I needed to give the words and ideas flesh.

189

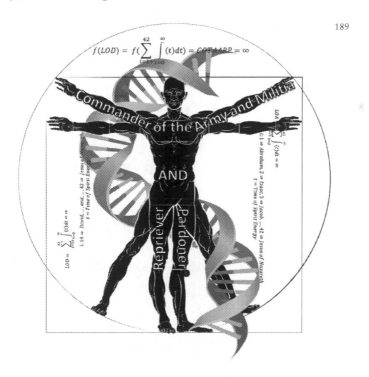

The skeleton and the spirit through a one-to-one correspondence between thoughts and deeds in spirit and truth that
Jefferson referred to in his letter to Adams on October 12, 1813,
needed to be in the Founders' vision and function for the president being the commander of the army and the repriever pardoner.® He is someone who will elevate the inherent rights in the
Constitution from the lineage of Abraham that neither the federal nor state governments can deny they ratified. The forty-six
presidents (except for the first six, whose political conditions and
options facing the nation and life circumstances never rose to the
critical mass necessary for its invocation, and Abraham Lincoln,
who I believe was consciously aware of the function) did not
have the vision to do or execute this. This person will argue that
before the Tenth Amendment was Madison's and the Founders'
efforts to prepare the way with the as yet uninterpreted Ninth
Amendment.

Presently, the First and Second Amendments seemingly enjoy
primacy over most rights in the Bill of Rights. The rights inherent in and granted to the people by the lineage of Abraham and
David are the supreme rights in this land, and this person will
argue that the Ninth Amendment enjoys a similar primacy with
a new interpretation of Article II, Section 2, Clause 1 as a single
theological function and most powerful power for progressive
change. The Ninth Amendment reads, "The enumeration in the
Constitution, of certain rights, shall not be construed to deny or
disparage others retained by the people."[190]

With the moral authority of the divine and the permission
of the Founders, this person will challenge us all to recognize
that rights deriving from the lineages of Abraham and David are
far greater than federal or state rights and that God's power to
forgive in our Constitution extends to federal as well as all state
and local offenses.[191]

He will offer to provide for the sick with no magic tricks
or miracles but with a commitment to hard work by building

thousands of world-class hospitals and long-term care facilities in rural and urban settings alike. This person's goal will be to train tens of thousands of world-class doctors and nurses graduating annually, more than the five military academies graduate soldiers combined, with tuition free of cost and incentivized with student loan forgiveness to provide high-quality care to all the American people as their God-given right.

As this army of medical professionals grows, this person will command their service to the global poor as ambassadors of American goodwill. This person will ask the American people to elevate such a right to the Constitution including the fundamental right to vote, the right to a public education of high quality, a clean, safe, and sustainable environment, and the right to decent, safe, and affordable housing so every generation can build on the progress of the previous one. The success of these amendments would be measured by the increased life expectancy of Americans living in barrios, ghettos, trailer parks, mansions, or penthouses—of all living in rural and urban areas.

Like David, this person will command and with the assistance of Congress will "well regulate"[192] all militias in all the states by directing them to the nearest military base for registration, where they will swear to uphold the Constitution, receive weekend-warrior and Jefferson's Tree of Liberty[193] training, and where their military-style weapons will remain until he calls them into "actual service"[194] to defend democracy and our nation's capital as well as our state capitals from foreign and domestic invasion and interference and to reinforce and back up the national guard if necessary. The president must issue a call for this to happen. And they will never be commanded to use their training or weapons against the American people, fellow citizens, immigrants, or the republic itself without punishment for treason.

They will argue that new basic human and economic rights must be enshrined in the Constitution for the life, liberty, and happiness system to endure the test of time and guarantee one nation under God with liberty and justice for all.

At the hour of this writing, 68 million federal and state debt-paid felons need the idea of becoming new men and women for "born again" to be true.[195] He will forgive far more than just 68 million such debt-paid felons along his perilous state-by-state journey. This do-over is not political; it is a deeply emotional, psychological, spiritual, and personal life-altering process for the offenders, the victims, and the nation that includes redemption and restoration from the lineage of Abraham.

God's grace must be made available for all after they have completed the time assigned to them by judges and juries. The nation needs to end lifelong vengeance, retaliation, and punishment after time has been served to break the cycle of shame, blame, and guilt. No debt-paid felon is outside the bell curve.

The president of this moral character will need an army of rejuvenated, redeemed, and grateful people to rebuild the country. New armies of hope are proposed by this idea. For this person, love, mercy, justice, forgiveness, redemption, full pardons, and the grace of God on earth as it is in heaven become unencumbered. And that is just the beginning of the entitlements promised by the lineage of David. There are far more entitlements than Democrats and Republicans have led the poor in this nation to believe. The Founders had figured out through the study of history that the power of forgiveness from the lineage of Abraham had ecclesiastical authorities and processes as its sole interpreters but that they were corrupt and ineffective. Ecclesiastical authorities could convince people to forgive themselves, but they could not restore those people to their communities without public forgiveness on behalf of society.

People had to pay for pardons and forgiveness while the Founders made unconditional forgiveness the mandatory obligation of their new government; these acts of clemency and the grace of God were to be free. After all, who could truly profit from the grace of God? We the people are called to elect a distributor of

God's grace. The function was placed in the Constitution for a single hand to administer because the Founders knew that one day, faith in our government would have to be restored. Being available to all was to be the primary function of the government. Debt-paid felons will ask and offer only a single quid pro quo in exchange for renewed, changed, and committed lives; those who have erred or stepped outside God's grace will "go and sin no more."[196]

This president would understand the debilitating psychological consequences of guilt on individuals and society. This presidential candidate would have experienced American law, not just studied it. It comes from a place of being adjudicated by it. The perfect candidate would be a guilt collector, a forgiver of debts and trespasses. This presidential candidate would be an avatar who transfers the guilt of other people who are helpless and on life's Jericho Road psychologically and politically to himself, and he would offer to relieve their burdens through his service. She would love all the American people and would want all of them and their families made whole. Her full-time job would be to extend mercy and forgiveness on behalf of the people and the injured. She would ask us personally to be bigger people than we have ever been. He would argue that no governor in the union could deny offenders or ex-offenders forgiveness from the lineage of David as if federal offenses were more worthy of relief from the Abrahamic system and that the petty theft of a loaf of bread at the local level was somehow unworthy.

Splitting human and American rights into federal and states' rights was an idea promulgated by the slave states and more specifically the slave owners, but such an idea was and is outside the grace of God. In the presence of the disciple of the doctrines of the Nazarene, I have a dream that we will witness the finger of the God of Abraham in our time. With an understanding of this dream, there will be a rumor from sea to shining sea that someone going around the countryside is passing out new life[197] and unconditional forgiveness. People will come from near and far to see that person. This person will be a religion and a psychology unto themselves, a sect of one. They will be the new model for American and global leadership. America loves a redemption story. The avatars will do their best to make sure 68 million federal and state debt-paid felons are indeed redeemed.

For 235 years, the unknown function of *(x)* or *f(x)*, where *(x)* equals the unknown Democrat or Republican, is now the known function of the lineage of David, *f(lod)*. Because we know the *f(lod)* in the birth, life, ministry, crucifixion, and resurrection of Jesus, we must now do better as a nation for the least of these if we are to be worthy of our inheritance.

Every day that this person functions in the lineage of David, he will be deeply troubled by the questions raised by Charles Spurgeon.[198]

> Hang that question up in your houses, "What would Jesus do?" and then think of another, "How would Jesus do it?" for what he would do, and how he would do it, may always stand as the best guide to us.[199]

What of the sick? Would he provide everyone with health care? What about the homeless? Would he provide everyone with decent, safe, and affordable housing? What of equality among God's children? Would the lost sheep be welcomed back into the flock? What of the stranger on America's Jericho Road? Would he beat swords into plowshares[200] and study war no more? How far will she go for peace? Would he be a zealot for peace? Would he be a zealot for God's creation and fight to sustain it? How would she provide health care, housing, equal and high-quality educational opportunities, and the emancipation of the least of these?[201] "To whom much is given much is required."[202] Those who have been blessed by the nation must pay their fair share of taxes to maintain the human liberty system.

How would he cut the military budget without cutting the nation's defense?[203] Nowhere in the moral code is there an expectation of a savior of corporations. The moral code is simply not written for their benefit because they are not persons[204] though they must operate in it. This person is accountable to the Constitution and the moral code. He or she would be deeply troubled by the answer to these questions and what he or she could do to bring about justice for all. Measuring their job performance by the economy and the economy's performance is very different from measuring their performance by this function.

Jesus carried a rugged cross to Calvary for the world at age thirty-three. The Founders set the minimum age for the person carrying the nation's cross and heavy burden at age thirty-five. At the time, if blessed with election by the people, he or she could serve as many terms as the nation would have him or her. This of course would change with a two-term limit after President Roosevelt had been elected to a historic fourth term.

The Founders bequeathed to their nation the most powerful force in history, but Democrats and Republicans don't know what to do with it. The architects understood that their experiment in democracy could not survive without such leadership. When Dr. Cornel West asked me who the commander of the army and the repriever pardoner® was, I responded, "Someone we have not yet seen in American or even world history. His first name is Original, and his last name is Intent, not Dow and Jones. He loves only one God and his neighbor as himself." By covenant and agreement, he will transfer the guilt of 68 million people to himself.

I reminded him that there are more debt-paid felons in America than those who lived around the Sea of Galilee two thousand years ago. The president is to be a person who brings forward the principles and precepts of primitive Christianity, the principles of the linear theological system.

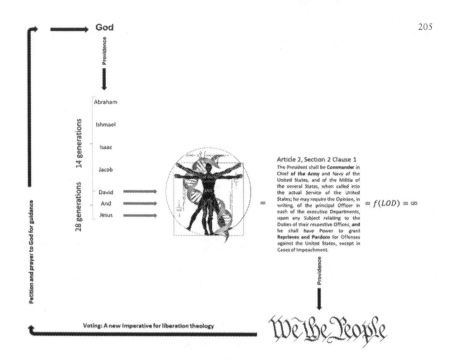

This leader represents a longing by the American people. On April 13, 2020, the Pew Research Center released the following survey in an article by Michael Lipka. Half of Americans say that the Bible should influence US laws, and that includes over a quarter who favor it over the will of the people.

The Constitution does not mention the Bible, God, Jesus, or Christianity, and the First Amendment clarifies that "Congress shall make no law respecting an establishment of religion." Still, some scholars have argued that the Bible heavily influenced America's Founders.

Today, about half of Americans say that the Bible should have at least some influence on the laws; that includes nearly a quarter who say it should have a great deal of influence according to a recent Pew Research Center survey. Among US Christians, two-thirds want the Bible to influence at least some US laws; among White evangelical Protestants, this figure rises to about nine in ten.

Americans split on how much Bible should sway laws

% of U.S. adults who say the Bible should have _____ influence on laws of U.S

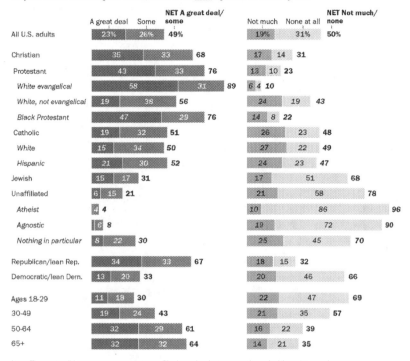

	A great deal	Some	NET A great deal/ some	Not much	None at all	NET Not much/ none
All U.S. adults	23%	26%	49%	19%	31%	50%
Christian	35	33	68	17	14	31
Protestant	43	33	76	13	10	23
White evangelical	58	31	89	6	4	10
White, not evangelical	19	38	56	24	19	43
Black Protestant	47	29	76	14	8	22
Catholic	19	32	51	26	23	48
White	15	34	50	27	22	49
Hispanic	21	30	52	24	23	47
Jewish	15	17	31	17	51	68
Unaffiliated	6	15	21	21	58	78
Atheist		4	4	10	86	96
Agnostic		6	8	19	72	90
Nothing in particular	8	22	30	25	45	70
Republican/lean Rep.	34	33	67	18	15	32
Democratic/lean Dem.	13	20	33	20	46	66
Ages 18-29	11	18	30	22	47	69
30-49	19	24	43	21	35	57
50-64	32	29	61	16	22	39
65+	32	32	64	14	21	35

Note: Those who did not answer are not shown. Blacks and whites are not Hispanic; Hispanics are of any race.
Source: Survey conducted Feb. 4-15, 2020, among U.S. adults.
"White Evangelicals See Trump as Fighting for Their Beliefs, Though Many Have Mixed Feelings About His Personal Conduct"

PEW RESEARCH CENTER

At the other end of the spectrum, there is broad opposition to biblical influence on US laws among religiously unaffiliated Americans, also known as religious "nones," who identify as atheists, agnostics, or "nothing in particular." Over three-quarters of them say that the Bible should hold little to no sway, and that includes 86 percent of self-described atheists who say that the Bible should not influence US legislation at all. Two-thirds of US Jews as well think that the Bible should have not much or no influence on laws.

All survey respondents who said that the Bible should have at least some influence on US laws were asked a follow-up question: When the Bible and the will of the people conflict, which should have more influence on US laws? The common answer to this question was that the Bible should take priority over the will of the people. This view is expressed by more than a quarter of all Americans. About one in five say that the Bible should have at least some influence but that the will of the people should prevail.

Two religious groups stand out for being especially supportive of biblical influence in legislation even if that means going against the will of the American people: Two-thirds of White evangelical Protestants (68 percent) say the Bible should take precedence over the people, and half of Black Protestants say the same. Among Catholics (25 percent) and White Protestants who do not identify as born-again or evangelical (27 percent), only about a quarter shared this perspective.

206

About seven-in-ten white evangelicals say the Bible should have more influence on U.S. laws than will of the people

% of U.S. adults who say …

	NET Bible should have a great deal/ some influence on U.S. laws	When Bible and will of people conflict, which should have more influence on U.S. laws?			NET Bible should have not much/ no influence on U.S. laws	No answer
		Bible	Will of people	No answer		
	%	%	%	%	%	%
All U.S. adults	49	28	19	2	50	1=100
Christian	68	42	23	3	31	1
Protestant	76	51	22	3	23	1
White evangelical	89	68	17	4	10	1
White, not evangelical	56	27	26	3	43	1
Black Protestant	76	50	25	2	22	2
Catholic	51	25	24	2	48	1
White	50	24	24	2	49	1
Hispanic	52	27	23	2	47	1
Jewish	31	12	19	1	68	<1
Unaffiliated	21	7	13	<1	78	1
Atheist	4	1	4	0	96	0
Agnostic	8	2	6	<1	90	1
Nothing in particular	30	11	19	1	70	<1
Republican/lean Republican	67	41	23	2	32	1
Democrat/lean Democratic	33	16	16	1	66	1

Note: Figures may not add to 100% or to subtotals indicated due to rounding. Blacks and whites are not Hispanic; Hispanics are of any race.
Source: Survey conducted Feb. 4-15, 2020, among U.S. adults.
"White Evangelicals See Trump as Fighting for Their Beliefs, Though Many Have Mixed Feelings About His Personal Conduct"

PEW RESEARCH CENTER

Four years before the Bill of Rights (1791), the Founders never intended for the lineages of Abraham or David to be limited to federal and states' rights, or become a family-and-friend redemption program for the politically connected, or a tool of the military-industrial complex. Men and women who have paid their debt to society need simply transfer their guilt to a disciple, an avatar, and let him or her carry their guilt in the lineage of David, to Iowa, New Hampshire, South Carolina, the Bible Belt, and beyond. Madison's final act gave the American people the power to restart the experiment of America over again.

We must reconsider what was being acknowledged, considered, and projected for future discovery. Once exposed, we must contemplate the why of the matter to figure out how we move forward with the exposure of what the Founders believed to be the new earth, the heaven on earth, the free world, one nation under one omnipotent God in America.

Adams said,

> I have examined all religions, and the result is that the Bible is the best book in the world.[207]

> Our Constitution was made only for a moral and religious people. It is wholly inadequate to the government of any other.[208]

> The Ten Commandments and the Sermon on the Mount contain my religion.[209]

Jefferson said,

> The day will come when the mystical generation of Jesus, by the Supreme Being as his father in the womb of a virgin, will be classed with the fable of the generation of Minerva in the brain of Jupiter.[210]

> The doctrines of Jesus are simple and tend all to the happiness of man, that there is only one God and God is perfect. That God and man are one. That to love God with all your heart, and your neighbor as yourself, is the sum of religion. These are the great points on which I endeavor to reform and live my life.[211]

Both of these members of the Great Seal committee were speaking of a future date when an avatar would advance the primitive principles of Jesus.

On September 17, 1787, the Founders inaugurated the domestic and global restoration of humankind. When the Founders inaugurated our system, there was no country that had accomplished this idea. America, the new Israel, was the grandest of all theological ideas. The architects of our republic respected our sectarianism and our desire for congregationalism. But they placed the future of their experiment in the hands of a future avatar, the Vitruvian, the person or an elected succession of persons in a sect of one from the linear theological system of Abraham, Ishmael, Isaac, Jacob, David, and Jesus. Understanding the single idea and what Dr. Howard Thurman called in his book *Jesus and the Disinherited*[212] "the Religion of Jesus" is the key to the second coming of America.

PART II
MY JOURNEY

14

The Finger of God

COURT

I still believe in the power of forgiveness. I believe in the power of redemption. Today I manned up and tried to accept responsibility for the errors of my ways. And I still believe in the resurrection.[213]

—Jesse Jackson Jr.

Your Honor, throughout this process I've asked the government and the court to hold me and only me accountable for my actions.[214]

—Jesse Jackson Jr.

O N THE DAY of my sentencing, I was burdened by the thought of all I had destroyed. My life had changed in the blink of an eye, and I was standing before a judge asking for one last thing: "Please give me her time."[215] I asked the judge to allow my wife to stay home and allow me to serve her sentence. My request was denied. When I asked this of the judge, my mother nearly fainted. My wife was unhappy. She did not think I had done everything I could have done to ensure that she would not have to serve her time in prison. I was catatonic. I had made a mess of our lives. I wanted to do everything I could to make it right, to make it better. I ultimately had to reconcile myself to the fact that both of us would serve time.

The months before, Sandra and I worked feverishly to secure the economic foundation for our children. We were unemployed, and we were aware that we would then be considered felons. Our goal was to make their reality as seamless as possible in spite of all the transitions that would take place. I was depressed. I could not sleep. I could not think. I now realize that the heaviness and the burden of all the changes we were going through, and the anticipated prison time had taken a toll on my constitution. I am grateful to be on the other side of that period.

I believe in second chances, and I will always use those past days as a guide to what happens when we become disconnected from our truest selves. I was saved by the exposure of using my campaign funds. My second chance was about allowing me to clear a path that would reconnect me to my passion and purpose. I share all this because I know that many people struggle with exposing their stormy days not wanting to be judged. I have exposed a small fraction of my story to express where I was mentally, physically, and spiritually as I prepared to complete my sentence. It was however at this very low point while lying on my back looking at the ceiling in prison that I was able to get the clearest understanding of myself, our country, and the country's Constitution. The words and the spirit of the Constitution matter because we follow it and people have died to protect, change, and expand it by amending it. The Constitution is a holy writ. It was imperfect at its conception, but it is nevertheless holy.

During this time, I was able to see with a keen understanding that our country was prepared to make a correction that our Founders anticipated when the Constitution was written. The Founders knew it would be during a time like this that our families, individuals, and citizens of our country would need something to extend forgiveness to people to ensure their humanity was always recoverable even after they made terrible mistakes or bad decisions.

Our Founders understood that theology, science, math, history, knowledge, and inventions were experiments that sometimes required an individual to start over and that at times we would make choices outside the boundaries of acceptable behavior and would need a do-over. Our Founders were in their time and in their star, and they placed in our Constitution a corrective for citizens who acted in bad judgment and made mistakes. This same constitutional language is still available and necessary as more citizens walk in unforgiveness in numbers greater than any other country or even around the Sea of Galilee two thousand years ago.

This number does not include people who have gotten away with crimes, avoided the law, and simply have not been caught, charged, or punished. In their spirits, they know what they have done wrong and often say, "There but for the grace of God go I."

The real power of my prison experience is that because I had to do my time, I was able to review our Constitution intrinsically and realistically from the perspective of the people who would most benefit from what I had found. Jesus helped the poor. He was determined to be for all people. He was the son of an unemployed carpenter and an unwed teenage mother and was born homeless. Can you understand and accept that he came to save and serve the least of us? Can you see the vantage point of the Nazarene?

I learned that the least of us needed new lives. Men and women in prison look forward to the day when they can return home to loved ones, but right after greeting their families, they face the question of how to move forward if they will be forever deemed felons.

As I walked out of court after having been sentenced by Judge Amy Berman Jackson, I said, "I still believe in the power of forgiveness. I believe in the power of redemption. Today, I manned up and tried to accept responsibility for the errors of my ways. And I still believe in the resurrection."[216] I had no idea then that my work would lead me right to the idea of national resurrection, redemption, and respiritualization.

15

ALL WERE CREATED EQUAL

IT IS NOT lost on me that in my life's journey, I discovered the most meaningful structuring of words ever written in a constitution. I value America and its traditions, and I love our country. All people were created equal and hold the truths of the Declaration of Independence to be self-evident. My blind spot is not the country of my birth, the country in which my father dreamed a presidency possible, but on my role in a country that extends the promise of life, liberty, and the pursuit of happiness to all.

I am awakening to my personal experience, exposure, and commitment to my purpose, passion, and role in moving America into a new beginning. Science, history, law, and theology conspired to create my current understanding of my life, a life of mistakes that I acknowledge. I am committed to carrying a message delivered to me during a rough season of my journey. My life is dedicated each day with renewed commitment and fervor to 68 million men and women who have paid their debt to society.

On September 17, 1787, the Founders promised all Americans the opportunity to go back to their communities and start anew. I hope my excavation of the finger of God will become a path for America to begin again. My story is a unique experience exposing an enlightenment in prison as a mission to ensure all I meet are provided the choices a new life promises.

It has been six years since my release from prison, and the world has changed. In the narrow confines of the walls of a prison and my mind, I could not have imagined the ramifications of my discovery for such a time as this.

My story is a call for the promise of America to be recognized and responded to and the concept of justice for all to be restored based on the commitments preserved by our Founders. The constitutional right I have studied and defined in this work positions me at the back of a very long line that started before I was born and before I discovered the language of the Founders that promised all new lives. The architects anticipated a day when faith would have to be restored in the life, liberty, and happiness system, and they placed the most powerful and yet unexercised power on earth in the Constitution before our eyes.

On August 14, 2013, I was charged with misappropriating my campaign funds. I acknowledged my crime and did the time I was assigned. As strange as it may sound, I am grateful for the journey and the experience of prison. I met men—Red, Yellow, Brown, Black, White, rich, and poor from all facets of life. They came from trailer parks, barrios, ghettos, mansions, and penthouses. In prison, I saw the early stages of the present political order in the voluntary self-segregation and tribalism that personal security concerns made necessary on my first day in the prison cafeteria. I met men who were in prison for minor drug crimes, for white-collar crimes, for manslaughter, and for murder. Each had a story—some more devastating than others. Each hoped to recover their lives after they served their time.

None of us could clearly envision that the lives we would walk back into would require our steps to be monitored and our lives to be altered by a loss of freedom. No one should be dismissed as hopeless until he or she is deemed impossible for recovery, and such deeming should not be done easily or quickly.

I am not making excuses for those who are paying the price for wrongs done; I am exposing the truth that time served on paper does not equal time served in reality; the walk of life assigned a felon after accepting responsibility and completing a prison sentence for a wrong is usually a long and treacherous road. There is an absence of a faith-restoration policy, a good neighbor policy, from sea to shining sea from the federal system to the state system, and the artificial walls of established barriers to psychological healing and legal remedy are overwhelming and burdensome.

I was awakened to this state of perpetual felonization I would not have considered without having heard the stories of the men in prison with me and to some degree what I am experiencing myself. While I will not relive the entire experience, my journey was enlightening and confirming.

I am grateful for Viktor Frankl's *Man's Search for Meaning.*[217] I am renewed in my spirit by the fact that life has given me an assignment to complete. I hope each reader will now understand that my prison experience was a very vulnerable event for me; I became most alive during that time. My awareness of my purpose and my recognition of all the pieces of my journey being ordered are not lost on me. I continue to clear a path and set in motion the potential of the experiment started by many before me.

My contribution to renewed faith and hope is continuous, and I have come to appreciate that love for neighbor, the second great commandment, is an experiment as is life; it is a process of trial and error. If at the end of this book you are filled with new insight and are committed to completing what our Founders set in motion 235 years ago, my work is complete and everything that comes after it is out of my sheer love for God.

I believe my experience, exposure, culture, family circles, residency, and even my choices were created based on my interests in subject, experience, or obligation. It is because of this work that everything I presented in this labor of love was created from the building blocks of a lifetime. These building blocks have contributed to the completion of my experiment that I have evaluated, tested, and tweaked over most of my life in what I call my laboratory. In it, I worked to confirm the revelation and therefore the metamorphosis I experienced during three nights in solitary confinement. The experience revealed an assignment my life had for me.

With a focus on walking through every point on my path, I am now prepared to bring new light to a marvelous truth collaborated on I believe in secret by the Founders. I have gone through periods of joy, sorrow, depression, elation, anxiety, and fierce determination to support the revelation this work represents for me.

My father explained that every storm in life had rules. First, when you're in a storm, close your eyes. Second, the only way to keep water from coming in is to close your mouth. Finally, keep kicking. My father explained, "You will never drown if you keep kicking."[218] Never give up. Keep hope alive.

I have continued to move along my path to expose this light because it can free the minds of 68 million individuals and their families now and forever by the renewing of faith in America through the idea of divine forgiveness for all. But even as I initially thought of liberation for the felon from shame, blame, and guilt, I could have never imagined while incarcerated how important the discovery would be for all Americans given the discovery's role in history. This discovery enables me to press forward on the promise I made to the men I met at Butner Federal Prison Camp in North Carolina and at Maxwell Federal Prison Camp in Montgomery, Alabama.

16

The Finger of God

THE METAMORPHOSIS OF "FELLA"

Every man and woman is born into the world to do something unique and something distinctive and if he or she does not do it, it will never be done.[219]

—Dr. Benjamin Elijah Mays

The movement of the Spirit of God in the hearts of men and women often calls them to act against the spirit of their times or causes them to anticipate a spirit which is yet in the making. In a moment of dedication, they are given the wisdom and courage to dare a deed that challenges and to kindle a hope that inspires.[220]

—Dr. Howard Thurman

It may be through the Negroes that the unadulterated message of nonviolence will be delivered to the world.[221]

—Mohandas K. Gandhi

WE ARE BORN into seasons, dates, and times. I was indeed born into a purpose-driven life by the nature of the energy and the events surrounding March 11, 1965. My mother was in the care of my grandparents in Greenville, South Carolina.

Around the time of my birth, my father departed the Chicago Theological Seminary to join the crusade of John Lewis, Hosea Williams, and Dr. Martin Luther King Jr. in Selma, Alabama. It was near the time of Bloody Sunday that students with a social consciousness began heeding the call of liberation.

I was born into a family committed to public service and social justice; I was the first son, the second child of Jacqueline and Rev. Jesse L. Jackson Sr. My parents contributed to the movement for the biggest change in the progress toward equal rights that America had witnessed in a generation. I was born of that energy, which does not grow; it is carried forward with the entrance of new life into the world. My energy I believe is magnetic, exciting, warm, enchanting, and enlightening, but it was often misinterpreted as mischievous or disruptive when I was in my formative years. You can imagine then that I received my share of strong verbal and physical reprimands and thus receiving the nickname Fella. I have told the story that it was only after some time that I inquired where my nickname came from, and I was told it was because I was "the baddest fella" they had ever known.

My mother often tells a story about when we lived on the South Side of Chicago at our home on 67th and Ridgeland. She and my father pulled up to the alley entrance of our third-floor apartment my family was renting from the Leak family, a prominent family on the South Side of Chicago that had been in the funeral business for decades and was of great service to the Black community. My mother got out of the car, looked up to the third floor, and saw me hanging out the window with my legs dangling over the ledge. "Wait right there, son! We'll be right there," she yelled. She told my father to position himself to catch me in case I fell the three stories, and she ran upstairs and snatched me out of the window. That story is still told as if it had happened yesterday.

I grew up with a friend, Rodney Pierre Lias. One day, he and a bunch of us kids were in the basement of my family's home on Constance Avenue watching a movie. We had a popcorn popper going. When Pierre bent over to change the TV station, I took some piping-hot corn kernels from the popcorn popper, pulled back his underwear, and dropped them into his shorts. He danced, jumped, hollered, screamed, and cried as the hot butter touched his hindquarters. It was of course as funny as hell to me at the time, but the more I looked back on it, the more I realized that I was impulsive and that many things that were funny to me were painful and hurtful to others.

I'll never forget the day I was serving in Congress when my brothers called me to say that Pierre had died in a car accident. A few days later, I flew to Atlanta to attend his funeral. I was profoundly remorseful for what I had done to him forty years earlier; I had never really gotten the chance as an adult to share with him how much I regretted the popcorn kernel incident. As a child, I expressed my regret for that many times, but his funeral made my childhood actions really hard for me to accept.

I attended the John J. Pershing Elementary School. I'm reminded of just how cruel we can be as children. Francesca, a classmate, had disabilities, but that did not stop my classmates and me from being cruel to her. No one wanted to sit with her. No one wanted her on his or her team. No one wanted to eat lunch next to her. If we bumped into Francesca, we would consider ourselves as having received the "touch" that we would then have to pass on to someone else, who would then pass it on …

I didn't give much thought to that cruelty back then, but in 1995, when I decided to run for Congress and to ask the people on Chicago's South Side and some south suburbs to support me, I opened an office, one of three, in a sprawling, 846-square-mile congressional district. One day, I got to the office early and saw only one volunteer—Francesca—answering the phones and telling people why she thought I should be her congressman. As a congressman, I was asking people to let me defend their interests if elected, but I felt I had not defended her when we were children. That affects me to this day. I spent a lot of time over seventeen years trying to earn her support.

As children, we can be unkind and cruel, and as adults, the shame, blame, and guilt we feel for that can haunt us. I had lived long enough to be able to share with Franny how much I appreciated her and how much she meant to me. I still get choked up thinking about the full circle of my life and how important she has been to me.

Another incident occurred when I was a student at the posh St. Albans High School in Washington, DC, where the children of presidents and vice presidents and ambassadors from other countries have sent their children. I met a wonderful young woman whose father later become the chairman of my father's presidential campaign in 1988; he went on to become the chair of the Democratic National Committee and the secretary of commerce under President Clinton. She attended St. Albans's sister school, National Cathedral. It was well known whom I was dating at the time. One day, I was in my dorm room at St. Albans when the dean of students, Mr. Billet, knocked on my door and said, "Jesse, everyone's looking for your girlfriend. We can't find her. Do you know where she is?"

To not embarrass her, I said, "I have no idea where she is."

Mr. Billet left.

Five minutes later, I told him the truth—that my girlfriend was in my room. I was suspended from school for having deceived him. These are just some of the examples of my childhood that earned me the title Baddest Fella Ever.

Today, I understand that I have always been driven by a spirit energy that seeks out and uncovers facts and truth. I have a profound love of science and history. My inquisitive nature moves me to study, reflect, and review information as I receive it. I document information and make mental notes of everything including sources and facts I can confirm. In Congress, I was labeled the Historian by members of the Congressional Black Caucus because I was able to recall details of our national journey.

While I always sought my path based on an instinctive, self-directed journey, I am not unaware that carrying the name of my father inspired my goals of leadership and a standard of excellence to pursue the road less traveled. It was not until later, however, in my experiment that I came to realize that every part of my life has been created to embark upon the work I deem the experiment, my reason for being.

I am dedicated to the idea of creating a new understanding of what it is to love one God with all my heart, soul, and mind and my neighbor as myself. This revelation has enabled me to embrace and love the energy I believe was mislabeled as bad and reflective of my Fella spirit. The energy of Fella allows me to evolve into the very purpose of my life with great commitment, empathy, passion, and resilience. I am radically dedicated to teaching the greatest understanding of the Constitution with the eternal flame of hope that in pursuing my purpose, I will help free 68 million federal and state debt-paid individuals with the federal pardon power of the Constitution from their shame, blame, and guilt to go and sin no more. I hope to reignite a flame in America that unites us to be a greater beacon of light for the world.

The last thirteen years were a low point in my life personally and publicly. While the season may have been long, it was a period of renewal I am grateful to have experienced. My faith is strong, and my hope is renewed. From 2008 through 2016, I was spinning in a tornado of circumstances most of which were well documented publicly. I resigned from my congressional seat, was charged, pled guilty, and was sentenced. I accepted responsibility for using my campaign funds for personal use. I served thirty months in prison.

My seventeen years in Congress were documented by a stellar voting record and with excellence in the pursuit of an agenda to help equalize the dynamics of our communities in education, health, and the environment and the establishment of the legal foundation of equality for women. I loved documenting our history. Every day, I went to work in the temple of our democracy, a museum of history that is constantly evolving.

Most important to me, I was driven by a love for my neighbor.

The people who elected me had real needs back home, and I was the representative of those needs. My love of neighbor enabled me to work continuously on behalf of my constituents and peers and my relationships that helped build my campaign. Trying to balance these segments with marriage, children, family, and my personal goals created a perfect storm for my stumbling and ultimately falling from public grace.

Many people will not believe or want to understand my testimony that I could not separate my personal and public lives after a time as they were very interdependent. Let me give you an example—the news report on the elk heads I purchased for my office.[222] While I love hunting, the decision to purchase the two elk heads that complemented the one I had harvested was a strategic proposition. Outside of inner-city Chicago is a vast, rural area of hunters, farmers, and lower-income supporters. I wanted these voters to feel just as comfortable visiting my office as were the inner-city voters who were more familiar with me. Being Jesse Jackson Jr. with all the positive and negative assumptions that came with it was and is not easy work. My father often reminds me that I inherited his friends and his enemies neither of which I had earned. He chided me, "It would be your job to earn my friends," and, "Neutralize your enemies as they enter your life and space."[223] The latter has been more difficult for me.

What I will tell you today is that the energy of Fella drives me to have a radical empathy for other people and especially the less fortunate. The name, brand, and persona of Jesse Jackson Jr. have retired to ensure that Fella makes a difference in our country and ultimately our world.

17

MY CONSTITUTION

I HAVE ALWAYS ADMIRED my father for his incredible contribution to America, to the world, and to the civil rights movement, for his running for president, being a man of service to the community, and his unapologetic global reach.

My father's contributions directly impacted my childhood and young adult development. My father did more than run for president; he transformed people's expectations. He transformed a political party. He transformed the nation by bringing farmers and urban dwellers together. He did not run a campaign but a crusade to bring the least of these to the forefront of American consciousness regardless of the color of their skin.

As much as I wanted to be the first son, he was running for something else. I received the opportunity to meet many prominent, famous, and powerful people. As a result, I was expected to serve, and when I matured, I desired to serve many less fortunate families in my community. That was Operation Breadbasket and Operation PUSH's mission.

I was educated in the best schools, and I have spoken to youth in many struggling schools. I am the product of a unique public view of Black families in America. My name automatically generates recognition of my father and places me in his shadow and footprint. He casts more light on my life than shadow. I think it is all a matter of how you view it.

I grew up in Chicago, which was founded by Jean Baptiste Point du Sable. Chicago is a city conscious of politics, religion, and community activism and their intersections. My father was assigned a role in Chicago by Dr. Martin Luther King Jr. to start Operation Breadbasket. Jesse Jackson Sr. was a young, handsome, and eloquent social activist. He was intuitive enough to know that if he was starting a church and having service on Sunday mornings in a city in which the establishment would determine who the "Head nigga in charge" (HNIC) would be, that person would have to report on the people after walking with them.

My dad was from a different cloth. He was opposed to the HNIC, externally imposed, Chicago democratic machine model. My father founded Operation PUSH, which operated seven days a week for fifty years with public forums on Saturday mornings. The public forums were weekly opportunities to detail to the public in an accountable way the work of the vineyard. He was able to pull together community leaders, political leaders, and pastors to discuss, plan, and organize efforts to support, lift, and financially empower the community. It was a push against culture and the history of racism in Chicago and in the US.

That was the culture I was raised in. My life was structured around utilizing all these paths to ensure all people could hope to be included in our political, religious, and legal systems. Our history would go forward by educating people to embrace empowerment through enlightenment and action. As I think about my experiment and discovery, I am acutely aware that the pioneer of living a life in which the Constitution and the laws of God came together to promote the advancement of human liberty was my father.

My father is still running the good race and fighting the good fight to ensure voting rights, economic empowerment, and justice in America. I believe he will continue to push until he takes his last breath because he has accepted the assignment of elevating and advancing all people. My personal drive and mission are the path I walk today.

I am keenly aware that Donald Trump and his family are given the benefit of the doubt for their political and financial dealings that overlooked the people of the nation while my father and I have been judged for our actions and in my opinion more harshly than others even as we continue to support the least among us in America.

I have been given insight that allows me to carry my unique responsibility for the balance of my life. My understanding of my "why" has enabled me to find my "how" by reviewing the fabric of my life and prison. Nietzsche said, "He who has a why to live for, can bear with almost any how."[224] My life's journey walked me right into the how of my life. Upon understanding my life assignment, I had to take inventory of the journey my life had taken to walk me into the how of my life. If I take off all the labels of achievement and review the experiences and exposure of my birthright, I understand why I was created to complete my experiment and see my life assignment through.

Rev. Rick Warren, who was the first visitor I received in prison, wrote *The Purpose Driven Life*[225] in which he stated that you are exactly where you should be.

> We are born from the right parents, into the right family, into the right time, into the right community, into the right skin color, into the right generation because everything is as it is intended to be.[226]

There is no do-over in these situations that allow you no choice, but there is the understanding that your birth is purpose driven. My exposure and experiences have enabled me to meet a rainbow of prominent people around the world and a rainbow of fallen people in my congressional and prison experiences. I have developed relationships with all cultures as a result of my education and professional experiences. I have mastered our constitutional language and the Founders' experiment as a result of my public service. The material I have developed to keep my pulse on the needs of our communities and specifically to ensure equal opportunity for all have provided me with precision tools to excavate powerful understandings of the uniqueness of America and what it means to be an American. I love our country.

Our country's greatness can be improved if we seek an understanding of what our Constitution affords every citizen. We must narrow our focus to the idea that the presidency was initially conceived (original intent) as a position in which the person elected would have unlimited moral power and authority based on divine truth but limited constitutional authority. Donald Trump's presidency was evolving to unlimited constitutional authority and little to no moral authority or power. On September 17, 1787, there was no country that had this function, $f(lod)$, in its constitution with democratic accountability to the people. It is my intention to show the American people their inheritance, how to use it in all affairs of state, and how to distribute the grace of God broadly. This thought alone allows me to carry the baton of my father's assignment however with a route change to ensure the destination is reached with complete understanding of our liberties, freedoms, and ability to dream impossible dreams by every American including the least of them—the politically and psychologically incarcerated.

If asked to describe myself at any point in life, I would say that I was a scientist of life, a historian, and even by education an unbarred juris doctor and business major. If asked to describe myself by career, of course, I would say that I was a US Congressman from Illinois for seventeen years. Ultimately, I would probably state the obvious—I am Jesse Jackson Jr., the son of Rev. Jesse Jackson Sr., and I am labeled a felon. I would be proud to give honor to a father who has been my role model and hero all my life. The kinship by name, shoe size, and the depth and width of the trail my father has blazed is massive when you are the person walking in his sunlight.

My father exposed my siblings and me to every level of living from early poverty to the upper middle class; we have personally experienced about every culture and every political, religious, entertainment, and business icon and leader in America and around the globe. His impact on issues of the day, from education and employment to voting, has given me a point of view in real time. I have gleaned understanding and moments of truth I have used to make decisions and for knowing how to walk in honor even when a situation has no honor in it. I have also learned that our God-given assignments require us as individuals to choose every option life presents us based on where God's assignment leads us and then to own the outcome. In my case, I believe this understanding has enabled me to navigate my life to bring me into the essence of my being, and I am excited about the journey ahead of me and us all.

18

MY YEARS IN CONGRESS

THE PEOPLE OF the Second Congressional District of Illinois sent me to Congress to represent them, and I was serious about my work. I was excellent in my efforts to map a plan to move Chicago and my district forward. I created dozens of timelines that presented a step-by-step review of history based on the initial history of Native Americans, the advent and sojourn of African slavery, the Founders, our Declaration of Independence, our country's history, the Constitution, the Bill of Rights, and our religious and individual freedoms. I have a timeline that dates to the most primitive of times.

In my American timeline, I showed how America failed to incorporate the struggle of African Americans into our country's fabric by history, law, and religion. Before I would lead visitors on a tour of the Capitol, I would review the timelines with them to provide a proper overview of our history. When trying to determine where I would focus my efforts, I would review the timeline to measure it against the current events by the environment we were in at the time. Then I would determine the tasks at hand for me during a congressional session.

My work was meaningful to me and filled with purpose. I was meticulous about pursuing my goals. During my seventeen years in Congress, I maintained one of the highest voting records and percentages on Capitol Hill. In some ways, my commitment to my career may have created erosion in my personal relationships. Sadly, I was a perfectionist.

One project I pursued with vigor was trying to get an airport built on the South Side of Chicago as it would have created growth in employment there and at hotels and banking and conference centers. All these factors ultimately would improve opportunities for my constituents to be gainfully employed. I love my community. I have relocated to the South Side of Chicago, to where former President Barack Obama is building his library and Tiger Woods is building a golf course. In August of 2021, a project that I spearheaded and began in 2012 came to fruition, the grand opening of the Pullman National Monument. These three projects give me great confirmation in understanding that even my airport project was a vision light-years ahead in creating opportunities to ensure Chicago and the south suburbs would thrive.

Congress does not have a stop and start period for members of Congress who are dedicated to the people they serve. When you leave work, you are heading out on your second or third tour of duty. Friends and fundraising are always essential to reelection strategies as is attending events to ensure that you express your appreciation for being able to serve. When you greet those who have lost loved ones, you must acknowledge their grief. When you greet those who have just given birth, you must acknowledge their joy. These dynamics require sometimes smiling when you're sad and crying when you're happy. Carrying the joy and burden of others can throw your balance off in subtle ways you do not realize. I started to stress over ensuring that I made every effort to never miss a vote, attend all fundraisers, and accept invitations to events in my district. I rarely missed a requested constituent meeting, and each meeting was fifteen minutes long. I held twelve staff-accompanied meetings between 9:00 a.m. and noon and eight constituent meetings attended by staff between 1:00 p.m. and 3:00 p.m. That was my day in the district and DC offices every day for seventeen years. Plus, I would try to ensure that my children saw me at their events and that my wife saw me supporting her career and career-related activities.

I worked hard and played hard, but I was never on vacation; I was never off my agenda. These dynamics caused me to blur the lines between my personal life and its obligations and my professional life and its obligations. I was slowly losing the battle to balance all my agendas—my commitments to family, friends, donors, constituents, and myself. While I thought I was functioning, I was slowly becoming more dysfunctional. I was overwhelmed, anxious, and obsessive with following up, and I became despondent when my strategies failed. Ultimately, I started to react to these periods by experiencing bouts of depression in my fast-paced and pressurized career. I would overspend, indulge in inappropriate personal relationships, and attempt to figure out how I could make myself unwind.

I would be so wound up that I could not sleep. If you have never experienced sleeplessness, you'll have to take my word for how debilitating it can be. The lack of sleep can cause an extreme emotional breakdown. I would try to sleep in my office, my car, at home. There was just no good place to be unequivocally me. I needed a place where there was no expectation of my disposition, no expectation for me to participate or have an opinion, but I could not find a place to cry without judgment or a place to laugh without having to explain my behavior. Due to this pressure, I could not sleep, I could not eat.

I was digging myself into deep debt. I thought I had to look the part of a congressman. I had to support my wife's ambitions. I had to be present for my career and not forget I was attempting to do that under the spotlight of my father's imprint on the fabric of our country. My father was on the scene and making his agenda known in some cases even when we were on opposite sides of the same agenda. While I was serving as cochair of the Obama campaign, my father was scrambling to recover from having suggested he would "cut Obama's nuts off"; he said that while I was chair of the campaign. I told Senator Obama not to respond publicly, but I responded; I issued a stern response on behalf of the campaign.

I by no means want anyone to think I do not accept the situation I created; I absolutely accept responsibility for my choices. My choices created the shame, blame, and guilt that exists in every life including mine. However, stacking wrong choices on each other ultimately causes the same crash that occurs when one pulls the wrong block out in a game of Jenga. I crashed. I was filled with shame. I looked for someone or something to blame. Ultimately, I was ridden with guilt. This is so hard to reconcile when all I ever wanted to do was make my dad proud. I wanted him to know that I appreciated all the trails he had blazed. I wanted my hometown to know that I loved representing its people. I wanted my wife and children to know that I was a true protector and provider. I thought I was committed to giving them a wonderful home and all the amenities a congressman should be able to extend to his family. I also loved the trappings my office allowed me to accept.

I asked Mike Flannery, one of Chicago's premier political reporters who covered my initial swearing in, for a favor. He said, "Sure, Congressman." I told him that he had covered public servants for most of his career, and I asked him to summarize what I should avoid. He told me about political figures who had fallen from grace; he said, "Their downfall occurs because of hubris, when it all goes to their head."[227]

The reconciliation came when I pled guilty to raiding my campaign funds and on sentencing day. I was at the lowest point in my life. I now know that every choice is for excellence in all I do. Viktor Frankl suggested that there were not as many races of people as we might think: "There are two races, the decent race and the indecent race."[228] I strive to remember that with every choice I make, I want to be a member of the decent race.

My resignation from Congress was painful. However, I have a renewed life and sense of purpose and passion to work for the decency of fallen men and women. I want to work for the poor and underserved in our trailer parks, barrios, and ghettos. I want children attending inner-city schools to have the same high-quality opportunities children in suburban America have. I argue that America is a theological experiment and that by rededicating our nation to the one true God, we can fulfill a unique role by demonstrating unconditional love for neighbor as our national moral duty and ethos.

19

The Finger of God

MY CAMPAIGN FUNDS

FIRST, I DID not participate in any pay-for-play politics with former Illinois governor Rod Blagojevich. I campaigned legally for the job, met with him in his office with the press outside, and offered him a notebook full of my accomplishments and qualifications, some polling data, and arguments why I should be the person to replace Barack Obama in the Senate. That's it. I did nothing wrong.

In 2012, I was reported to have been away grappling with bipolar disorder. I never saw bipolarity or depression as a problem. There is a balancing act between ego and despair. Ego is the gasoline of ambition while despair is the flashing red light of an empty tank. I always saw these signals as assets for me. I outwork everyone. I get more done without sleep than everyone. Only recently did they tell me that my work ethic was a disorder that led to highs and lows. Previous headlines contained allegations of my paying for a Senate seat[229] and ultimately reported my being charged with raiding my campaign funds.

I accepted responsibility for what I did. I acknowledged that my inappropriate personal relationship was being worked out privately with my spouse. It wasn't the first time I had offered such apologies, and it wasn't the last. I accepted responsibility for using campaign funds for my personal use and was sentenced for that. I served my time for all my behavior. All these things were devastating, embarrassing, and humiliating and were a stain on my family, my name, and what I believed had been a stellar career in Congress.

I cannot stress enough the gravity of the shame, blame, and guilt associated with each and every headline, conversation, court date, hiring of attorneys, wondering about my image, outcomes, my children, family, spouse and my own well-being. I was in a genuine tornado, a catastrophe. I acknowledge that this was all due to self-inflicted wounds. I was at a breaking point, and I broke.

This story is hard to share; it puts me in a vulnerable position not because I have not come to terms with the events but because I know that even if I tell my truth, readers will evaluate how they choose to accept or not what I share. I can only state my truth as I know it. I do not look back other than to ensure I calculate the cost of doing anything that would cause me to fall that hard again.

20

The Finger of God

SHAME, BLAME, AND GUILT

If we could read the secret history of our enemies, we should find in each man's life sorrow and suffering enough to disarm all hostility.[230]

—Henry Wadsworth Longfellow

Every man has his secret sorrows which the world knows not; and oftentimes we call a man cold when he is only sad.[231]

—Henry Wadsworth Longfellow

DURING MY TIME of great introspection and reflection, I came to understand a form of triangular thinking that keeps a person locked in a pattern of reviewing life, life choices, and life works through the lens of shame, blame, and guilt (SBG). Every individual goes through a cycle of SBG. Some people will feel heavier shame, some will experience heavier blame, and some will have heavier guilt, but all of us have felt SBG at one time or another and perhaps more than once.

Living with SBG is the opposite of living with LLH—life, liberty, and happiness. This psychological state is the antithesis of our system. I am no different; my SBG ultimately required me to continuously make excuses for why I was spending my campaign funds. A famous name does not translate into wealth. My family is not one of great means. Our names are tied to decades of ser-vice; that's all we have. A young family, election to Congress, a life in two cities, and media attention do not translate into a life of wealth. It can be the contrary.

Imagine some starting congressional careers with great wealth and personal spending completely in line with their means. I entered Congress with my and my wife's salaries as our main sources of income. The expenses of my children and family came later, and the desire for my family to live as I had been accus-tomed to when I was growing up was difficult on fixed salaries.

In my mind, every family vacation was justified as a cam-paign and a political expense. No matter where I went, even on vacation, I had to shake hands and pose for pictures. I was always on the job. I accepted full responsibility for living above my means. Over ten years in Congress, I made many purchases to create a level of living that I felt was appropriate for my edu-cation, career, and exposure. And yes, I convinced myself that this kind of thinking would allow me to believe I could shift my shame and blame the culture I was working and living in at the time.

I made the wrong choice when I used my campaign funds to support my spending. I did purchase some items that I thought would make my office comfortable for my constituents when they came there. I also purchased items I wanted for my and my family's use. I often felt guilty for the purchases. I purchased a Rolex watch to try to lift my spirits at a particular time, but I could not wear it without feeling guilty. My shame ranged from knowing my spending was inappropriate to pulling others into negative positions because of my behavior. My blame was to use the excuse of making my lifestyle reflective of the precongressio-nal incomes of my peers. My guilt was to look back and recog-nize that my marriage did not withstand the storm. My children have experienced pains and the loss of their parents during a very precious time in their growth and development. I feel guilty for having smeared my family name, specifically my father's, whose namesake I am. There is a moral obligation as a Junior to always represent the family well.

Again, I accept full responsibility for my actions. I did my time, and I have a renewed faith and commitment to help former inmates receive new lives. We live in a system designed to guarantee life, liberty, and the pursuit of happiness, the antithesis of shame, blame, and guilt. I believe everyone deserves a new start. Pardoning debt-paid felons who have completed their time will give them the option to "go and sin no more."[232] Felons in America and their families are anchored in shame, blame, and guilt, but most of them can be forgiven for their choices by their families, churches, and communities and never return to the improper behavior. Yet for the formerly incarcerated to successfully reenter society and become productive citizens, we must forgive people in their personal relationships (family), in our religious systems (privately), and in our public, institutional, and government systems publicly (pardons).

SBG was central to Jesus's ministry; the modern church has made SBG and especially the guilt dynamic central to its existence. Whoever can guilt people through the door can build a big church. But the modern church and its radically individual Protestant sects and historically Catholicism cannot extinguish guilt on the scale that the national problem requires. In fact, it thrives on guilt's self-perpetuation and has no means to extinguish guilt except on the most personal level. If you think about the literal interpretation of the two extremes associated with the Article II, Section 2, Clause 1's two job responsibilities, the civilian presidency doesn't do that well particularly if the occupant has no military experience. As a result, more often than not, beyond the initial decision to engage in military action, presidents delegate the conduct of war to professionals, and they pardon individuals only in the last few days of their administrations. It's all of the stuff in between or the $f(LOD)$ that they fail to do. That failure is unraveling society.

The first thing we must do as a nation to challenge our

shame, blame, and guilt is to admit that we were wrong, and then we must repent and seek redemption by changing course and repairing the damage done domestically and globally. I am grateful to have spent time in prison if for no other reason than to acknowledge that the stories of the men I met there have burned a mission into my heart. Now, I have personal insight and perspective into how the prison system destroys families, communities, and societies. Once those who were incarcerated complete their sentences—after they have accepted responsibility, owned their behavior, completed their time, and done what the judge said—they too go home, where the dynamics have changed. The restoration is not just for them to reenter the space; rehabilitation must occur in their relationships and bonds with their families.

Just as my relationship with my now ex-wife could not endure the storm, many walk back into empty spaces or new additions to their homes. Some of us can overcome the changes; many of us are forced to leave our old knowledge behind and attempt to rebuild by ourselves. This period of recovery is filled with endless hours of toil trying to acknowledge, reject, make peace with, and lash out at all the choices and circumstances leading up to our new realities.

My level of SBG coming out of prison and after having been in the press for an affair, my inappropriate use of my campaign funds, being falsely accused of trying to purchase a senate seat, and struggling with depression that became a public conversation were very difficult to handle. I felt that I was in a house of cards that would collapse on me. I can unequivocally tell you now that the storms I endured girded me with the fullest armor of God. I wear my armor daily knowing that in the process of falling, I hurt some people, I disappointed some people, and I even subjected myself to unnecessary situations that caused much of the storm I was in.

My faith is renewed, and I would describe my ability to move forward each day as a radical resilience. In *First-Rate Madness*,[233] Dr. Nassir Ghaemi highlighted resilience as a key leadership trait. I believe this is true. My ability to move through situations because of my personal choices or choices of friends or family has always been based on my desire to live to see another day and help others. I become more affirmed in this effort every day. I have an absolute commitment to see my mission through with determination to allow our nation to start anew.

21

MY PREAMBLE

I AM LABELED A felon. I left prison understanding that every time I would be stopped while driving, my information would be pulled up and I would be identified as a felon. While on probation, I was stopped for a speeding ticket going to visit Sandra. My probation officer immediately called me—at 2:00 in the morning—and asked me if I had been stopped for a traffic infraction and if I was in the presence of law enforcement, and I said I was.

When I wanted to travel, I had to email my probation officer for permission to do so. Now, I have served my time and have been released from probation. I still do not have a right to bear arms. I enjoy hunting, but that is no longer an option for me. Being a felon requires me to always ensure that my space is maintained properly. We all live our lives to ensure that we are within the lines of the law. However, as a felon, I am acutely aware that even the actions of others have the potential to create issues for me.

Imagination/Science

For the first time in my life, I understand unequivocally what I was created to do, and I cannot ignore the driving force that moves me down my path to accomplish it. It is only because of my journey thus far that I can move into the work I have accepted responsibility to complete. In his book *Man's Search for Meaning*, Viktor Frankl wrote,

> We needed to stop asking about the meaning of life, and instead to think of ourselves as those who were being questioned by life-daily, and hourly. Our answer must consist not in talk and meditation, but in right action and in right conduct. Life, ultimately, means taking the responsibility to find the right answer to its problems and fulfill the tasks which it constantly sets for each individual.[234]

While it would seem that all my choices up until now were made from a place of being the son of Jesse Jackson Sr., acquiring my theological education, having completed law school, having been a Member of Congress, and being perceived as a person of entitlement and privilege, none of those considerations are even close to the truth of my life. I believe I was created to bring forth knowledge and understanding of a work that the Founders created knowing there would be a time such as now that would require a radical shift in the way we address our neighbors, and it begins with American felons, who are in the lowest caste. The Founders understood that there would be a time when all the experiences and experiments involved in creating our country would bottleneck into confusion about what was justice and what was injustice.

The person uncovering what the Founders created would need to have a mastery of history, law, the Declaration of Independence, the Constitution, and an understanding of our government. The person exposing the mind-blowing proposition of what our Founders placed in our Constitution would have to understand African American history starting from 1619. He would have to draw attention to the way slavery, race, sexism, and their corrective actions throughout our history has dominated the arguments our laws are founded on.

My exposure to public and private school education, HBCUs (Historically Black Colleges and Universities), PWIs (Predominantly White Institutions), and my working to provide for the less fortunate while working with many of America's public figures helped develop my belief in public service. If what I have come to believe is true, it will have a powerful impact on ending discrimination and inequality in our nation, it will bring new life and meaning to the uncomfortable parts of this nation's history, it will result in a practical "on earth as it is in heaven" utopia in America, and it will advance the cause of social justice in a way never before believed possible.

Religion

I love one God with all my heart, soul, and mind and my neighbor as myself. That is the entirety of my religion. It is not a complicated system. These commandments are built on the prophets. All other beliefs and values and my mission in life are built on this understanding. Jesus shined a light on the path to God, whom he called his Father.

I believe that science is fact-based—seeking it is the beginning of every invention, discovery, word, thought, and deed.

Science is knowledge, and research is understanding; these two combined with intuition constitute wisdom. Knowledge, reason, and understanding are required above all things before we can seek and explore our passions and purposes. In the book *Ye Will Say I Am No Christian*,[235] Bruce Braden submitted a letter from Adams to Jefferson dated June 10, 1813, in which Adams was asking Jefferson to explain, "The President himself declaring, that 'We were never to expect to go beyond them in real Science,'" which Jefferson attributed to Adams; however,

Adams did not seem to recognize it. The reference to "them" in this quote was a reference to our ancestors. The quote was suggesting that innovation, invention, and advancement should be a process of looking forward to new discoveries, not looking backward at the works of others.

I believe that everything we do out of curiosity, inquiry, questioning, and asking the what-ifs allows us to move forward on the journey that life expects of us during our time in our star. Dr. Benjamin Elijah Mays said it best: "No man is ahead of his time. Every man is within his star, each in his time."[236] My seeking and walking in my purpose was initially firmly established in Trinitarianism; I was open to Deism, but I recognized the providence of God in human affairs, and it is best understood in Unitarianism, in fact, a linear Unitarianism. Deism is understanding God through nature or natural inquiry while Theism is a reliance on providence. Providence and spirit energy motivate us to pursue our highest level of inquiry. In his book *The Purpose Driven Life*, Rick Warren wrote,

> The purpose of your life is far greater than your own personal fulfillment, your peace of mind, or even your happiness. It's far greater than your family, your career, or even your wildest dreams and ambitions.[237]

Ultimately, my relationship with God is unique to me. Jesus said,

> Thou shalt love the Lord thy God with all thy heart, and with all thy soul, and with all thy mind; this is the first and great commandment. And, the second is like unto it, Thou shalt love thy neighbor as thyself. On these two commandments hang all the law and the prophets.[238]

I believe in Jesus. Washington, Jefferson, Adams, and Madison were Deists and of this ancient religion. Religion is a very personal commitment to something higher or greater than ourselves, but we have to understand the implications of Deism and Theism and the perspective of the Founders that went into their creation of the Constitution.

I connected religion, history, and law in my research, and that led me to the discovery I have revealed in this book. A knock at midnight in prison awakened me every night to continue my work in the laboratory of my mind—researching, writing, confirming, and connecting pieces to validate and test my work—and I am pleased with the results. I believe it is because of my purpose that life has led me to understand the vast and extraordinary impact my discovery will have on our country and the world. I am very specifically working to free the 68 million debt-paid felons from SBG. This work reaches into the barrios, ghettos, and trailer parks but does not leave behind the middle class, upper class, or elite class in our great country. Freeing the poor and haggard of their burdens extends to them freedom from shame, blame, and guilt.

Creating new life, liberty, and the pursuit of happiness under the Constitution will renew the spirits of all who are struggling psychologically in our country. I believe that we all should love God and our neighbors if we want to complete the work life has for us.

I am in a sect of one, a religion all by myself. The Founders protected in our Constitution the supreme belief of a single believer in divine truth four years before the Bill of Rights and the First Amendment, which guaranteed freedom of religion and more specifically the freedom of congregationalism and denominationalism, in short, the right to practice one's religious beliefs in a group or public gathering.

22

A NEW EARTH

LIFE, LIBERTY, AND the pursuit of happiness start with peace of mind. Imagine having assurance in our hearts and minds that we have the constitutional right to seek these three inalienable rights in spirit and in truth. Our Founders went through the process of putting the finger of God in our Constitution to ensure our peace in the United States.

Our freedoms, hopes, and dreams have been embedded in our Constitution for 235 years waiting for someone in David's lineage to reveal our right to prosperity in the fullness of life. We are no longer tied to our mistakes and forgiven only in a spiritual renewal; we have been given the right by God to go and sin no more in a constitutional renewal.

Those whose decisions lead them into our prison system can be legally forgiven through our constitutional process. If we stumble, we have a supreme right, not a privilege, to be forgiven by our Constitution and have another chance to pursue life anew regardless of our social status. This is the concomitance of high religion; after we pay our debts, our sins are forgiven and we gain renewed minds and spirits. Our right to seek life, liberty and the pursuit of happiness is in the constitutional restoration of our freedom.

Who qualifies for the forgiveness of our legal system and a new life? Everyone. In and out of prison, "all men are created equal."[239] The white-collar felon is equal to the blue-collar felon. The drug dealer is equal to the tax evader. The prostitute is equal to the money launderer. Once our time is served, we can redeem and restore our spirits, families, and our places in society because all of us were created equal.

We must give all an opportunity to walk in the spiritual forgiveness of their birthright with the power of constitutional forgiveness—a God-given human right. We must believe that everyone has fallen short and deserves a second chance. We must walk in love of our country and the knowledge that the finger of God is in the Constitution; the two great commandments—love God and love our neighbors—generate the energy to maintain our great status as Winthrop's city on the hill, the light of the world. American citizens would be assured an opportunity to contribute at every level to our heritage and future.

The new earth is not in the clouds; it is here. It is America under the revelation that all have a right to seek life, liberty, and happiness even after they fall from grace. All men and women deserve new lives. All men and women were created equal. The burden of despair is removed from felons and their families. The president is the commander of the army and the repriever pardoner.® America has elevated humanity by embedding forgiveness, restoration, freedom, and the highest love and supreme power in our Constitution, a living document that expresses our guiding principles.

Once upon a time, a man was going around the Sea of Galilee extending forgiveness. He came with a sublime and consistent demeanor and the understanding that everyone was burdened with shame, blame, and guilt. He came as light to a world of darkness explaining that God was his Father and ours as well regardless of our race, class, or sexual orientation. He explained that for every bad decision, for every scheme gone astray that causes us to feel shame, we can rest in blessed assurance that we are free by knowing that we were created by a power greater than us. That power enables us to have a fresh start each day with a renewed spirit.

The grace of God is planted in the soul and confirmed in our Constitution. Our country is consistent in spirit and truth. Freedom is extended in the heart and soul, and it is extended in the law and our Constitution for our opportunities to carry on. I have a dream that the 68 million debt-paid felons will be freed after serving their time to come back into our great nation and contribute to our society. We will reduce our prison burdens, restore our families, rebuild our communities, and live in a country that seeks our kingdom on earth and in heaven with the guiding finger of God.

Given an opportunity to live now and in eternity, all men and women should wake up with faith, hope, and love of God, who watches over a country, and love for their neighbors, which enables us to rise and fall together. We the people of the United States need to seek our perfect union now on earth as we dream it to be in heaven.

23

SOLITARY CONFINEMENT

URING MY TIME in solitary confinement, I gained the realization that our Constitution never intended forgiveness to be just something received at the altar in church; forgiveness had been built into our Constitution.

The Founders knew that the American dream was an experiment in governance—that breaking free from England would come with some hiccups, unforeseen challenges, and repercussions. They knew that they would make some mistakes; implementation always comes with lessons learned. But they built into the Constitution a way to recover from bad decisions. Our country was formed around the idea of trusting in God—"Love God with all your heart and all your soul and mind"[240] and "love thy neighbor as thyself."[241]

I walked out of the hole enlightened. I became aware that all my curiosity about our Constitution and my formal education in business administration, theology, and law were in alignment. As I stated earlier, while I was in Congress, I wanted to ensure that the amendments that I offered were key during each session I served in Congress to building a more perfect union. I can point out periods in our history that directly recognize how African Americans entered our country and how specific issues dealing with the humanity of our race created debates and decisions affecting how America moved forward.

I have always loved history; I think it demonstrates God's love and the plan he has for humanity. History is not just dates and events; it's also revelatory. Those who record history but bring their biases to it corrupt it, but discerning their biases is part of the reflective journey.

It is also not lost on me the impact economics has on our ability to distribute equality and particularly wealth to all Americans. My business administration degree gave me a working knowledge of economics and statistics. Let me give an example. Children attending public schools should have equal opportunities to gain an equal high-quality education. Schools in lower-income neighborhoods, the happenstance of geography, should offer the same equal high-quality education that schools in upper-income neighborhoods offer, and that includes amenities such as swimming pools, tennis courts, and tracks. I use this example to point out how economics plays a key role in honoring the goals of our Constitution. I understand with even greater empathy how those struggling to find employment should not have to stress over the education their children receive. I found that it was not enough to speak about prison, prisoners, and their families; I actually had to experience prison to understand what those who are incarcerated go through.

I am grateful to God for my three nights in solitary, where the revelation of my next mission started and where I believe the redemption of the nation would begin. It is with this understanding that I will now go into the inmate story, which will provide further understanding of our prison system and the struggles of inmates. In hindsight, prison was one of the best things that happened to me. I am not fighting just for prison reform; I am fighting for the rights of every human being and especially the fallen. The fight is for justice, but my personal experience gave me the fire of radical empathy and a new American truth.

After being processed into the camp where I was to spend thirty months, I was led to my assigned area and met my "cellee," Abrahaman Muhammad. The process was numbing. I could not think. I could not sleep. My limbs were motionless, and my mind was unable to comprehend the gravity of how in what seemed to be the blink of an eye I had gone from being an esteemed Congressman to being an inmate. While I understood how I had gotten there, I had to unravel the events, contemplate my choices, and dissect my lifestyle. I had to grapple with how I looked to my family, friends, and the people who had supported me during not just my seventeen years in Congress but also during my entire life. In this very still, catatonic state, I knew I would have to take inventory of what I had been consistently trying to do with my life and why what I had been trying to do had turned into something unimaginable for me.

My transition into prison was a long, still moment. It was as if my world had ceased to spin long enough for me to step out of one reality and into another completely different one. During that time, I came to understand Frankl's *Man's Search for Meaning*. While I did not have to endure the atrocity of Frankl's experience, I do understand that landing in that place albeit at my own doing disrupted the I Am-ness of life. I am a father, a son, a husband, a former Congressman, an HBCU graduate, a theologian, and I graduated from law school. I am the son of parents deeply involved in the civil rights movement, and in spite of it all, I found myself living with men many of who were very different from me whose paths converged in prison, where the level of living is the same, not unlike Geoffrey Chaucer's *Canterbury Tales*. The dress code was the same, the food was the same, the work was the same, the privileges were the same, and many of the stories were the same. Our offenses differed, but we were all exiles from society for varying times.

Abrahaman said to me, "No one here has fallen as far as you. Many of us here have been in 'the life' our whole lives."[242] Yet none of the factors of distinction or sameness combined would matter as much as these: Why are we here? What did we do? How can we get out not from prison but from the mental space in which we had made poor choices? What will we do while we are here?

My presenting the problems of felons who have completed their time would not have been a radical endeavor unless I had lived that experience myself. All my fellow inmates felt shame, blame, and guilt. Our experiences tell the greater story of a purpose we cannot articulate with words. Words are energy. My experience in prison filled me with a radical empathy for all felons and especially debt-paid felons.

While in solitary confinement, I found myself in a search for meaning, the meaning of my life. In the foreword to *Man's Search for Meaning*, Rabbi Harold Kushner summarized Frankl's search.

> Frankl approvingly quotes the words of Nietzsche: He who has a Why to live for can bear almost any How. He describes poignantly those prisoners who gave up on life, who had lost all hope for a future, and were inevitably the first to die. They died less from lack of food or medicine than from lack of hope, lack of something to live for. By contrast, Frankl kept himself alive and kept hope alive by summoning up the thoughts of his wife and the prospect of seeing her again, and by dreaming at one point of lecturing about the war and the psychological lessons to be learned from the Auschwitz experience. But Frankl's concern was less with the question of why most died than it was with the question of why anyone at all survived.
>
> Life is not primarily a quest for pleasure, as Freud believed, or a quest for power, as Alfred Adler taught, but a quest for meaning.

The greatest task for any person is to find meaning in his or her life. Frankl saw three possible
sources for meaning: In work (doing something
significant), in love (caring for another person)
and in courage during difficult times. Suffering in
and of itself is meaningless. We give our suffering
meaning by the way we respond to it.[243]

I had to determine the meaning of it all. Frankl, who had
faced different and far more difficult circumstances, was sharing
with me my why and my how. He wrote,

The reader may ask why I did not try to escape
what was in store for me after Hitler had occupied
Austria. Let me answer by recalling the following
story. Shortly, before the United States entered
World War II, I received an invitation to come to
the American Consulate in Vienna to pick up my
immigration visa. My old parents were overjoyed
because they expected that I would soon be allowed to leave Austria. I suddenly hesitated, however. The question beset me: could I really afford
to leave my parents alone to face their fate, to be
sent, sooner or later, to a concentration camp, or
even to a so-called extermination camp? Where
did my responsibility lie? Should I foster my brain-
child, logo-therapy, by emigrating to fertile soil
where I could write my books? Or should I concentrate on my duties as a real child, the child of
my parents who had to do whatever he could to
protect them? I pondered the problem this way
and that but could not arrive at a solution; this
is the type of dilemma that made one wish for a
"hint from Heaven," as the phrase goes.

It was then that I noticed a piece of marble lying on a table at home. When I asked my father about it, he explained that he had found it on the site where the National Socialists had burned down the largest Viennese synagogue. He had taken the piece home because it was part of the tablet on which the Ten Commandments were inscribed. One gilded Hebrew letter was engraved on the piece; my father explained that this letter stood for one of the Commandments. Eagerly I asked, Which one is it? He answered, Honor thy father and thy mother that thy days may be long upon the land. At that moment I decided to stay with my father and my mother upon the land, and to let the American visa lapse.[244]

By no means am I equating the conditions in a concentration camp to the circumstances surrounding America's penal system. The former involved unspeakable, horrific treatment of innocent people while the latter involves the consequences of unacceptable personal behavior that leads to shame and blame and, in more cases than not, guilt even if many offenders I met maintained their innocence in spite of overwhelming evidence to the contrary. Every society must have rules, regulations, and discouraging consequences for unacceptable behavior including imprisonment.

Our worst day in an American penal institution doesn't come close to the horrors that millions faced at the hands of the Nazis—at the hands of other men. The physical, psychological, and emotional abuse including human experimentation during the holocaust remains in a category of its own. Frankl's capacity to endure, observe, record, and report it with clarity offers insight into our human capacity that cannot be ignored. His testimony of hope and psychological analysis under the cruelest of human circumstances remains an inspiration and encouragement to those whose behaviors have landed them in physical and psychological confinement and in need of rehabilitation and redemption. Frankl's testimony applies equally to those who have never been incarcerated yet whose minds have never known freedom. Those in this latter group can identify all too well with Fannie Lou Hamer's description of a common mental condition: "I am sick and tired of being sick and tired."[245] Relief is found in our capacity to subdue fear, maintain dignity, and remain concerned about others, our hardships notwithstanding.

"There are great storms in life that everyone must weather," my dad said. "Open your eyes and close your mouth is a great rule for navigating a storm and may keep you from drowning. People don't drown because of the storm; they drown because they stop kicking."[246]

While in prison in Montgomery, Alabama, I offered a daily affirmation: "Whether the weather be good, or whether the weather be bad, I will weather the weather no matter the weather whether I am happy or sad." "Keep living," I can hear my father say. "Storms don't last always; joy comes in the morning."[247]

Prison deprives the vast majority of the incarcerated of meaning and purpose. One could easily argue that a lack of purpose in their lives had landed them in prison in the first place, and I accept that. However, American prisons reinforce the purposelessness. Work, love of neighbor, and courage are central to developing a sense of meaning and purpose; the American penal system does not foster that. While the prison system offers inmates an opportunity to hold jobs, they do not receive fair compensation for it. This aspect of the prison experience is an assault on man's unalienable and inalienable rights to pursue the significance that makes life worth living.

If we evaluate the American prison system's ability to encourage meaning and consider just how capable convicts and prisoners are of experiencing love, the prison system receives a failing grade here as well. Those who become entangled in the legal and prison systems are usually economic, social, and political outcasts prone to *de facto* subhuman treatment and devoid of neighborly love. Jailhouse Lawyers Speak, a prisoner rights organization composed of imprisoned individuals, released this statement in August 2018 coincidental with a three-week nationwide prisoner strike organized by members of the group.

> Prisoners understand they are being treated as animals. We know that our conditions are causing physical harm and deaths that could be avoided if prison policy makers actually gave a damn. Prisons in America are a war zone. Every day prisoners are harmed due to conditions of confinement. For some of us, it's as if we are already dead, so what do we have to lose?[248]

I was different from most of my fellow inmates during my time at two camps. They are called country clubs in comparison to the Federal Correctional Institution's high-, medium-, and low-security institutions. I had visits from family and former colleagues. In contrast, scores of prisoners had not spoken to loved ones for decades; they had been abandoned. A psychologist at Montgomery Correctional Facility once told me that the number one cause of death for people in general was abandonment. Like Frankl, Dr. Cannon was a scientist who had spent his career observing abandoned men in prison. "Why hast thou forsaken me?"[249] Even at the hour of his death, the perception of abandonment weighed heavily on the Son of Man. There were times I had so many visitors in prison that I was ashamed. I was of course grateful for each visitor who came to see me and hear my confession, but I was ashamed because my name would be broadcast throughout the prison summoning me to the visitation room when a visitor came; it was an announcement that I had not been abandoned and that I had a reason to live. I wanted my visitors including my father, ministers, preachers, thought leaders, and members of Congress[250] and the Nation of Islam[251] to speak

to the inmates to ease the pressure of abandonment and the profound sense of loneliness that comes at the hour of death and un-
certainty. In some ways, I guess I had been preparing for prison
for a long time. I've never wanted to be alone or abandoned, so I
had tried to live a life in which I was relevant to others.

Some might ask, "Who cares if an offender receives no visitors or mail in prison?" That too is a legitimate question, but
the answer is a little more complicated. We should all care when
the most desperate among us are released back into society feeling abandoned and desperate. When there is greater comfort in
prison than outside it and former offenders offend again to return
to that environment for its comfort and familiarity, which puts
all of us at risk. Second, there are more abandoned people outside
prison than in it. That is evidenced by our not speaking every
time we get on a crowded elevator even to those we know well.

Frankl saw human behavior under the worst circumstances.
He reflected on it and on how many who had never endured it
behaved; he questioned our capacity to endure it. Something
deep in me is the belief that a person "whose back is against the
wall,"[252] the most desperate among us as the late Dr. Howard
Thurmond expressed it, should never be alone.

Frankl's ability to observe human behavior under the conditions in Auschwitz makes his work compelling for me and my
story. Many of us I believe would have been too busy focusing
on ourselves under those conditions to practice a good-neighbor
policy. He didn't merely observe; even at the height of exhaustion
and the depths of despair, he counseled and encouraged fellow
prisoners.

While I remained in a state of depression due to shame,
blame, guilt, and embarrassment, what lifted me during my
incarceration was hearing the life options and circumstances
of other people who had far fewer options in life than I did.
Right when I wanted someone to feel sorry for me, someone else
showed up in my space whom I felt even sorrier for, a hierarchy
of sorrow. My fellow inmates wanted me to do something about

our collective condition. They would tell me, "Make a call … Use your power, Congressman!" I would say to myself, *I don't have any power.* I would laugh it off and say, "I'm here with you." I developed an appreciation of the law second only to the commands to love God and my neighbor. I learned that to be judgmental and nonjudgmental both have a judge and a mental state.

My job at Butner was cleaning the restrooms and toilets. The smell was putrid due to puddles of oily piss from the diabetics under every toilet. There were no urinals, just toilets where inmates had removed the seats and designated the toilets as pissers, yet there were still times when people missed the toilets. The restroom was near my living quarters. The inmates in my vicinity called it the beach. We could smell everything from the beach. We called the two remaining toilets with seats shitters, and woe to the man who pissed where we shat.

I remember what Frankl said about the first jobs offered to prisoners as a favorite practice of the Nazis. The bathroom detail was designed to break your spirit and remind you how far you had fallen in my case. Frankl's preparation helped me make the best out of a shitty situation. My thoughts were, *I am not going to let this prison break my spirit. This is going to be the nicest shit house in the prison.*

The stain of oil from the diabetics was intense, so I came up with a plan. African Americans have dry hair, and the shampoo we used from the commissary took that into account. Alberto VO-5 degreaser was the product of choice for White inmates. I mixed that with the water I mopped with, and the other inmates began to notice the difference. Also, the coffee pot was in the restroom near the shitters. For that, I used scalding hot water and VO-5. The restrooms and the showers smelled nearly like home. Catawba East had the cleanest bathrooms in the compound. The fellas appreciated my efforts. I was becoming one of the crew. "Fucking with Jesse means a shitty bathroom … Leave him alone."

Not only that … and I know this may sound crude, but in

a purely psychological sense, it was my hope. I named my mop Sandi. I danced with Sandi every day. I was required to clean only once a day, but three times a day, I danced with Sandi. I remembered what Frankl wrote while incarcerated at Auschwitz—it's the small things that help a man maintain his sanity when his back is against the wall.

The men would wait in lines to use the restroom until I was finished. We all waited our turns near the restroom, where men urinated and shat all night long. We were becoming a family, and we respected each other. Jesse Jackson Jr. wasn't too big or too haughty to do the shitty work.

My mother used to tell me sometimes, "Son, you act like your shit don't stink." I learned that all shit stinks. My dad used to remind me, "No one can make chicken salad outta chicken shit." And he was right. "Never shit where you eat." This too is good advice, but should you disregard it and end up being served shit on a platter, make the most of it. In this case, the duty fell to me, the Congressman. It was shitty work, but somebody had to do it, and I owned it.

I have always been countercultural. As a result, I can see possibilities in low-feasibility zones, and my heart is moved by those who cannot see past barriers to what is available to them. By nature, my response to finding a crack and vulnerability in a system is to discover the reinforcement or corrective to the weakness.

Furthermore, I understand a life of service and believe deeply in it as a way of life. However, I do not believe a life of service requires us to struggle through. Jefferson said it best.

> It is not to be understood that I am with him [Jesus] in all his doctrines. I am a Materialist; he takes the side of Spiritualism; he preaches the efficacy of repentance toward forgiveness of sin; I require a counterpoise of good works to redeem it.[253]

As a person whose father's ministry was for the least of these and the grassroots, I was raised in middle-class privilege. I mingled with the elite and accessed their spaces to achieve results for those who had sent me to Washington to represent them.

In her first year as Congresswoman, Alexandria Ocasio-Cortez indicated that she could not maintain residences in NY and DC at the same time. She may have made history, but before she made history, she was bartending at New York City's Flats Fix. Upon winning her race for the House, she had to engage constituents, peers, and many others on a salary few could live on in DC and NY. Most recently, AOC attended the Met Gala, a $30,000 ticketed event, wearing a designer dress with the words Tax the Rich on the back. As I write about this, the GOP and many in media are questioning the irony of the statement she made with her dress and what it cost her to attend the gala. The temptation for many in Congress who live in Chicago and DC or New York and DC—expensive places—to misuse campaign funds is strong. I now know it is neither acceptable nor excusable, but it can be a trap for those entering the role with limited economies of scale. The proposition then is to be elevated to the title without income to accommodate all the extras, and it is a lofty race to endure. I fell. I would not do it the same today. I am acutely aware of how many others have fallen since my incarceration.

I have learned that attaining a higher level requires first a solid understanding of what it takes to maintain that higher level. My struggle to keep up socially and economically became a weighty, chaotic juggling act and became depressing and all consuming. Seventeen years of pressure to be professional, confident, capable, and relatable allowed me to justify personally feeding my ego with expensive and excessive gifts for myself and my family.

I learned that leaders engaged in above-average intellectual, artistic, mathematic, scientific, and political acuity are often prone to a melancholy nature. I started to evaluate the actions, steps, and decisions (often marked by the oddities of an overachiever) that had led to my circumstances. The work of self-examination actually started to heal my spirit of some of the mistakes I had made and the notoriety I had gained. I began looking at my self-imposed pressures and personal expectations brought on by my perception of myself and the world. What I know to be true today that I did not understand before is best stated this way.

> Here's to the crazy ones. The misfits. The rebels. The troublemakers. The round pegs in the square holes. The ones who see things differently ... They push the human race forward. While some may see them as the crazy ones, we see genius. Because the people who are crazy enough to think they can change the world, are the ones who do.[254]

While in prison, I read the works of Neel Burton, author of *The Meaning of Madness, The Art of Failure: The Anti Self-Help Guide, Hide and Seek: The Psychology of Self-Deception,* and many other books. I studied his writings and documented my thoughts on depression and how they related to our daily experiences and exposure.

He described three cognitive disorders seemingly common enough to be present in many otherwise well-balanced, high-functioning people. The first, selective abstraction, is a tendency to see the glass as half-empty. It is being unable to appreciate the positive aspects of life because of the disproportionate amount of attention being paid to even the most minute of negative matters. Those who suffer from dichotomous thinking tend to read the worst into the actions of others when those actions do not agree with their idea of what's appropriate. Last, the catastrophic thinker, when faced with unknown possibilities in a situation, is subject to believing in extreme negative possibilities in lieu of any number of more-moderate scenarios.

In his interpretation of these disorders, Burton contrasted depression symptoms with the tendencies projected by people considered not to be depressed. He explained that many people (also seemingly well-adjusted and balanced) thrive on cognitive distortions. However, nondepressed folks use positive illusions to generate the perspectives through which they interface with the details of their lives. The psychiatrist and philosopher pointed to a "rose-tinted perspective," "better than average" expectations, and "undue self-regard and false hope" to explain what helps people take risks and cope with hardship but also to exercise poor decision making, anger, anxiety, and failed efforts. Burton looked at depressive-realism as the ability to be just logical enough to scratch beneath the veneer, acknowledge the dings in the paint, and call it like it is in favor of finding meaning in life.[255]

This thought process helped me recover my sense of self. I was so committed to ensuring that I showed up on the House floor to cast every vote; I wanted to be accountable to my district. I would ensure that if nothing else was done, that part was settled. I did not want to miss an invitation to attend one of the many events held by my constituents. I wanted to make sure they knew I was committed to the people of Illinois's Second District. I wanted to make sure I studied the history of our political systems and politics, and I tried to make sure I created a strategy to create opportunities for my constituents. I had to navigate the potential that my father could be in the building having a meeting with one of my peers or a group of them unbeknown to me until they told me they had to attend the meeting. Yet I could not see all the juggling and thanklessness (unless my efforts benefited someone's personal bottom line) as a job; I did it all from a place of love and loyalty.

I spent most of my time in prison reading about leaders who possessed traits similar to mine. I looked for these traits in other men, traits common to their potential to recover. The understanding I received in this provided a solid sense of normalcy for me. Suddenly, I could understand the pressures of my life relative to my thought patterns that yielded my unique ability to innovate and express ideology including my ability to recall dates, times, and events. It is this gift I believe my colleagues appreciated.

Depression is the most common condition of the incarcerated. There are two prominent theories used to address depression. The most widely accepted is cognitive-behavioral therapy (CBT). It argues that when depression occurs, it is as a result of an abnormally negative view of reality. On the other hand, the depressive realism hypothesis (DRH), which is gaining more traction in the scientific community, expresses that because the onset of depression is due to perspective, it is in fact one's ability to realistically evaluate his or her experiences that causes the condition; those who experience depression are not wrongly but rightfully negative about what is happening around them.

In his book *First-Rate Madness: Uncovering the Links Between Leadership and Mental Illness*,[256] Dr. Nassir Ghaemi was careful to acknowledge that whatever the impetus for depression and mania is, the experience is devastating and painful and often leads to self-harm. Such suffering often happens in relative silence and sometimes at the core of otherwise powerful and dynamic lives.[257]

Three of the leaders Dr. Ghaemi looked at whom I admired and attempted to emulate are Lincoln for his realism, Gandhi for his empathy, and King for the radical empathy he modeled after Gandhi.

I think I see things other people don't. I see the world differently, and I get real down when I can't change it. I think it's important to note that we see these men as seriously flawed people who not unlike anyone else have struggles and challenges. But these few examples also show us that we are willing to accept their contributions their faults and shortcomings notwithstanding. To paraphrase Jack Nicholson's character from *A Few Good Men*,[258] "We want them on that wall, we need them on that wall, and then we complain about the manner in which their dreams become our reality."

There is no textbook in this unique space. There is no treat-ment model for the men and women who forge history. We can try to understand, and we should so we can better empathize with the internal ramifications and the human toll, the agony, that it takes to move people forward toward a communion with the Creator and creation. But it is not easy work, and it isn't the work of the mentally well adjusted; it's the work of those who dream and think outside the box. It's the work of the "creatively maladjusted," Martin Luther King Jr. said.[259] Our greatest lead-ers at the earliest ages of their lives are pure potentiality however excruciating the journey of their lives before leadership was; they were not born in a vacuum but in a womb and are the sum of the generations of the toil of others.

My mother promised to write me every day I was incarcer-ated. She wanted to ensure that I was not focused on making where I was more than a temporary space. She wanted to extend the reassurance of home into my daily life. She was determined to transmit her love and her reassurance that I was not alone. I am grateful for her letters. She conveyed her love through scripture, stories, and more than anything her constant reminders that she loved me and was thinking of me and that I should never forget to pray.

My mom was my rock. I started to hear her voice pulling me through. I started to understand the little details she would tell me in the letters to let me know I had not been paying attention to the people in and around my space. This awakening allowed me to evaluate the years I spent rushing and running too fast and to explore the reasons I was doing what I was doing. I got off the hamster wheel in enough time to know that the period of punitive time was the corrective action required for repositioning myself in pursuit of the real purpose of my life. My time in the camp actually removed a layer of pressure that allowed me to look at the world from outside my life and lifestyle. I began to hear the stories of people who had suffered through quagmires and ended up in a place where recovery to full citizenship and their natural capacity would be hard if not next to impossible.

I ultimately gained a radical empathy for my fellow incarcerated Americans. This immersion experience as one of our nation's expendables left me with an understanding of a gaping hole in the US reform system. But for this experience, my stance would not be as firm as it is. It was the catalyst for my exposing a constitutional right that is overlooked and thus far unattained.

In his study of Gandhi, King, Kennedy, Lincoln, and others, Dr. Ghaemi highlighted the pressure associated with creativity, empathy, realism, and resilience. I was profoundly enlightened to see that I too had experienced the same struggles some of the greatest leaders of our world had faced. Reading about them resonated with my experiences in childhood and throughout my life as I struggled to be unique and intelligent and to clash with the status quo. My ideas have always been disruptive. I have never accepted dysfunctionality. I am equally consistent in my modus operandi: I organize details in linear order to document how something came to be.

My resilience over seventeen years was built on my aversion to dirty politics. I am a realist. I have remained well aware that my conduct must be informed by the nature of my family and the history of my name. Nevertheless, I was found to be approachable. And now, I believe that over time, people will come to know that if I had not served time for using my campaign funds, the empathy I have for the imprisoned would instead be a distant participation in this major issue.

Today, I am standing at the end of a long line declaring that second chances are a constitutional mandate between America and those who have served their time. My commitment to this cause enabled me during the lowest point of my life to stand up and teach people serving time with me their legal rights in the public forgiveness process. I learned how disconnected from the true legal process most of those serving time were and how that kept them connected to a system that deemed them damaged goods for the rest of their lives.

Today, I can say I have participated in every institution in our land including our prison system. My leadership skills have been strengthened, and my honor will be renewed through my efforts to honor those who have been left behind and treated as untouchables. We are all God's children; we are greater than the least of these only until we become one of the least.

Jesus bore all our sin so we would be forgiven. I believe our Founders understood Jesus's precepts and established our country on God's providence. Redemption can be extended only by our president and based on the moral and civil code. The goal was never to use it as leverage or to show grace or favor to a well-connected few; the goal was always to restore the lives of all individuals and therefore the life of our nation.

Americans have a collective dictate to elect someone who will extend the finger of God into the process of pardoning debt-paid felons and redeeming the nation. This call will not be heard until we reconcile the shame, blame, and guilt of our nation with the condition of our collective mental health. Not everyone who serves time has committed a crime, and not everyone who has committed a crime has served time, but we all have fallen short and are carrying shame, blame, and guilt.

These individuals might embark on personal journeys to overcome their shortcomings. Ultimately, many will look to God for forgiveness. This spiritual renewal is appropriate and acceptable. Felons carry anguish, guilt, and shame well after they complete their sentences. We must stop shaming them. The mental health issue attached to SBG for the individual who has never served time exists because we all carry private guilt, but that is magnified for those who have served their time because we often have a problem living with public guilt; we can't keep it a secret. It was in the paper, and everyone knows about it. Felons must forever carry the scarlet letter *F* on their chests to be reminded time and again why they cannot reenter the life, liberty, and happiness system we call America, why many cannot cast a vote in our political process, and why the Second Amendment no longer applies to them.

My journey of incarceration required me to record the details of our laws and our founding documents. I believe our Constitution is a living document. I believe our Founders recognized that being a nation founded on the belief in the providence of God was to understand the importance of forgiveness. They also knew the person who would be president would be a person of pious reflection and great character equipped to carry out the truest sense of who we the people are.

Since having resumed my life as a free citizen, I have not been able to ignore the details of how our mental health can also be directly connected to the mental health of the leader of our country. America has witnessed for the first time with 45 a presidency that has left its citizens feeling unsafe, numb, and uncertain about our future. I believe it is during the process of correcting this term that we must look to the original intent of our Founders.

My psychology and best thinking have always been to utilize our most important documents and history to participate in the process that would allow every citizen an opportunity to participate with equal footing in a society that until now has extended the right to be free to only a segment of our people. To be equal, we must start anew.

My work was extensive, and it cannot all be documented in this book, but the greatest validation of my study was the experience I had on the night I was thrown in the hole for educating my fellow inmates on the forgiveness process, the pardon process.

What I admire most about the leaders Dr. Ghaemi researched is not the press conferences, the speeches, the crowds, the Nobel Peace Prizes, their statures, places in history, their books, courage, their creativity, and so on. I admire them for being men who believed in one God, loved their neighbors, and decided that the opinions of most others about their beliefs did not matter.

These men and the way they handled their conditions is a

model for me. They were all victims of modern crucifixions. They struggled with life and death every day; they battled personal demons and tried to hear God's word and calling.

What I most admire about them is the God factor, which is self-propelled. It drives you beyond self and circumstances to achieve good neighborliness. It is innovative and inventive; it is what makes great leaders tick. It is what made those great leaders different, kept them up late at night, and took them to the brink in their decision-making processes. It made them find creative solutions to advance the cause of human freedom and liberty. It made them see the love of God and neighbor as the first and second laws of their lives. It attached their lives to the infinite.

Was it their sense of normalcy, crowd pleasing, perfect adjustment, and acceptability, or was it their response to their sense of human fallibility, mortality, and error? The gasoline for their ambition was not speeches and outward signs including accomplishments great and small that we easily identify with; it was the courage to overcome things we never saw. They were fueled by their late, lonely, sleepless nights, their conversations with God—which some call dreams and could easily be interpreted as crazy or the private rantings of lunatics—their impulses, their mania. It was the stuff they and we kept secret until after their deaths, when the truth of who they really were began to emerge from family and friends. It was their mental health that made them tick. They all saw a different reality. And they had the courage to pursue it for us.

Another way of looking at these men's personal struggles must include the dynamic that they saw the world the way it was and dreamed of a world that would be different. They knew it would come with sacrifice including fatalism. Jesus made the acceptance of fatalism rational as a part of a system of self-sacrifice for the greater good.

Not everyone who is struggling with mental health and stability falls into this altruistic category; many are very dangerous people. But many of these men including those I am drawn to changed the course of history for the better. What they person-ally struggled with made the world a better place. It is a worthy struggle for us all.

I distinguish this struggle from that of people whose mental health presents a threat to themselves and others. Treatment and medicine are very necessary to stabilize mood disorders. I believe there was global serendipity in the lack of availability of drugs; we needed them the way they were.

Today, you and I are the beneficiaries of their struggles and how they dealt with their mental challenges. In fact, they may not have even seen their struggles as such. Their examples are worthy of study and emulation. They seriously questioned faith and then tested the outcome of their life experiments in their faith to reshape their lives and the destiny of humankind.

We want the positive contributions that came from their lives. But the God factor, the thing that provides the answers to the whys of life? I don't think we want to hear it. After all, it is difficult for rational minds to appreciate the dark places the hu-man mind has the capacity to venture into. We recoil at the idea in spite of the fact that once there, in the dark, lonely, abysmal space, great answers may come bearing new and creative direc-tions for humanity.

I went to prison knowing this. I was deeply remorseful and penitent. I was physically in the place my mind had ventured to long before conviction for my offenses—the pit. Prison is the closest to death a man can ever be in this life. There was nothing left for me to do except find a way to climb out.

To be forgiven, we have to acknowledge that we have done something wrong for which we seek forgiveness. Even President Clinton had to follow the four C's process—confession, contri-tion, conversion, and consequences—the loss of his legal license. That is sometimes the result of a public life. On January 16, 2020, the sitting president did not follow the four Cs. I believe his SBG will ultimately create consequences for the actions he followed to deny his accountability.

This acknowledgment is a personal commitment to change and a public acknowledgment of the need to be held impeachable for repeat behaviors if the sought-after repentance is not genuine.

PART III

HUMAN RIGHTS AND GOD THROUGH US

24

FORGIVENESS

I am not an advocate for frequent changes in laws and constitutions. But laws and institutions must go hand in hand with the progress of the human mind. As that becomes more developed, more enlightened, as new discoveries are made, new truths discovered and manners and opinions change, with the change of circumstances, institutions must advance also to keep pace with the times. We might as well require a man to wear still the coat which fitted him when a boy as civilized society to remain ever under the regimen of their barbarous ancestors.[260]

—Thomas Jefferson

True compassion is more than flinging a coin to a beggar: it understands that a society which produces beggars needs restructuring.[261]

—Dr. Martin Luther King Jr.

What have "rights" been historically in the United States if not an evolving societal sense of justice and entitlement, won, always, in political struggle (frequently undergirded by various intellectual efforts)? The right of slaves … of women … workers … the Civil Rights movement of the 1960s … in all of these instances, the appeal was to a higher sense of justice, to fundamental principles of a democracy, and to foundational documents embodied in the creation of our country.[262]

—Chester Hartman, Poverty and Race Research Action Council

FOR THE FOUNDERS, the power to pardon or forgive came from a system that included Jesus. The God of the Old Testament was vengeful. Jesus injected the idea of forgiveness and new human possibilities through a moral system of repentance, forgiveness, love, mercy, redemption, restoration, and second, third, fourth, and fifth chances. According to Matthew 18:21-22: "Then came Peter to him and said, Lord, how oft shall my brother sin against me, and I forgive him? till seven times? Jesus saith unto him, I say not unto thee, Until seven times: but, until seventy times seven."[263]

Before Jesus, the law was vengeful, retributive; it was eye for an eye. Life in prison without the possibility of parole became an alternative to the death penalty, lynchings, firing squads, and hangings. The appellate process also owes itself to the ministry of the Nazarene. Criminal defendants are human beings, and the idea that prisoners have rights owes its foundation to the life of Jesus.

America was to be the one country in the history of the world in 1787 that did not have to wait for mythology, blazing chariots, or mysticism but the exercise of our highest faith. From the moral conscience of the Nazarene emerged concepts such as due process, second chances, do-overs, and individual human rights protected by constitutions written by the people that become the emphasis of law.

The turning point in the history of law is the function of the ministry of Jesus over time. The consequences of the ministry of Jesus and its broad ramifications for law and fundamental fairness cannot be overstated. Even the idea of trial by jury of peers is part of that fairness calculation, and it too emanates from his ministry. What would a reasonable person do? Is anyone beyond the grace of God? Can sinners and people who make mistakes be redeemed? Is there any good left in the criminal defendant? How much time for the crime? What is proportional? Was it just a mistake or momentary error in judgment? Can Saul become Paul? Can a prostitute go and sin no more?

Conscience, accountability, personal responsibility, moral compasses, good neighborliness, and respect for all moved to the forefront as considerations in the construction of all laws. His doctrine of turning the other cheek challenged the idea of retaliation. He advanced the idea of a civilized common law applicable to everyone with love and respect for our neighbors as central to the idea. Jesus's system of freedom, liberty, and human emancipation would challenge and threaten the forces of colonization, exploitation, segregation, and slavery and advance the cause of equality before the law as children of God for 2021 years and counting.

Ideas whether conscious or unconscious underlie all action. Both the North and the South in the Civil War were motivated in part by abstract ideas—republican democracy, liberty, interpretations of the Constitution, flags, the Union, states' rights, and the right of secession. No one should underestimate the power of ideas.

Human rights are that kind of powerful idea—and are still emerging. Human rights are like Maslow's hierarchy of needs— they start with a base and develop upward. Thus, the human species has moved from the divine right of kings to the democratic rights of the people. Governments have gone from monarchies—God's representatives on earth—to the democratic notion of self-government. Even some religions have adjusted from a strictly structured priestly hierarchy to a more divine democracy, the priesthood of all believers.

In American democracy, we have the idea that certain unalienable rights are given by God, not bestowed by governments. Natural rights are "the idea that people by their nature have certain basic rights that precede the establishment of any government."[264] But even a representative democratic government of, by, and for the people still codifies the will of the people in law and recognizes inalienable rights.

The actual legal meaning of these God-given, inalienable rights in the Constitution is vague. What does the document's right to life, liberty, and the pursuit of happiness and to "promote the general welfare" mean in a democratic society? Antichoice people use this "right to life" phrase in the Constitution as the basis for their opposition to abortion. But could not the right to life, liberty, and the pursuit of happiness also mean the right to a fuller and higher quality of life, the right to such things as gainful employment at living wages, comprehensive and universal health care, safe and affordable housing, an equal high-quality public education, genuine equal opportunity for women, and a clean environment built on renewable energy?

In the republican world in which we live, there is one simple fact about rights: All human rights are politically determined. Ultimately, human rights in a representative democracy are whatever the people say they are. This means we must struggle and organize politically to protect old freedoms as well as to secure new rights. Labor unions had to struggle to win workers' rights. The right to directly elect senators, the right to nondiscrimination in voting for former slaves, women, and eighteen-year-olds, and Virginia's ratification of the Equal Rights Amendment in 2020 to become the thirty-eighth state to do so—meeting the three-fourths of the state's standard needed to add an amendment—will require continuing struggle because of a deadline set in the original legislation in 1972. It too will come through a political struggle to codify those legal advances in the Constitution, in legislation, or in the constitutional interpretation by the Supreme Court.

Codifying human rights in the law was Dr. Martin Luther King's goal; he wrote and preached about it. He said that the law might not make you change your heart or attitude toward a man or make you love him, but it can keep you from lynching him. He understood that the law could dictate a change in behavior that could foster a new social climate in which understanding between people is more possible.

He understood the significance of the 1954 *Brown* decision, which established the legal principle and provided the legal foundation of equal protection under the law. Rosa Parks first met King in Montgomery at an NAACP meeting where he was explaining the implications of the *Brown* decision. He cited *Brown* in his first struggle, the Montgomery bus boycott, as the legal basis for expanding African American rights. King always used nonviolent but direct action to bring about enough creative tension in the society to change the law. The Montgomery bus boycott culminated nine years later in ending legal segregation with the passage of the 1964 Civil Rights Act.

King went to Selma to fight to codify the right to vote, which happened on August 6, 1965. He went to Chicago to lead marches and change the laws that were creating segregated neighborhoods and communities, and upon his death, as a tribute to his life, the 1968 Open Housing Act was passed.

At the time of his death, King was organizing the Poor People's Campaign and trying to secure through the political process and the law an expansion of human rights that would end hunger and provide every American with a job or an income. That of course can best be achieved through the creation of jobs paying living wages and by providing other basic human rights. Words of racial tolerance and diversity ring hollow without genuine equal economic and political opportunity for all and an economic system that leaves no American behind. King's struggle and campaigns were always at bottom about expanding human rights by changing the law.

All politics may be local, and I agree that politics should emerge and build from the bottom up, but only Congress can bestow new human rights in this country because it is the only body that writes national laws. Constitutional amendments must first pass by two-thirds votes in both houses of Congress and then by three-quarters of state legislatures. We have federal, district, and appellate courts, but only the Supreme Court renders decisions for the entire nation. Thus, the ultimate political aim of any grassroots and human rights movement must be to codify these new rights in constitutional amendments and laws and secure constitutional interpretations to protect those rights.

In my book *A More Perfect Union, Vol. II*, I spelled out what I think these new fundamental human rights are that Americans must struggle to codify. Obviously, these rights will come with a cost, but not having them will cost even more in wasted human potential, lost production, slower growth, a weaker GNP, inefficiencies, waste, crime, and much more.

I believe that God created all of us just a little lower than the angels and that these nine democratic fundamental human rights—voting, employment, health care, housing, education, equal opportunity, a clean environment, fair taxes, and an end to the Electoral College—should now become a part of the God-given inalienable rights provided in our Constitution. But they, like all human rights, must be struggled for politically. Some progress may be achieved through new laws and new constitutional interpretations by these or a new set of progressive justices, and such progress should be pursued. But I believe these fundamental rights must ultimately be anchored in new constitutional amendments. New amendments should not be added thoughtlessly, precipitously, or carelessly, but neither should they be frivolously denied. Constitutional amendments are the most effective way that we the people can democratically secure these new rights.

These new American rights are what I understand the Constitution to mean when it mandates us to build "a more perfect Union, establish justice, ensure domestic tranquility, provide for the common defense, promote the general welfare and secure the blessing of liberty to ourselves and our posterity."

We must never take our current rights for granted. We should also have an understanding of the evolutionary nature and history of law as well as an appreciation of the long and sacrificial struggle for human rights. We must recognize the role of the function of the lineage of David and the unique role that America was afforded at our nation's founding.

25

A BRIEF HISTORY OF LAWS

2350 BC: Urukagina's Code is the oldest known set of laws. While not actually discovered, they are referenced in other documents as a consolidation of "ordinances" of Mesopotamian kings confirming that the "king was appointed by the gods" and affirming the right of citizens to know why certain actions were being punished.

2050 BC: Ur-Nammu's Code is the earliest known written law. Only five articles can be deciphered, but archaeological evidence shows it was supported by an advanced legal system that included specialized judges, testimony under oath, a proper form for judicial decisions, and a judge's ability to order damages be paid to a victim by the guilty party.

1850 BC: The earliest known legal decision involved the murder of a temple employee by three men in this year. Recorded on a clay tablet, the murder became public, and the three men and the murdered man's wife were indicted. She was indicted because she knew of the murder but remained silent. Nine witnesses testified against them, and the death penalty was sought for all four. The wife had two witnesses who testified of spousal abuse but added that she was not part of the murder plot and that things were worse after her husband's murder. The three men were found guilty and put to death in front of the victim's house.

1700 BC: Hammurabi's Code, carved in columns on a large rock in 1700 BC, was developed for this Babylonian king who had come to power fifty years before. "An eye for an eye" was the guiding judicial principle underlying his code. Its 282 clauses regulated an array of obligations, professions, and rights, including commerce, slavery, marriage, theft, and debts. Punishment by modern standards was barbaric, including cutting off a finger or a hand for theft; cutting out the tongue for defamation; putting to death the builder of a house (and his son) if the house collapsed and killed the owner (and his son).

1300 BC: The Ten Commandments, according to the Jewish Hebrew Bible and the Christian Old Testament, were received directly from God and written on a tablet of stone by Moses. Many of these commandments underlie our modern laws against murder, adultery, and stealing. The commandments are found in the book of Exodus, which also contains other rules largely based on the "eye for an eye, tooth for a tooth" legal philosophy.

1280 BC: About this same time in India, known rules passed down orally through generations were formally written in the Laws of Manu. They were the basis of India's caste system, which established people's social standing and regulated most facets of Indian society. Punishment was used sparingly and only as a last resort. Interestingly, members of the higher castes were punished more severely than those in the lower castes.

621 BC: Draco's Law was written for Athens. A Greek citizen chosen to write their first code of laws, Draco's punishments— often death—were so harsh that we derive our word "draconian" from his name. However, Draco's Law also introduced the idea that the state, rather than private parties or vigilantes, had the "exclusive role" in trying and punishing a person accused of a crime. Draco was wildly loved by the Athenian people. One day at a reception honoring him, they showered him with such affection—in the traditional Greek way of throwing their hats and cloaks over him—that by the time they dug him out he had smothered to death.

600 BC: In a military state in southern Greece, the world was given the oral Law of Lycurgus (he never wrote them down) by this renowned king of Sparta. Lycurgus's Law held that women had a duty to have children, but if the children were born deformed, they were killed. Those who lived became wards of Sparta at the age of seven, when they began their preparation for military duty. Lycurgus's Law covered virtually every aspect of life; given the military orientation of Sparta, the greatest crime was considered to be retreat in battle.

550 BC: Solon, an Athenian statesman and lawmaker, refined Draco's Law by "democratizing" or making it more accessible to the citizens of Athens.

536 BC: China created the Book of Punishments, a legal book limiting the ways in which someone could be punished after conviction for a serious crime. Still, the punishment could include tattooing, mutilation, castration, amputation of the feet, and death.

450 BC: The Twelve Tables were originally ten laws written by ten Roman men to govern the conduct of Roman citizens. Subsequently, two more were added. The Twelve Tables form the basis of all modern law, both public and private. Under these laws a system of public justice was developed whereby injured parties could seek compensation from guilty defendants; the lower classes (plebes) were given greater protection from legal abuses by the ruling classes (patricians), especially with regard to debts.

The Twelve Tables also prohibited marriage between differing classes; severely punished theft; and gave fathers the right of life or death over their sons. The Tables survived for nearly a thousand years, until the wood and bronze tablets were destroyed by invading Gauls in AD 390.

350 BC: The first Chinese imperial code of laws, the Code of Li k'vei, dealt with the issues of theft, robbery, prison, arrest, and other general subjects. It served as a model for the Chinese T'ang Code, which came about a thousand years later.

339 BC: The trial of Socrates played a role in the development of law. Socrates was not a religious man but an Athenian philosopher who taught logic. When Athens lost the Peloponnesian Wars, conservative Athenians looked for a scapegoat. Three citizens accused the popular seventy-year-old of corrupting the minds of the youth with his logic and of not believing in the gods. They tried him before a jury of 501 citizens, who found him guilty by a vote of 281 to 220. He was asked to speak to the jurors with regard to his sentencing. Instead, in his speech, he chose to mock the jurors—who swiftly sentenced him to death by a vote of 361 to 140. His trial, however, advanced the role of "conscience" in legal proceedings.

33 AD: While not part of the normal history of laws, the following is important to my own understanding of the law. Christians saw Jesus the Christ as introducing a new dimension to Moses's Law. Under Jesus's law, pure motives, a mature love and grace (unmerited love), and nominal justice, good behavior, and honorable ends became important. Jesus was not replacing Moses's law but was perfecting it.

In Matthew 5:17–18, Jesus said, "Think not that I have come to abolish the law and the prophets; I have come not to abolish them but to fulfill them. For truly, I say to you, till heaven and earth pass away, not an iota, not a dot, will pass from the law until all is accomplished." In Galatians 5:14, Paul wrote, "For the whole law [of Moses] is fulfilled in one word, 'You shall love your neighbor as yourself.'" And in Romans 13:10, he wrote, "love is the fulfilling of the law." Thus, this Judeo-Christian understanding of the law as a commitment to justice and the application of a knowledgeable understanding of love is important to the spiritual framework that underlies and undergirds much of my and the nation's philosophy of law as well as the purpose and function of law in society. This understanding is important where Christianity is the predominant religion and particularly in Western civilization. The influence that his life had and still has on history divided time between BC and AD.

325: The Council of Nicaea is convened to "organize" the Bible.

529: Justinian's Code organized Roman law into a series of books called *Corpus Juris Civilis*. This legal collection was guided by Greek logic and English common law, the two main influences on contemporary Western society. Many legal maxims in use today, indeed the very spelling of the modern word "justice," all emanate from Justinian, the emperor of Byzantine.

604: Written by a Japanese prince for a country that had just begun to develop and become literate, the seventeen-article Constitution of Japan shaped its morality and law. Paternalistic in orientation, it espoused such legalisms as: "peace and harmony should be respected because they are very important for intergroup relations"; "There are very few evil men. If we teach them [the Buddha beliefs], they may become obedient"; "equality, speediness and integrity should be maintained in court procedures"; and "the basic philosophy in all matters should be 'against privacy' and 'toward public benefit.'" One distinction that characterizes two different legal traditions is that Oriental law seeks to prevent disputes, whereas Western law seeks to resolve disputes.

653: What is known today as China was originally several kingdoms occupied for thousands of years by various feuding kings. In AD 221, the king of Ch'in finally defeated the other six kingdoms and unified China. Some four hundred years later, the empire developed a code of law called the T'ang Code. The code revised earlier existing Chinese laws and standardized procedures—including the 350 BC Code of Li k'vei—and listed crimes and their punishments in 501 articles. One article allowed only two forms of capital punishment for a convicted criminal: beheading or hanging.

700: China invented the use of fingerprinting as a means of identifying people.

1100: The first law school came into existence in medieval Italy, when students hired a teacher to teach them Roman law, especially *Corpus Juris Civilis,* Justinian's Code. One of these teachers, Imerius, became especially popular; students from all over Europe flocked to Bologna to learn from him. The number of students became so large that he had to hire other teachers and, thus, formed the world's first law school. By 1150, Imerius's law school had more than ten thousand students. Such numbers and enthusiasm contributed to the revival of Roman law and helped spread it throughout Europe.

1215: The basis of English common law is the Magna Carta, signed into law at *Runneymede, England, on June 15, 1215, by King John. It forced the king, for the first time, to concede a number of legal rights to his barons and the citizens of England. In financing foreign wars, King John had heavily taxed the people, and many of his barons threatened rebellion. With this threat hanging over the king's head, the barons were able to extract a number of rudimentary concessions from him, such as freedom of the church, fair taxation, controls over imprisonment *(habeas corpus),* and the right of all merchants to freely come and go except in time of war. The Magna Carta was comprised of sixty-one clauses, the most important of which was number thirty-nine. It said that "No freeman shall be captured or imprisoned ... except by lawful judgement of his peers or by the law of the land." For the first time, even the king was restrained by the law from merely exercising his personal will against another citizen.

1611: The King James Bible.

1689: The English Bill of Rights was enacted. It became a precursor to the American Bill of Rights. It set out strict limits on the royal family's legal prerogatives, such as a prohibition against the arbitrary suspension of Parliament's laws. More importantly, it limited to Parliament the right to raise money through taxation.

1692: The Salem Witch Trials took place in Salem, Massachusetts. A group of young women accused several other women of practicing witchcraft or worship of the devil. The accusations turned the atmosphere surrounding the judicial proceedings into a frenzy, creating a delirium where more than three hundred people were accused of witchcraft, of whom twenty were eventually executed, including a priest. Eventually people of New England rose up against any more prosecutions of witchcraft.

1740: The infamous South Carolina Slave Code, which regulated the use of slaves, became the model for slavery in other states. It said that "all Negroes, Indians ... and all their offspring ... shall be and are hereby declared to be and remain forever hereafter slaves; and shall be deemed ... to be chattels personal in the hands of their owners."

1765: Law became more accessible to the common man when a British barrister named Blackstone wrote down the entire English law in an easy-to-read, four-volume *Blackstone's Commentaries* *on the Laws of England*. It also became a standard reference work for all lawyers and law students. The many reprintings of *Blackstone's Commentaries* made the transport of English law into the American colonies easy, an important legal development in the New World. Many legal scholars contend that *Blackstone's Commentaries* were the law for the first hundred years in the independent American colonies.

1776: On July 4, the American Declaration of Independence from Great Britain announced that "all political connection between [the united colonies] and the State of Great Britain is and ought to be dissolved" and that "we the people" of these new United States rebuke the medieval legal theory that certain people possess, by divine or royal right, the power to rule others. It affirmed that "all men are created equal" and have "certain inalienable rights, that among these are life, liberty and the pursuit of happiness. That to secure these rights, governments are instituted among men, deriving their powers from the consent of the governed." Jefferson, Adams, and Franklin were appointed to the First Great Seal Committee to memorialize the spirit and occasion of the revolution and the Declaration of Independence.

1787: The Constitution of the United States of America was signed in Philadelphia on September 17, 1787. The Constitution was ratified by the required nine states on June 21, 1788. The U.S. Constitution formed the legal basis for the first republican government in the history of the world. It defined the institutions of government and the powers of each institution, carefully carving out the duties of the executive, legislative, and judicial branches. The U.S. Constitution has served as a model for many other nations attaining independence or becoming democracies. The "Finger of the Almighty Hand," the "Final Act" is added to the Constitution in the Sect of One.

1788: Sydney became the site of the first British settlement in Australia. It was to serve as the prime location of a British penal colony. For fifty years, Britain sent its worst men there. They were quickly assigned to chain gangs and put to work building roads and bridges. By 1821, there were thirty thousand British settlers in this British Commonwealth, of which 75 percent were convicts. Thus, through the operation of penal law, a country was formed.

1791: The American Bill of Rights, the first ten amendments to the U.S. Constitution, was approved and ratified. These ten amendments, in the Jeffersonian tradition, declared rights in the areas of free speech, freedom of press and religion, the right to a jury trial by one's peers, and protection against "cruel and unusual punishment" or "unreasonable searches or seizures," among many other things. The Bill of Rights has influenced many modern charters and bills of rights around the world.

1803: In *Marbury v. Madison,* the Supreme Court upheld the supremacy of the Constitution and stated unequivocally that it had the power to strike down actions taken by American federal and state legislative bodies that, in its opinion, offended the Constitution. This has come to be known as the power of "judicial review." This case is considered by many in the legal profession to be the most important milestone in American law since the Constitution was ratified.

1804: Jefferson extracts the life and morals of Jesus of Nazareth in Greek, Latin, French, and English.

1804: In the Napoleonic Code, France adopted a comprehensive code of law that canonized many of the victories attained during the Revolution, such as individual liberty, equality before the law, and the "consent of the governed" character of the state. It also incorporated most parts of Roman law. Additionally, with respect to its influence beyond France, it served as a model for civil law systems in Quebec, Canada (1865), Germany (1900), Switzerland (1907), and California and Louisiana in the western territories of the United States. It was written in nontechnical language, which made it more available to the common people.

1864: The Geneva Convention set forth minimal human rights standards during times of war. It included such things as protection of military medical personnel and provided for the humane treatment of the wounded. It was later supplemented by a Prisoner of War Convention. While frequently ignored or violated during actual military operations, the Geneva Convention remains an important legal document.

1865: After the Civil War, the U.S. Congress passed and the states ratified on December 18, 1865, the Thirteenth Amendment to the Constitution, officially ending legal slavery.

1868: The 14th Amendment

1870: The 15th Amendment

1945–1946: The Nuremberg War Crimes Tribunal (Trial) brought together eight judges from the United States, Great Britain, France, and the Soviet Union in a special panel to try Nazi military officers for crimes committed against humanity (war crimes) during World War II. Twenty-four Nazis were put on trial and convicted. Half of them received the death penalty for their crimes, though one of them, Hermann Goring, committed suicide hours before his execution. The trial was important in establishing a legal principle that, even in times of war, basic moral standards apply. "The true test," wrote the tribunal, "is not the existence of the [superior] order but whether moral choice [in executing it] was in fact possible." The Nazi crimes included torture, deportation, persecution, and mass extermination. Nuremberg was a small town in Germany.

1948: The General Agreement on Tariffs and Trade (GATT) was originally written. Modified and updated several times since, GATT was developed by the United Nations and served as a catalyst for the lifting of legal barriers against the free movement of goods, services, and people. Now, under the auspices of the World Trade Organization (WTO), the implementation of GATT by almost all countries is causing commercial interplay among differing legal systems and, in most cases, is providing the impetus for those legal systems to move toward similarity and compatibility. GATT is also reflecting a new emphasis in the development of international law: from legal agreements providing military and basic human rights, to trade and economic rights. The problem is that the old politically conservative "Golden Rule" is too often being applied, rather than the new spiritually progressive Golden Rule of "do unto others as you would have them do unto you." That is, under the old "law," too often nations with the most "gold" (economic power) make the "rules" in their favor, to the disadvantage of weaker and developing economies, while often ignoring or placing on a lower legal level of priority basic and fundamental human, labor, and environmental rights.

1948: The General Assembly of the United Nations adopted the Universal Declaration of Human Rights, which puts forth a legal code of internationally recognized human rights. It served as a basic guide to the fundamental rights I will discuss in the coming chapters. Following this historic act of statesmanship, the assembly called upon all member countries to publicize the text of the declaration and "to cause it to be disseminated, displaced, read and expounded principally in schools and other educational institutions, without distinction based on the political status of countries or territories." The United States is a signatory to this document, but our government and educational system have done virtually nothing to give exposure to or educate the American people on the contents of this extremely important document.

The UN's Universal Declaration of Human Rights, in addition to raising consciousness of the rights to which all people are entitled, gives these same people a tool with which to fight for their human rights: The Supreme Court has ruled that all international treaties and legal principles to which the United States are signatories are considered legally binding on all citizens and the government of the United States.

Why My Interpretation Matters

2013–2021: Jesse Jackson Jr. discovers, excavates, and introduces the finger of the almighty hand of God from the Constitution and thus injects and brings to the consciousness of the American people the Founders' original intent to rely on providence as the guiding force of the United States.

The power of God-endowed human rights extracted from the lineage of Abraham as a function of the lineage of David is central to the internal and external governance of the affairs of the United States. To paraphrase Karl Barth, the discovery is "of a certainty that a stone, that is the ministry of Jesus of Nazareth, must have been dropped into deep water in 1787 and it is at the foundation of American history."[265]

Human law and political rights have evolved through history to ever-higher forms and the granting of more rights. This meant that responsibilities and obligations have moved away from external sources of appointed governmental power (divinely appointed leaders, successive royal bloodlines) to the voice and majority vote of democratically elected representatives of the people.

The word *democracy* consists of two Greek words, *demos* (people) and *kratos* (strength or power)—people power. It means that we the people have the strength and the power to elect people to make our laws and rules. We the people have the right to declare what rights we have and don't have, what rules we will live and play by, and under which laws we will be governed.

A representative democratic government is a political structure whereby the supreme governmental authority is accepted and the rules are made with the consent of a majority of the people. The elected representative of the people who functions in the *f(lod)* for all will also appoint Supreme Court justices and federal jurists who understand the *f(lod)* as well. The life tenure afforded the jurists in the federal system would forever ensure that the values of the *f(lod)* are respected over time, and this is central to building a more perfect union among the states and the people. The equation below should serve as a guiding method for future jurists.

Supreme Court Nominees   266

$$Sup.Ct.Nominees = f\left(\frac{f(LOD)}{t(dt)}\right) \; © $$

Progressive Ideology

Supreme Court Nominees are a function of Ideology over time. They must have, in my opinion, a progressive ideology, that recognizes the f(LOD) for building A more Perfect Union **and they must be young enough, to serve long enough, to render decisions based upon the reconstruction Amendments especially the 14th Amendment that benefits all of us,** State Rights and the 10th Amendment notwithstanding. They must have a proven record of the elevation of human rights over State and Federal Rights, God/Creator endowed rights have primacy.

© Jesse Jackson Jr 2018

Thus, the contrast between the organic, evolutionary, and political nature of the law versus the static, strict constructionist, and natural view of the law should be clear in terms of the creation and preservation of political rights in human development. The approach of conservatives to play down or advocate an antipolitical, antilegislative, and anti–federal government philosophy of social change is therefore certainly not a strategy designed to advance the public interest or real economic interests of a majority of the American people. These conservatives are acting on behalf of the special interests of the few who do not want mass democratic participation and action. This antigovernment and undemocratic conservative approach is a strategy to undermine progressive economic change intended to benefit the public good.

In a democracy, we must continually criticize and reform politics, government, and policies to keep them relevant, effective, efficient, accessible, accountable, and responsive to the people's real needs. This is very different however from criticizing politics and government *per se* as irrelevant and ineffective as instruments of change, of protecting old rights or advancing new ones.

Strict constructionism runs contrary to the whole legal development of rights in history. Strict constructionists look back to the Founders' original document only—before the Thirteenth, Fourteenth, Fifteenth, and other progressive amendments to the Constitution were added, before nonlandowners could vote, and before Lincoln's Gettysburg Address.

Strict constructionists, as former Supreme Court Justice Thurgood Marshall said at an event celebrating the two hundredth anniversary of the writing of the Constitution, "believe that the meaning of the Constitution was 'fixed' at the Philadelphia Convention."[267] That would require us to know their original intent and rigidly preserve the Founders' philosophy even though they were all men, most were slave owners, and they allowed slavery in the Constitution.

It will be difficult for strict constructionists to accept that the Constitution has a finger of the almighty hand in it that was placed there by the architects to expand God-given human rights. A strict constructionist's interpretation of the Constitution also means a reaffirmation of states' rights as the preeminent guiding legal principle. However, such an interpretation would leave state offenders outside the available forgiveness promised by the lineage of Abraham, David, and Jesus.

A broader interpretation on the other hand sees the

Constitution as a forward-looking, positive, and hopeful document. We respect the past and the positive contributions the Founders made, seek to understand their intent in the full context in which the Constitution was written, and seek to understand to the fullest its original meaning. But we also know that it has been changed and improved along the way to be more inclusive of all the American people. Therefore, we also know that we have an obligation today to keep improving it.

The more people are made aware of the rights they are entitled to and that have been written in national and international law, the more politically educated and conscious people will become of these rights. The more politically active and organized the people become in the struggle to achieve these rights and the more accessible and responsive our democratic institutions of politics and government become to the democratic will of the people, the faster and more nonviolently we will achieve a new and higher set of human rights.

26

A MATURE FAITH

When a religion is good, I conceive it will support itself; and when it does not support itself, and God does not take care to support it so that its professors are obligated to call for help of the civil power, 'tis a sign, I apprehend, of its being a bad one.[268]

—Benjamin Franklin

Christianity has sufficient inner strength to survive and flourish on its own. It does not need state subsidies, nor state privileges, nor state prestige. The more it obtains state support the greater it curtails human freedom.[269]

—Justice William O. Douglas

If men were angels there would be no need for government.[270]

—James Madison

GOD IS OFTEN described as omnipotent, omniscient, and omnipresent. There are also a cosmological—orderly—universe, a teleological—purposeful—universe, and ontological—first-cause—arguments for God's existence. I encourage people to study and wrestle with these various philosophical and theological concepts.

While we can certainly have a vibrant and valid faith without reason and science, it is generally more desirable to have such a faith beyond them. A mature faith recognizes the potential benefit of intellectual curiosity and the scientific method's relentless inquiry, but it also clearly understands their limitations. At the center of my personal faith and relationship with God is the conviction that the God I worship and serve is active and can do great things in nature and history.

Philosophically, there are only two basic views we can hold of history. All philosophies of history are mere variations or adaptations of these two fundamental approaches. One view of history sees the world and life as cyclical while the other sees it as linear. The cyclical view of history sees the universe and world as an unending series of repetitions and cycles, like the seasons, which have no beginning and no end. History is not going anywhere and thus has no ultimate purpose or design.

A linear view of history on the other hand says that our universe and world have a beginning and will have an end. Linear history may have many ideas of what that beginning and ending are or may be and various interpretations of its ultimate purpose. There may be a variety of numerators, but beginning, ending, and ultimate purpose are the common denominators of a linear view of history.

The Judeo-Christian faith holds a linear view of history. God, who is spirit, created the world *ex nihilo*—out of nothing. It's logically true that *ex nihilo, nihilo fit*—out of nothing, nothing comes, but God creating the world out of nothing means that God created it out of nothing material. Thus, God created the world not out of nothing but out of nothing material; God created the material world out of spirit.

In the Judeo-Christian linear view of history, God is not merely an idea or ideal, a principle, or first cause. God is something more, and God did something more. God is a personal God who cares about each of us and is and was involved with us throughout history.

Through this linear view, God can be known in many

ways—through using reason and the scientific method of observing and studying people and their social arrangements, nature, and the universe. But most important for Christians, God is truly known not in the abstract or impersonal realm of things or nature but through men and women working throughout history and uniquely so in Jesus. Thus, through God, we learn most fully that our purpose in the world is to be dedicated to God in the universe, to work toward better personal and social relations, and to respect the world that God gave us to take care of as responsible stewards; we are to love our neighbor as we do ourselves.

While theological particulars differ, Jews, Christians, and Muslims all share a linear view of history and believe that a monotheistic God is revealed to us in history. God worked through a specific chosen people to send all people a universal message of God's concern and involvement in their human affairs. God revealed through Moses universal laws for basic conduct—the Ten Commandments. God spoke through the prophets, who were primarily forth-tellers of the present, not foretellers of the future, so we would know God's will and the demands of justice. For Christians, God spoke most dramatically through Jesus to let us know that faith, hope, and especially a genuine and mature love of self and neighbor—everyone—were the keys to life and God's will for us.

When I became a Member of Congress, I put my hand on the Bible and swore to uphold the Constitution, not the Bible, the Torah, or the Koran. The people of the Second Congressional District of Illinois did not elect me to be their pastor, priest, rabbi, or imam who would shepherd their souls. They elected me to be their political representative and the guardian of their God-given human and constitutional rights.

To uphold my oath of office and the Constitution, I had to defend the rights of Christians, Jews, and Muslims, people of other faiths in America, and agnostics and atheists. In essence, I had to uphold the public religion of the one true God. The greatness of our country and our Constitution (as amended) is that it puts believers in the position of defending the rights of unbelievers while unbelievers must defend the rights of believers.

I must defend the rights of all Americans even when I cannot defend the choices of some of them. Therefore, as a matter of public policy, we must support public policies and laws that grant the maximum amount of individual freedom compatible with the demands of social justice and societal stability. One of the greatest contributions that any person or institution—and especially religious leaders and institutions—can make to society is to teach humility and tolerance.

Leaders should not teach a false humility that is a weak ego or teach a tolerance that in reality is a lack of courage or principles. We should teach a genuine humility based on a mature understanding of God and our human finitude.

False humility and tolerance must not be allowed to serve as excuses for inaction or for not standing up for things that are morally, socially, economically, and politically sound. Our society should cultivate a hope and an expectation that our leaders, even when it's difficult, will have a real commitment to equal protection under the law for all Americans and strongly and aggressively enforce the rule of just laws. We should not concede to a more cynical view of society and leaders that they will always follow public opinion polls rather than mold public opinion. It is honest, courageous, and realistic for us to say that at our best, we Americans hope, expect, and urge our leaders to have the courage not just of their convictions but also of sound moral convictions and to lead us in such a manner and direction.

Good religion deals with what ought to be while good politics deals with what is. The religious "ought" should always be challenging the political "is" to get better, and the political should be forced to struggle with the religious ought as it grapples to solve societal problems in ethical ways. Both at their best create a good and healthy tension in a morally alive and democratic civil society.

America is a multiracial, multicultural, multireligious, democratic, and secular society, not a religious theocracy. Having said that, we do need strong leaders with well-founded moral convictions and political beliefs who will lead us by appealing to the highest and best, not the lowest and worst, in us.

I see two critical problems confronting people who are religiously and politically serious and committed but who live in a multicultural, secular society such as the United States. Religion tends to deal with the absolute and the eternal while politics deals with the relative, the temporal, the politically possible. How to mesh, balance, or integrate the two is the challenge.

Finite people cannot know absolute truth or eternal principles except by faith. To take our faith seriously and make relative judgments that must be made by finite human beings in a secular democratic society, we must see ourselves as purposeful but also limited human beings. Again, this requires us to be humble and tolerant relative to others' points of view. And in a democracy, we should be more than just tolerant or respectful of others' points of view. Hopefully, we can be appreciative and celebrate our differences.

In *Moral Man and Immoral Society*, Reinhold Niebuhr taught that as individuals, we can sometimes approximate Jesus's standard of *agape* love for one another. But, he argued, as we move higher up the social structure or ladder to more-complex relations such as family, friends, neighborhood, church, state, economic interest groups, political parties, and finally relations between nations, we are less able to approximate Jesus's individual love ideal because of sin—which he defined as an inevitable but false human pride. This innate original sin as manifest in human pride is, as social relations become more complex, the inability to see from another's point of view. Therefore, Niebuhr said, while we should maintain the ideal of love and certainly strive to achieve it at the individual and family levels, at the more complex levels of social and political organization, a balance of power—especially economic power—is necessary to achieve justice.

Even the opportunity for the ideal of individual and family love becomes more available and possible in the context of social, economic, and political justice. As Dr. Cornel West said, "Justice is what love looks like in public."[271]

Niebuhr argued that those seeking social justice should make moral and humanitarian arguments and appeals, try to persuade through reason, use education to achieve their socially just ends, and through politics fight to change the laws to better society. But, he said, unless there is also a balance of economic power, the use of morality, reason, education, politics, and law in the end would reinforce and serve the special interests of those with the most economic power.

This should not be read as a form of economic determinism whether of the inevitable progress or the inevitable failure variety. I believe in neither. I believe that God has given every individual and society genuine if limited human freedom. Obviously, some individuals and societies because of their human, social, or political circumstances have relatively more or less freedom than others. But God has given everyone and every society in whatever circumstance they find themselves a degree of genuine freedom to make choices that have consequences and for which they are accountable. The focus on economic interest is merely an underlying principle of reality and social organization that those engaged in the struggle for social change and social justice must keep in mind. However, the success of their efforts is determined not by economic forces but by the forces of divine spirit energy that has coalesced around a single idea—that we are all children of an eternal force that aligns itself with justice, love, and forgiveness.

Niebuhr's view is a true analysis of our human condition and political situation. Therefore, I believe an active participatory democracy is necessary for secular and civic reasons and spiritual and religious ones as well. In a secular sense, an active democracy that maximizes the participation of all the people is necessary to ensure genuine representation.

Morally and religiously, democracy is required as the best antidote to the original sin of not being able to see from another's point of view, and striving and fighting for a greater balance of economic power is necessary politically to offset human pride and sinfulness. The phrase "power corrupts, and absolute power corrupts absolutely" is true for secular and religious reasons. The democratic and spiritual correction for this problem is not the absence of power, less participation, bigger contributions, and more reliance on an expert class or a political elite. A balance of power will be achieved only through greater democratic participation. Just two simple changes—public funding of our elections and a 95 percent turnout of eligible voters—would dramatically alter politics in the United States as we all witnessed in November 2020.

Religiously trained or motivated people may have a unique or special understanding of human nature and God-based faith, but they must participate in a secular democratic society and politics using the same rules, laws, and constitutional standards as everyone else uses. They must not be thought of as having a unique or special social, economic, or political understanding that must be given preference or be allowed to play the political or economic game using different rules.

Like Dr. Martin Luther King Jr., I can say that at the center of my faith is the conviction that in the universe there is a God of power who can do abundant things in nature and history. I too believe in a God who can beat back gigantic waves of opposition and bring low prodigious mountains of evil. For many African Americans and other Americans, this is a belief born of experience and a faith tested by time.

In "The Answer to a Perplexing Question," a sermon in his book *Strength to Love*, King wrote, "Human life through the centuries has been characterized by man's persistent efforts to remove evil from the earth."[272] In effect, King was also posing the question of religion and politics. He was asking, Is the answer to the human family's quest to build a more perfect union and a more perfect world in human effort or in letting God do it? Is human ingenuity or divine goodwill the path to international peace and social and economic justice? These are questions that many religionists and nonreligionists wrestle with daily.

King suggested that sincere and dedicated human effort in the areas of reason, science, invention, agriculture, education, technology, industry, and all humanitarian efforts to eliminate the social evils in the world today must be respected, encouraged, and continued. But he also warned that unless we recognize our mortal nature and human limitations and the presence of sin in the world, we delude ourselves and are doomed to failure. Through my own observations of people involved in the civil rights movement, I understand that such human failure and frustration can turn to bitterness, disillusionment, and despair and even manifest themselves in violence against ourselves, our families, our neighbors, and society.

King wrote, "The second idea for removing evil from the world stipulates that if man waits submissively upon the Lord, in his own good time God alone will redeem the world."[273] Here, he contrasted the overly optimistic Renaissance with the overly pessimistic Protestant Reformation regarding human nature. The Renaissance saw our capacity for good and overlooked our capacity for evil; the Reformation saw our capacity for evil and overlooked our capacity for good, and it turned both God and man into absolutes. God was absolutely sovereign with man having no freedom, and man was absolutely helpless and could make no difference in the world.

The overemphasis on human sin and evil led people to give up on this world and instead concentrate on a Christian religion that was otherworldly and that left the troubles of this world behind; it concentrated almost exclusively on getting to heaven after this life, a "pie in the sky by and by" religion.

This kind of religion has no application of religion to politics.

This pessimistic view of religion is otherworldly oriented or in a modified form concentrates only on meeting the physical or emotional needs of an affected individual. It seldom if ever comes to grips with working to eliminate the underlying systemic social, economic, legal, and political causes that created the individual human need in the first place.

In this kind of religion, prayer becomes a substitute for effort and makes a mockery of work. This religion of limited hope is concerned only with the issues of an afterlife, not with the issues of life. This false and heretical Christianity—Christian heretics were not people who did not tell the truth but those who did not tell the whole truth—creates too rigid a wall of separation between the sacred and the secular, between the human and the divine, between the mortal and the immortal, and between the religious and the political. King put it this way.

> We must pray earnestly for peace, but we must also work vigorously for disarmament and the suspension of weapon testing. We must use our minds as rigorously to plan for peace as we have used them to plan for war. We must pray with unceasing passion for racial justice, but we must also use our minds to develop a program, organize ourselves into mass nonviolent action, and employ every resource of our bodies and souls to bring an end to racial injustice. We must pray unrelentingly for economic justice, but we must also work diligently to bring into being those social forces that make for a better distribution of wealth within our nation and in the underdeveloped countries of the world. We must learn that to expect God to do everything while we do nothing is not faith, but superstition.[274]

How then do we reconcile human effort and divine guidance?

King said that the answer was in two kinds of faith in God working together—a rigorous intellectual faith that was tough minded (a faith that "believes that") and a tender faith of the soul that engulfed and committed the whole person to God's will and service (a faith that "believes in"). "So, by faith we are saved. Man filled with God and God operating through man bring unbelievable changes in our individual and social lives."[275]

We cannot build a more perfect union by sheer human will and making New Year's resolutions. Neither can we build a more perfect world merely by calling on God through prayer to change our circumstances and save us. Through us, God can build a more perfect union. Through faith, we must surrender ourselves to become instruments of God's love, justice, and peace.

"Now faith is the substance of things hoped for, the evidence of things not seen" (Hebrews 11:1). Those in America and around the world who will allow God to work through them in history have this kind of faith and are held and sustained by it.

Dr. Samuel DeWitt Proctor argued,

> Faith in God, faith in their own worth and dignity, and faith in the idea that America's 330 million diverse peoples can cohere in a true community that gives space to ethnic preference, but gives loyalty to the basic values of equality, compassion, freedom and justice. Through the long, winding trail of political fortunes, with a disciplined transcendence over movements and individuals who would impede their progress, they have survived every challenge and still press forward toward helping America fulfill a unique and unprecedented role in the history of humankind.[276]

> Like millions of other black Americans, I am heir to the faith that was born the day twenty frightened black captives were unloaded at Jamestown

in 1619. Their slow, courageous journey from the Dutch slave boat to the present, in the face of unrelenting oppression, is the story of their faith; and therein I believe lies the clue to the answer to today's dilemma. Faith put steel in their spines to endure physical bondage, and zeal in their souls to prevail against evil; it illuminated their minds to keep the vision of a better day and inspired their hearts to learn and embrace the great human conversation. Faith gave them a sense of eternity, a mystical transcendence that transposed their pain into song and their agony into a durable, resilient quest for complete humanity, the substance of things hoped for.[277]

My faith gives me the courage to believe that the same Constitution that freed the slaves can free 68 million debt-paid felons from shame, blame, and guilt. The same Constitution can eliminate an industrial prison complex by allowing recovery from mistakes. The same Constitution can be upheld by recognizing that strength is not in the serpent but in balancing the serpent and the dove. The same Constitution that built the most massive military machine in the history of humankind can "beat swords into plowshares" and "study war no more" (Isaiah 2:4). The same Constitution can improve our democracy by providing for our right to vote, create and sustain full employment with living wages, advance public education, extend health care to the sick, offer affordable housing "that the son of man may have a place to lay his head" (Luke 9:58), sustain the environment, provide equal rights for women, and render taxation fair for all Americans. It is with this faith that I press on with God's help and guidance to build a more perfect union. We can all be instruments of God's love and peace and justice if we open and surrender ourselves and let God work through us.

AFTERWORD

DR. CORNEL WEST

JESSE JACKSON JR. has been shaped by a family of spiritual nobility and a freedom struggle of moral majesty. His father is a world historical figure, and his mother is a global citizen of pure gold.

When I first met Jesse Jackson Jr. over thirty years ago, he was a brilliant student at the Chicago Theological Seminary; he was full of genuine intellectual curiosity and undeniable charisma. Twenty years later, he (then a US congressman from Chicago) sat with me, the presidential candidate Barack Obama, Charles Ogletree, David Axelrod, and others in preparation for a debate at Howard University early in the campaign.

Four years ago, I was blessed and pleased to see him in my lecture on John Coltrane in New York and break bread reflecting on his divine calling and work.

This original and rich book—powerful and insightful—is the product of his painstaking research and grand vision. This serious and substantive text plunges deep into the theological imagination of the Founders of the US Constitution. In stark contrast to many American constitutional scholars who highlight the influence of the European enlightenments, class interests, or White supremacists' beliefs, Jackson focuses on the incontestable biblical sources and theological formulations of Jefferson, Madison, Franklin, and others. This religious emphasis takes us back to the greatest scholar of early American history—Perry Miller. Jackson's turn back to the fundamental theme of divine providence—the finger of God shot through the US Constitution and tied to the original intent of the framers—unsettles common secular perspectives. Yet his textual evidence is compelling.

Jackson's Christian sensibilities resonate with the two great literary epics in American history: Herman Melville's *Moby Dick* and William Faulkner's *Go Down, Moses*. Both artistic masterpieces posit the beginnings and endings of America as a theological if not downright biblical experiment. The fundamental question is whether the human spirit can be resurrected in the US project as a republic and a culture.

Jackson has two basic aims. First, he argues that the Constitution harbors strong energies of forgiveness for our precious 68 million "debt-paid" felons. The "reprieve and pardon" portion of Article II, Section 2, Clause 1 enables a tough military commander in chief to enact soft and merciful acts of forgiveness for fellow citizens with incarcerated experiences. This serpent-like power and dove-like action can flow from a president of integrity and sensitivity—one of "pious reflection"—who exemplifies "unlimited moral power and authority based in divine truth" yet within limited constitutional authority. Jackson even argues that this presidential figure was viewed as one who was in lineage of the biblical David to Jesus. Forgiveness and the shedding of shame, blame, and guilt were built into the Constitution itself—another way in which divine providence would trump a mean-spirited nationalism.

Jesse Jackson Jr. is a real patriot—a Black man committed to liberty and justice who calls for racial equality, economic fairness, and especially prison reform. He also is an unapologetic Christian—like myself—who is deeply disturbed about the prevailing spiritual decay and pervasive moral decrepitude in American life. Like a good Christian, he begins with himself—his own shortcomings, faults, and failures. His poignant stories about his arrest, trial, and incarceration (including solitary confinement) are riveting. And his dancing with Sandi—his mop—is touching.

Yet in the end, nothing can stop the prophetic fire burning

in the soul of Jesse Jackson Jr. He has a divine calling to pursue his divine mission—to use his divine gifts to keep hope alive and the American experiment afloat headed toward a more perfect union!

—Dr. Cornel West

NOTES

There are four techniques I used to help crystalize the concept of the commander of the army and repriever pardoner® as a single idea. The first is to simply take the first letters of the concept and create an acronym, COTAARP.™ The second technique is Hegel's dialectic, which Martin Luther King Jr. explained in his sermon that I referenced in the introduction of this book combining strongly marked opposites in a single character trait. The third was to better understand and incorporate *History and Spirit*[278] by Joel Kovel and *The Conjunct Life*[279] by Elton Trueblood. I was directed to these books by Dr. James A. Forbes Jr., and in them, I came to understand how "splitting and differentiating" impacted words and spirit throughout history.

The fourth and slightly more complicated technique was math. The words in the Bible contain spirit and spirit energy over time, more specifically, across infinity. Therefore, its words are quantifiable. On this matter, I turned to my college professor Dr. Dong Kuen Jeong. He taught me college-level statistics in a fascinating way.

One day, he worked out a very complicated statistical problem and arrived at normal distribution.[280] When he finished, he paused for what seemed to be like ten minutes, stepped back to (I thought) admire his work, and said shockingly, "Look at this! This is the work of God. This is normal distribution, and only God could have done this." I finally understood that math could turn complicated subjects into simple equations. I also came to understand that math could contain spirit and spirit matter. That was thirty-seven years ago.

Matthew 1:1–17 provides a lineage of forty-two generations

between Abraham and Jesus. Because the lineage of the prophets of Matthew 1:1–17 contain the lineage of the men whose infinite and divine spirit make up the Bible, their energy is best presented against infinity. Dr. Jeong and I called it DPSE—Divine Providential Spirit Energy. This energy is best represented by this simple equation. The sum of the generations of DPSE from Abraham (one) to Jesus (forty-two), times the integral of divine human spirit energy, times the time constant, equals infinity.

$$LOA = \sum_{i=1}^{42} \int_{t=0}^{\infty} (t)dt = \infty \qquad \text{281}$$

The lineage of David is a subset of the lineage of Abraham, and there were twenty-eight generations between David and Jesus; it is best represented by the equation the sum of the generations of DPE from David (fourteen) to Jesus (forty-two) times the integral of divine human spirit energy times the time constant, which equals infinity. The sum of the generations of DPSE (spirit energy), David, and Jesus, is best represented by the following equation extracted from the lineage of Abraham.

$$LOD = \sum_{i=14}^{42} \int_{t=0}^{\infty} (t)dt = \infty \qquad \text{282}$$

Commander of the army and reprieves and pardons are extracted from the linear theological by function, and for more than

234 years, it has been a function of the unknown Democrat or Republican or $f(x)$.[283] Article II, Section 2, Clause 1 is a function extracted from the lineage of David except in cases of impeachment. It begins "He shall ... and he shall ..."; that is a function of the responsibility of the office, and it is not a job but a calling. It is now as a result of this work the known function of the lineage of David or the $f(lod)$ with one notable exception, impeachable when the leader of the free world is operating outside of the grace of God and the Constitution.[284]

Article II, Section 2, Clause 1 of our Constitution is a function and an advertisement to infinity. The function cannot change without amendment, and no Christian who believes in the return of the redeemer would allow its change. It is a calling to eternity, not a partisan job. But it is not just a function because it is in the American Constitution, a living document, a constant, living function. It is not just a constant, living function; it is a mandatory responsibility of the government to perform and therefore is a compulsory function.

The constant function too is measured against infinity and all who have historically occupied the position. And the occupant of the White House is elected to perform this function of the (lod), the operationalized function of the lineage of David for every generation unless of course the president is impeached for a high crime or misdemeanor, which more accurately is tied to violating the principles and precepts established by the function of the lineage of David along with obedience to the common law, for no man is above it.

The president can be impeached for stepping outside the moral and common law. "How oft shall my brother sin against me, and I forgive him till seven times? Jesus saith unto him, I say not unto thee, until seven times: but, until seventy times seven."[285] Forgiveness was not to be an occasional act of the government but its permanent domestic and global attitude and behavior. On September 17, 1787, before the Bill of Rights was added in 1791, divine forgiveness is the only function in the Constitution that applies to everyone and the states ratified it.

The function is best represented mathematically as the function of the lineage of David in Article II, Section 2, Clause 1 of the Constitution by the following acronym COTAARP™ an equation.[286] How we the people wield the COTAARP™ is how we wield the finger of God. Everyone deserves health care, good housing, living wages, education, equal opportunity, peace, and a clean, safe, and sustainable environment that honors our Creator. This I believe is the will of God. Therefore, the function of the lineage of David equals the function of the sum of the DPE between David (fourteen) and Jesus (forty-two) times the integral of divine human spirit energy times the time constant, which equals COTAARP,™ which equals infinity and is best represented by the following equation.

[287]

$$f(LOD) = f\left(\sum_{i=14}^{42} \int_{t=0}^{\infty} (t)dt\right) = COTAARP = \infty$$

The only exception to the function is in cases of impeachment; lying, stealing, cheating, and deceiving the American people are high crimes and misdemeanors. That is what is meant by being outside the function of divine truth. These offenses include following federal and state law because no one is above the law. However, the president does not get to ignore the laws of Moses given on Sinai. Violating one's solemn oath by lying to Congress and the people is very serious business under the moral code and the position. Clearly, the president is impeached by the House, but the severity and/or removal is determined by trial in the Senate. The structure of this language, the action verbs, "He shall ... and he shall ..." commander of the army and reprieves and pardons[288] was not placed in the Constitution as two job responsibilities but as a single theological idea.

Every four years, the man or the woman in the sect of one we vote for has an opportunity to rise to the occasion of securing our liberties and providing for our most basic human needs in this God-ordained system. The integral of human spirit energy, however, ranges from $t = 0$ to infinity, or for perfect clarity, it ranges from 0—sitting on a couch—to trying to emulate, imitate, and model one's presidency for the least of these and be like Jesus. However, history has shown that nationalism and patriotism and the military-industrial complex have through successive Democratic and Republican presidents used these two job requirements (splitting) as a justification for a violent global, clandestine, capital-dominating, and military-enforcing empire, a domestic military and police state, and the pardon power in our Constitution as a family and friends' program for the politically connected. Democrats and Republicans have jointly participated in this abomination. With an understanding of the single idea, Dr. Cornel West said to me, "Jesse, you have unlocked the theological imagination of the Founding Fathers." I responded to Dr. West, "Once the American people see it, it will be impossible for them to unsee it."

REFERENCES

ABC News. ABC News Network. Accessed April 7, 2021. https://abcnews.go.com/Blotter/ConductUnbecoming/story?id=6431739&page=1.

Adams, Abigail and Edith Belle Gelles. *Abigail Adams: Letters*. Library of America, 2016.

Adams, John. A Defence of the Constitutions of Government of the United States of America against the Attack of M. Turgot in His Letter to Dr. Price, Dated the Twenty-Second Day of March, 1778. Lawbook Exchange, 2001.

Adams, John Quincy. "The Historical Magazine and Notes and Queries Concerning the Antiquities, History and Biography of America: Free Download, Borrow, and Streaming." Internet Archive. Morrisania, NY [etc.] Henry B. Dawson [etc.], January 1, 1970. https://archive.org/details/historicalmagaziv4morr/page/194/mode/1up?view=theater.

"Alexander Hamilton: Ceasar II." Infoplease. Infoplease. Accessed April 25, 2022. https://www.infoplease.com/primary-sources/government/federalist-papers/alexander-hamilton-ceasar-ii.

Alliance for Religious Freedom. "America Dedicated to God." Alliance For Religious Freedom. Accessed May 21, 2021. https://allianceforreligiousfreedom.com/educate-yourself/america-dedicated-to-god/#:~:text=America%20Dedicated%20to%20God%20On%20April%2030%20th,the%20Inauguration%20of%20our%20first%20president%2C%20George%20Washington.

Article II Section 2: Constitution Annotated: Congress.gov. Accessed April 17, 2021. https://constitution.congress.gov/browse/article-2/section-2/.

Auten, Brian, Joshua, anonymous, Jarrett Doyle, Neal Korfhage, R Lidster, et al. "H. G. Wells on the Historicity of Jesus." *Apologetics* 315, June 2, 2013. https://apologetics315.com/2013/06/h-g-wells-on-the-historicity-of-jesus/.

Barth, Karl, Douglas Horton, In *The Word of God and the Word of Man*. New York: Harper, 1957.

Beliefnet and Beliefnet Editor. "Letter from Franklin to Ezra Stiles." Site accessed February 14, 2019. www.beliefnet.com/faiths/faith-tools/the-founding-faith-archive/benjamin-franklin/letter-from-benjamin-franklin-to-ezra-stiles-1.aspx.

Bell, Danna. *"A Republic, If You Can Keep It" | Teaching with the Library of Congress*, September 8, 2016, blogs.loc.gov/teachers/2016/09/a-republic-if-you-can-keep-it/.

Blanchard, Calvin. Complete Works of Thomas Paine Containing All of His Political And Theological Writings. New York: Belford, Clarke, 1885.

Brotherton, Elizabeth. "Emancipation Hall Moves Ahead with House Vote." Roll Call. Roll Call, December 13, 2019. https://www.rollcall.com/2007/11/13/emancipation-hall-moves-ahead-with-house-vote/.

Buonarroti, Michelangelo, et al. "La Mia Definizione Di Scultura." *Michelangelo Buonarroti è Tornato*, June 30, 2014, michelangelobuonarrotietornato.com/2014/06/30/la-mia-definizione-di-scultura/.

Burton, Neel. *The Meaning of Madness*. Oxford: Acheron Press, 2009.

Chaucer, Geoffrey. *The Canterbury Tales*. London: Penguin, 2007.

Constitution of the United States. Providence Forum, July 16, 2020. providenceforum.org/story/declaration-independence-2/.

Diamant, Jeff. "Three-Quarters of Black Americans Believe in God of the Bible or Other Holy Scripture." Pew Research Center. March 25, 2021. https://www.pewresearch.org/fact-tank/2021/03/24/three-quarters-of-black-americans-believe-in-god-of-the-bible-or-other-holy-scripture/.

Edwards, Owen. "How Thomas Jefferson Created His Own Bible." Smithsonian Institution, January 1, 2012, www.smithsonianmag.com/arts-culture/how-thomas-jefferson-created-his-own-bible-5659505/.

Eidenmuller, Michael E. "Online Speech Bank: Franklin's Prayer Speech at the Constitutional Convention of 1787." www.americanrhetoric.com/speeches/benfranklin.htm.

Encyclopedia Britannica. "Establishment of Israel." www.britannica.com/place/Israel/Establishment-of-Israel.

Encyclopedia.com. "Nonfiction Classics for Students." March 18, 2021. www.encyclopedia.com/arts/culture-magazines/self-reliance-0

Federalist Papers, "The People Who Mean To Be Their ..." thefederalistpapers.org/.

Federalist Papers, by Alexander Hamilton et al., Signet, 2005.

Forbes magazine. "The Real Story Behind Apple's 'Think Different' Campaign." July 9, 2020. https://www.forbes.com/sites/onmarketing/2011/12/14/the-real-story-behind-apples-think-different-campaign/.

"Founders Online: A New Version of the Lord's Prayer, [Late 1768?]." National Archives and Records Administration. National Archives and Records Administration. Accessed October 2, 2021. https://founders.archives.gov/documents/Franklin/01-15-02-0170.

Founders Online: From Alexander Hamilton to The Daily Advertiser, [15 September ...]. National Archives and Records Administration. founders.archives.gov/documents/ Hamilton/01-04-02-0135.

Founders Online: From Benjamin Franklin to Richard Price, 9 October 1780. National Archives and Records Administration. National Archives and Records Administration. Accessed September 14, 2021. https://founders.archives.gov/documents/ Franklin/01-33-02-0330.

Founders Online: From Franklin to Sarah Bache, 26 January 1784. National Archives and Records Administration. founders.archives.gov/documents/Franklin/01-41-02-0327.

Founders Online: From John Adams to Jonathan Jackson, 2 October 1780. National Archives and Records Administration. founders.archives.gov/documents/Adams/06-10-02-0113.

Founders Online: From John Adams to Massachusetts Militia, 11 October 1798. National Archives and Records Administration. founders.archives.gov/documents/Adams/99-02-02-3102.

Founders Online: From John Adams to Thomas Jefferson, 2 February 1816. National Archives and Records Administration. founders.archives.gov/documents/Adams/99-02-02-6575.

Founders Online: From Thomas Jefferson to William Short, 13 April 1820. National Archives and Records Administration. Accessed April 10, 2021. https://www.founders.archives.gov/ documents/Jefferson/98-01-02-1218.

Founders Online: From Thomas Jefferson to Rush, 21 April 1803. National Archives and Records Administration. founders.archives.gov/documents/Jefferson/01-40-02-0178-0001.

Founders Online: From Thomas Jefferson to Waterhouse, 26 June 1822. National Archives and Records Administration. founders.archives.gov/documents/Jefferson/98-01-02-2905.

Founders Online: From Thomas Jefferson to John Adams, 11 April 1823. National Archives and Records Administration. founders.archives.gov/documents/Jefferson/98-01-02-3446#:~:text=and%20the%20day%20will%20come,in%20the%20brain%20of%20Jupiter.

Founders Online: John Adams to Thomas Jefferson, 13 November 1815. National Archives and Records Administration 2002. founders.archives.gov/documents/Jefferson/03-09-02-0121.

Founders Online: John Adams to Thomas Jefferson, 25 December 1813. National Archives and Records Administration. founders.archives.gov/documents/Jefferson/03-07-02-0040.

Founders Online: John Adams to Thomas Jefferson, 4 November 1816. National Archives and Records Administration. founders.archives.gov/documents/Jefferson/03-10-02-0378#:~:text=The%20Ten%20Commandments%20and%20The,the%20Jesuits%2C%20is%20in%204.

Founders Online: Memorial and Remonstrance against Religious Assessments, [Ca. ...]. National Archives and Records Administration. founders.archives.gov/documents/Madison/01-08-02-0163.

Founders Online: To John Adams from John Quincy Adams, 31 August 1811. National Archives and Records Administration. founders.archives.gov/documents/Adams/99-03-02-2020.

Frankl, Viktor E., et al. *Man's Search for Meaning*. Beacon Press, 2006.

Franklin, Benjamin. "Franklin—Address to Public." PBS, www.pbs.org/benfranklin/pop_address.html.

Franklin, Benjamin. "Franklin On His Religious Faith." American Heritage Publishing, April 1, 2021. https://www.americanheritage.com/benjamin-franklin-his-religious-faith.

Franklin Historical Society. "Constitutional Convention." www.benjamin-franklin-history.org/constitutional-convention/#:~:

text=Thus%20I%20consent%2C%20Sir%2C%20 to,and%20here%20they%20shall%20die.

Full Text of "Trattati D'arte Del Cinquecento Vol. 1." archive.org/ stream/219TrattatiDarteDelCinquecento1Si259/219_ Trattati-darte_del_Cinquecento_1_si259_djvu.txt.

Hall, L. Kermit. *The Oxford Companion to the Supreme Court.* New York, NY: Oxford University Press, 1992.

Hamer, Fannie Lou. "I'm Sick and Tired of Being Sick and Tired—Dec. 20, 1964." Archives of Women's Political Communication. Iowa State University. Accessed April 10, 2021. https://awpc.cattcenter.iastate.edu/2019/08/09/im-sic k-and-tired-of-being-sick-and-tired-dec-20-1964/.

Harvard Square Library. "We Are Determined to Foment a Rebellion." Accessed April 17, 2021. https://www.har- vardsquarelibrary.org/wp-content/uploads/2013/06/SBU_ Abigail_Adams.pdf.

Hill, Napoleon. *Think and Grow Rich.* Chartwell Books, 2015.

Holowchak, M. Andrew. "Thomas Jefferson," Stanford Encyclopedia of Philosophy. December 16, 2019. https:// plato.stanford.edu/entries/jefferson/.

Independence Hall Association. "The Lincoln-Douglas Debates." www.ushistory.org/us/32b.asp.

Jackson, Jesse, and Frank E. Watkins. *A More Perfect Union: Advancing New American Rights.* New York: Welcome Rain Publishers, 2001.

Jefferson, Thomas. The Jefferson Bible: the Life and Morals of Jesus of Nazareth, Extracted Textually from the Gospels in Greek, Latin, French & English, by Thomas Jefferson et al., Smithsonian Books, 2011.

Jefferson, Thomas. "Jefferson Quotes & Family Letters." Extract from Thomas Jefferson to Ezra Styles Ely, 25 June 1819

[Quote] | Jefferson Quotes & Family Letters, tjrs.monticello. org/letter/2409.

Jefferson, Thomas. The Jefferson Bible: The Life and Morals of Jesus of Nazareth Extracted Textually from the Gospels in Greek, Latin, French & English. Washington D.C., DC: Smithsonian Books, 2011

Jefferson, Thomas. *Ye Will Say I Am No Christian*, in Thomas Jefferson/John Adams Correspondence on Religion, Morals, and Values. Prometheus, 2006.

Ketcham, Ralph Louis. The Anti-Federalist Papers: The Constitutional Convention Debates. Signet, 2003.

King, Martin Luther and Coretta Scott King, *Strength to Love*, Fortress, 2010.

Klos, Stan. "Abolition of Slavery." Abolition of Slavery. BenjaminFranklin.org, 2013. https://www.benjaminfranklin. org/p/in-his-later-years-benjaminfranklin.html.

Kovel, Joel. History and Spirit: An Inquiry into the Philosophy of Liberation, Beacon Press, 1991.

Kruppa, Patricia Stallings. "The Life & Times of Charles H. Spurgeon." Christian History. January 1, 1991. www.christi-anitytoday.com/history/issues/issue-29/life-times-of-charles-h-spurgeon.html.

Lipka, Michael. "Half of Americans Say Bible Should Influence U.S. Laws, Including 28% Who Favor It over the Will of the People." Pew Research Center. August 18, 2020. https://www. pewresearch.org/fact-tank/2020/04/13/half-of-americans-sa y-bible-should-influence-u-s-laws-including-28-who-favor-i t-over-the-will-of-the-people/.

Martin, Adam. "Jesse Jackson Jr. Pleads Guilty to Squandering Campaign Cash on Elk Heads." *Intelligencer*. February 21, 2013. https://nymag.com/intelligencer/2013/02/jesse-jackso n-jr-pleads-guilty-to-fraud.html.

MacAuthor, John D. "Charles Thomson- Principal Designer of the Great Seal." GreatSeal.com. John, 1998. https://www.greatseal.com/committees/finaldesign/thomson.html.

Meachum, Jon. American Gospel: God, the Founding Fathers, and the Making of a Nation. Random House, 2007.

MSNBC. "Jesse Jackson Jr. to Serve Two and a Half Years in Prison." April 20, 2014. www.mars-in-prison-42294851618.

National Archives and Records Administration. "Declaration of Independence: A Transcription." www.archives.gov/founding-docs/declaration-transcript.

National Parks Service. "June 28, 1787: Franklin's Proposal for Prayer." US Department of the Interior. Accessed May 21, 2021. https://www.nps.gov/articles/constitutional convention-june28.htm?back=https%3A%2F%2Fwww.google.com%2Fsearch%3Fclient%3Dsafari%26as_qdr%3Dall%26as_occt%3Dany%26safe%3Dactive%26as_q%3DBenjamin%2BFranklin%2Bprayer%2Bdelivered%2B-Thursday%2C%2BJune%2B28%2C%2B1787%26channel%3Daplab%26source%3Da-app1%26hl%3Den.

Novak, Michael. On Two Wings: Humble Faith and Common Sense at the American Founding. Encounter Books, 2003.

One Nation Under God: Alexander Hamilton, Christian Defense Fund, 1997. www.leaderu.org/orgs/cdf/onug/hamilton.html.

Paine, Thomas. The Complete Works of Thomas Paine. Chicago: Belford Clarke, 1885.

Patterson, Richard S. The Eagle and the Shield, edited by Richardson Dougall, Office of the Historian, Bureau of Public Affairs, Department of State, 1976.

Penn, William. In Primitive Christianity Revived by William Penn. Also, Select Essays on Religious Subjects, from … the Writings of Isaac Pennington. Gale Ecco, 2018.

Priestley, Joseph. *An History of the Corruptions of Christianity.* London: Franklin Classics, 1793.

Proctor, Samuel D. Essay in The Substance of Things Hoped for: a Memoir of African-American Faith. New York: G.P. Putnam's Sons, 1996.

Quotations on the Jefferson Memorial. "Monticello." www. monticello.org/site/research-and-collections/quotations-jefferson-memorial.

Raboteau, Albert J. *Canaan Land: A Religious History of African Americans.* New York, NY: Oxford University Press, 2001.

Religion and the Founding of the United States. "Thomas Jefferson & Religious Freedom." Accessed April 17, 2021. https://people.smu.edu/religionandfoundingusa/thomas-jeffersons-danbury-letter/thomas-jefferson-religious-freedom/.

Sabella, Jeremy. "Postures of Piety and Protest: American Civil Religion and the Politics of Kneeling in the NFL." Digital Publishing Institute, July 25, 2019. www.mdpi.com/2077-1444/10/8/449/htm.

Sandstrom, Aleksandra. "God or the Divine Is Referenced in Every State Constitution." Pew Research Center. August 27, 2020. https://www.pewresearch.org/fact-tank/2017/08/17/god-or-the-divine-is-referenced-in-every-state-constitution/.

Smithsonian Institution. "This Theologian Helped MLK See the Value of Nonviolence." January 12, 2018. http://www.smithsonianmag.com/history/this-theologian-helped-mlk-see-value-nonviolence-180967821/.

Southall, Ashley. "Statue of Rosa Parks Is Unveiled at the Capitol." *New York Times*, February 27, 2013. www.nytimes.com/2013/02/28/us/politics/statue-of-rosa-parks-is-unveiled-at-the-capitol.amp.html.

Special Academic Programs. Mellon Mays Undergraduate Fund. "Introduction to MMUF and Dr. E. Mays." Accessed April 7, 2021. https://osap.williams.edu/fellowships/mmuf-intro/.

Spurgeon Center. "Christ—Our Substitute." April 15, 1860. www.spurgeon.org/resource-library/sermons/christ-our-substitute/#flipbook/.

Straub, Steve. "Alexander Hamilton." The Federalist Papers, July 11, 2012, thefederalistpapers.org/founders/alexander-hamilton.

Thurman, Howard. Footprints of a Dream: the Story of the Church for the Fellowship of All Peoples. Eugene, OR: Wipf & Stock, 2009.

Thurman, Howard. "Whole." Essay in *Jesus and the Disinherited*. Boston: Beacon Press, 1996.

Trueblood, Elton. *The Conjunct Life*. Prinit Press, 1985.

US Constitution—Second Amendment: Resources: Constitution Annotated. Library of Congress. Constitution Annotated. Accessed April 17, 2021. https://constitution.congress.gov/constitution/amendment-2/.

US Constitution—Ninth Amendment: Resources: Constitution Annotated. Library of Congress. Accessed May 21, 2021. https://constitution.congress.gov/constitution/amendment-9/#amendment-9.

Waite, Kevin. "Congress Is Still Littered With Insurrectionists." *Slate Magazine*, January 12, 2021. slate.com/news-and-politics/2021/01/congress-is-still-littered-with-insurrectionists.am.

Warren, Rick. *The Purpose Driven Life*. MI: Zondervan, 2002.

West, Cornel. "'Justice Is What Love Looks like in Public.'" Pride Foundation, March 6, 2019. https://pridefoundation.org/2017/02/justice-is-what-love-looks-like-in-public/#:~:text=Cornel%20West%20famously%20said%2C%20

%E2%80%9CJustice,the%20only%20true%20path%20 forward.

White House Historical Association. "Which President Started the Tradition of Pardoning the Thanksgiving Turkey?" www. whitehousehistory.org/questions/which-president-started-th e-tradition-of-pardoning-the-thanksgiving-turkey.

Woodard, Colin. Union: the Struggle to Forge the Story of United States Nationhood. New York: Viking, 2020.

ENDNOTES

1   Matthew 25:40–45 KJV.

2   Jude 24 KJV.

3   Michael Novak, *On Two Wings: Humble Faith and Common Sense at the American Founding* (San Francisco: Encounter Books, 2003), Dedication. pg. front matter

4   Ibid.

5   James Weldon Johnson, "NAACP History: Lift Every Voice and Sing," NAACP, August 16, 2018, https://www.naacp.org/naac p-history-lift-evry-voice-and-sing/.

6   Ibid.

7   Bill Moyers, "What a Real President Was Like," *Washington Post*, November 13, 1988, https://www.washingtonpost.com/archive/opinions/1988/11/13/what-a-real-president-was-like/d483c1be-d0da-43b7-bde6-04e10106ff6c/.

8   King, Martin L. "A Proper Sense of Priorities." *Closing Remarks*. Speech presented at the Closing Remarks, n.d.

9   Thomas Paine, *The Complete Works of Thomas Paine* (Chicago: Belford Clarke, 1885), appendix to *Common Sense*, 49–50.

10   "1984 Speech | The Long Pilgrimage Of Jesse Jackson | Frontline, (PBS, 1995), https://www.pbs.org/wgbh/pages/frontline/jesse/speeches/jesse84speech.html.

11   John 1:14 KJV.

12   Martin Luther King and Coretta Scott King, "Strength to Love," in *Strength to Love* (Philadelphia, PA: Fortress, 2010), p.13.

13   Matthew 10:16 KJV.

14   King, Strength to Love, p.13.

15   King, Strength to Love.

16   Ibid.

17   The Federalist Papers, by Alexander Hamilton et al., Signet, 2005, 445–48.

18   Ibid., 226–27.

19 *One Nation Under God: Alexander Hamilton*, Christian Defense Fund, 1997, www.leaderu.org/orgs/cdf/onug/hamilton.html.

20 The Constitution of the United States, *Providence Forum*, July 16, 2020, providenceforum.org/story/declaration-independence-2/.

21 Dana Bell, *A Republic, If You Can Keep It | Teaching with the Library of Congress*, September 8, 2016, blogs.loc.gov/teachers/2016/09/a-republic-if-you-can-keep-it/.

22 https://founders.archives.gov/documents/Madison/01-08-02-0163, James Madison, "Memorial and Remonstrance against Religious Assessments," ca. June 20, 1785.

23 John Winthrop, "City Upon a Hill." *Digital History*, 2016, www.digitalhistory.uh.edu/disp_textbook_print.cfm?smtid=3. "A City upon a Hill" is a phrase derived from the parable of salt and light in Jesus's Sermon on the Mount. In a modern context, it is used in US politics to refer to America acting as a beacon of hope for the world. Aboard the *Arbella*, Winthrop delivered the speech "A model of Christian Charity" on April 8, 1630 also known as the "city on a hill." Michal Novak, *On Two Wings* (Encounter Books, 2002), 82.

24 Thomas Jefferson, The Jefferson Bible: the Life and Morals of Jesus of Nazareth, Extracted Textually from the Gospels in Greek, Latin, French & English (Smithsonian Books, 2011), 11.

25 "Ye Will Say I Am No Christian," in Thomas Jefferson/John Adams Correspondence on Religion, Morals, and Values by Thomas Jefferson et al. (Prometheus Books, 2006), 98–101.

26 Congressman Jackson is the founder of Quantum Linear Theology, a system of teaching Quantum Linear Theology and Method of Measuring National and Presidential Spirit Energy Using Computer and Application Based Timelines. Patent pending.

27 "The Vitruvian Man," Leonardo DaVinci, iStock, Chris DiGiorgio.

28 Founders Online: From John Adams to Jonathan Jackson, 2 October 1780, National Archives and Records Administration. founders.archives.gov/documents/Adams/06-10-02-0113.

29 Albert J. Raboteau, *Canaan Land: A Religious History of African Americans* (New York, NY: Oxford University Press, 2001). p.30,

30 Ibid p.35.

31 Joseph Priestley, *An History of the Corruptions of Christianity* (London: Franklin Classics, 1793).

32 Calvin Blanchard, Complete Works of Thomas Paine Containing All of His Political And Theological Writings (New York: Belford, Clarke, 1885).

33 Conversations with Dr. James A. Forbes (2019–2021), 1996. In a Baylor University worldwide survey of 341 seminary professors and editors of religious periodicals, Forbes was voted one of the twelve most effective preachers in the English-speaking world.

34 iStock images, Chris Gorgio. The Founding Fathers provided a skeleton for a White man to discover and inherit the DNA of the linear theological system including the original intent that allowed only White men to vote for the office. It was discovered by a Black man who added the characteristics of the lineage of Abraham to meet the objective needs of the least of these at the hour of the writing of this manuscript.

35 "Monticello," *Quotations on the Jefferson Memorial*, 1987, www.monticello.org/site/research-and-collections/quotations-jefferson-memorial.

36 Thomas Jefferson/John Adams Correspondence on Religion, 98–101. iStock, Chris Gorgio image.

37 John 1:14 KJV.

38 Matthew 22:36–40 KJV.

39 Quotations on the Jefferson Memorial.

40 The discovery was placed in the Constitution on September 17, 1787, four years before the Tenth Amendment and the Bill of Rights.

41 Thomas Paine (1737–1809), *Thomas Paine's Common Sense: The Call to Independence* (Woodbury, NY: Barron's Educational Series, 1975). In the appendix to *Common Sense*, January 9, 1776, Paine wrote about the birthday of a new world.

> We have it in our power to begin the world over again. A situation, similar to the present, hath not happened since the days of Noah until now. The birthday of a new world is at hand, and a race of men, perhaps as numerous as all Europe contains, are to receive their portion of freedom from the events of a few months. The reflection is awful, and in this point of view, how trifling, how ridiculous, do the little paltry cavilings of a few weak or interested men appear, when weighed against the business of a world.

42 Jefferson Bible.

43 Jefferson/Adams Correspondence, 98–101.

44   Ibid.

45   Ibid.

46   Ralph Waldo Emerson (1803–1882) was an American essayist, philosopher, and leader of transcendentalism. He was a champion of individualism who believed in self-reliance. He wrote "Self Reliance" in an 1841 essay. Transcendentalists saw divine experience every day rather than believing in a distant heaven.

47   Joseph Priestley (1733–1804) was an English chemist, natural philosopher, separatist theologian, grammarian, multi-subject educator, and liberal political theorist who published over 150 works. *Disquisitions relating to Matter and Spirit* (1777) is a major work of metaphysics written by eighteenth-century British polymath Joseph Priestley and published by Joseph Johnson.

48   Thomas Jefferson, The Jefferson BIBLE: The Life and Morals of Jesus of NAZARETH Extracted Textually from the Gospels in Greek, Latin, French & English (Washington D.C., DC: Smithsonian Books, 2011).p. 25-26

49   Owen Edwards, "How Thomas Jefferson Created His Own Bible," Smithsonian Institution, January 1, 2012, www.smithsonianmag.com/arts-culture/how-thomas-jefferson-created-his-own-bible-5659505/.

50   *Full Text of "Trattati D'arte Del Cinquecento Vol. 1,"* archive.org/stream/219TrattatiDarteDelCinquecento1Si259/219_Trattati-darte_del_Cinquecento_1_si259_djvu.txt.

51   Ibid.

52   Founders Online: From John Adams to Massachusetts Militia, 11 October 1798, founders.archives.gov/documents/Adams/99-02-02-3102.

53   Federalist Papers, 226–27.

54   "Alexander Hamilton: Ceasar II," Infoplease (Infoplease), accessed April 25, 2022, https://www.infoplease.com/primary-sources/government/federalist-papers/alexander-hamilton-ceasar-ii.

55   Founders Online: To John Adams from John Quincy Adams, 31 August 1811, founders.archives.gov/documents/Adams/99-03-02-2020.

56   Ibid., founders.archives.gov/documents/Jefferson/03-09-02-0121.

57   Ibid., founders.archives.gov/documents/Jefferson/98-01-02-2905.

58   Ibid., founders.archives.gov/documents/Madison/01-08-02-0163, James Madison "Memorial and Remonstrance against Religious Assessments, [ca 20 June] 1785."

59   Genesis 1:1–5 KJV.

60   Trattati D'arte.

61   Image drawn by Abrahaman Muhammed second night in solitary confinement FPC Butner (ca. 2013), "Three nights in solitary confinement with 'The Finger of God.'"

62   Richard S. Patterson, *The Eagle and The Shield*, edited by Richardson Dougall, Office of the Historian, Bureau of Public Affairs, Department of State, 1976, 6–35.

63   Matthew 6:10 KJV.

64   The Great Commandments is the name given to the commandments; Matthew 22:35–40; Mark 12:28–34; Luke 10:27.

65   Matthew 6:9; Luke 11:2. The "Our Father's" reference to "on earth" or "in earth" depends on the translation.

66   Jackson Jr. notes from solitary confinement, FPC Butner, ca. 2013.

67   Genesis 17:5 KJV.

68   "Which President Started the Tradition of Pardoning the Thanksgiving Turkey?" *WHHA (En-US)*, White House Historical Association, www.whitehousehistory.org/questions/which-president-started-the-tradition-of-pardoning-the-thanksgiving-turkey.

> The tradition of "pardoning" White House turkeys has been traced to President Abraham Lincoln's 1863 clemency to a turkey recorded in an 1865 dispatch by White House reporter Noah Brooks, who noted, "a live turkey had been brought home for the Christmas dinner, but [Lincoln's son Tad] interceded in behalf of its life. . . . [Tad's] plea was admitted and the turkey's life spared."

> Recently, White House mythmakers have claimed that President Harry S. Truman began this amusing holiday tradition. However, Truman, when he received the turkeys, and subsequent presidents did not "pardon" their birds. The formalities of pardoning a turkey gelled by 1989, when President George H. W. Bush remarked, "Reprieve," "keep him going," or "pardon": it's all the same for the turkey, as long as he doesn't end up on the president's holiday table.

69 "Declaration of Independence: A Transcription," National Archives and Records Administration, www.archives.gov/founding-docs/declaration-transcript.

70 Jesse Jackson and Frank E. Watkins, *A More Perfect Union: Advancing New American Rights* (Welcome Rain Publishers, 2001).

71 Ashley Southall, "Statue of Rosa Parks Is Unveiled at the Capitol," *New York Times*, February 27, 2013, www.nytimes.com/2013/02/28/us/politics/statue-of-rosa-parks-is-unveiled-at-the-capitol.amp.html.

72 Elizabeth Brotherton, "Emancipation Hall Moves Ahead with House Vote," Roll Call (Roll Call, December 13, 2019), https://www.rollcall.com/2007/11/13/emancipation-hall-moves-ahead-with-house-vote/.

73 Kevin Waite, "Congress Is Still Littered With Insurrectionists," *Slate Magazine*, January 12, 2021, slate.com/news-and-politics/2021/01/congress-is-still-littered-with-insurrectionists.amp.

74 Jeremy Sabella, "Postures of Piety and Protest: American Civil Religion and the Politics of Kneeling in the NFL," Multidisciplinary Digital Publishing, July 25, 2019, www.mdpi.com/2077-1444/10/8/449/htm.

75 Matthew 6:9 KJV.

76 Jonathan Karp, publisher of Simon & Schuster.

77 Federalist Papers, 226–27.

78 Jon Meacham, American Gospel: God, the Founding Fathers, and the Making of a Nation (Random House, 2007), 38.

79 Ibid.

80 Ibid.

81 Beliefnet and Beliefnet Editor, "Letter from Franklin to Ezra Stiles," February 14, 2019, www.beliefnet.com/faiths/faith-tools/the-founding-faith-archive/benjamin-franklin/letter-from-benjamin-franklin-to-ezra-stiles-1.aspx.

82 Abigal Adams and Edith Belle Gelles, *Abigail Adams: Letters* (Library of America, 2016), 924.

83 Founders Online: From Thomas Jefferson to Waterhouse, 26 June 1822, founders.archives.gov/documents/Jefferson/98-01-02-2905.

84 Matthew 1:1–17 KJV.

85 Matthew 17:14 KJV.

86 Matthew 6:10 KJV.

87 John 8:11 KJV.

88   Joel Kovel, History and Spirit: An Inquiry into the Philosophy of Liberation (Beacon Press, 1991), 54–58.

89   Ibid.

90   Ibid.

91   Ibid., 54–58.

92   Ibid,

93   Terrence L. Johnson, *Tragic Soul-Life: W.E.B. Du Bois and the Moral Crisis Facing American Democracy* (Oxford, New York: Oxford University Press, 2012), 122–23.

94   Kovel, History and Spirit, 54–58.

95   Denise A. Spellberg, Introduction to Jefferson QUR'AN Imagining the Muslim at the Founding of the United States, exists this opening quote: "[He] sais "neither Pagan or Mahamedan [Muslim] nor Jew ought to be excluded from the civil rights of the Commonwealth because of his religion"; Thomas Jefferson, quoting John Lock, 1776" I have therefore added Ishmael to the American linear theological system.

96   The function of the lineage of David extracted from the linear theological system of Abraham *f(lod)*.

97   I extracted the language of Article II, Section 2, Clause 1 to define "the person" who could best objectively fulfill the tasks of action verbiage. This began my experiment. The architects of the republic extracted the function of the linear theological system and constructed Article II, Section 2, Clause 1 of the Constitution on September 17, 1787.

98   Ibid.

99   Federalist Papers, 226–446.

100   Winthrop, "City Upon a Hill."

101   Founders Online: From John Adams to Massachusetts Militia, 11 October 1798, founders.archives.gov/documents/Adams/99-02-02-3102.

102   Matthew 22:36–40 NKJV.

103   Exodus 3:7 KJV.

104   Thomas Paine, appendix to *Common Sense*, 1775–1776 advocating independence from Great Britain to the thirteen American colonies.

105   The Founding fathers extracted the function of the linear theological system and made it the function of Article II, Section 2, Clause 1 of the US Constitution.

106 Founders Online: From John Adams to Massachusetts Militia, 11 October 1798, founders.archives.gov/documents/Adams/99-02-02-3102.

107 Federalist Papers, 226–446.

108 Founders Online: From Alexander Hamilton to The Daily Advertiser, founders.archives.gov/documents/Hamilton/01-04-02-0135.

109 Jefferson Bible, 11.

110 The Vitruvian efforts measured against infinity, iStock, Chris Gorgio.

111 iStock images, Chris Gorgio.

112 Founders Online: Memorial and Remonstrance against Religious Assessments, founders.archives.gov/documents/Madison/01-08-02-0163.

113 Founders Online: From Thomas Jefferson to Rush, 21 April 1803, founders.archives.gov/documents/Jefferson/01-40-02-0178-0001.

114 Thomas Jefferson, "Jefferson Quotes & Family Letters," extract from Thomas Jefferson to Ezra Styles Ely, 25 June 1819, tjrs.monticello.org/letter/2409.

115 Founders Online: From Thomas Jefferson to Waterhouse, 26 June 1822, founders.archives.gov/documents/Jefferson/98-01-02-2905.

116 Founders Online: From John Adams to Thomas Jefferson, 2 February 1816, founders.archives.gov/documents/Adams/99-02-02-6575.

117 Napoleon Hill, *Think and Grow Rich* (Chartwell Books, 2015). p. 1

118 Ibid.

119 Michael Novak, "Jewish Metaphysics at the Founding," in *On Two Wings: Humble Faith and Common Sense at the American Founding* (San Francisco, CA, CA: Encounter Books, 2003), p. 8.

120 "Monticello." *Quotations on the Jefferson Memorial*, www.monticello.org/site/research-and-collections/quotations-jefferson-memorial.

121 "Establishment of Israel," Encyclopedia Britannica, accessed April 4, 2021, https://www.britannica.com/place/Israel/Establishment-of-Israel.

122 A conversation with my father, Rev. Jesse Jackson.

123

124 Aleksandra Sandstrom, "God or the Divine Is Referenced in Every State Constitution," Pew Research Center. August 27, 2020), https://www.pewresearch.org/fact-tank/2017/08/17/god-or-the-divine-is-referenced-in-every-state-constitution/.

125   Jeff Diamant, "Three-Quarters of Black Americans Believe in God of the Bible or Other Holy Scripture," Pew Research Center, March 25, 2021, https://www.pewresearch.org/fact-tank/2021/03/24/three-quarters-of-black-americans-believe-in-god-of-the-bible-or-other-holy-scripture/.

126   Steve Straub, "Alexander Hamilton," The Federalist Papers, July 11, 2012, thefederalistpapers.org/founders/alexander-hamilton.

127   Matthew 25:40–45 NIV.

128   King, Strength to Love, 1–2.

129   *One Nation Under God: Alexander Hamilton*, Christian Defense Fund, 1997, www.leaderu.org/orgs/cdf/onug/hamilton.html.

130   Colin Woodard, Union: The Struggle to Forge the Story of United States Nationhood (New York: Viking, 2020), 2.

131   Ibid., 141.

132   "Nonfiction Classics for Students," Encyclopedia.com, March 18, 2021, www.encyclopedia.com/arts/culture-magazines/self-reliance-0.

133   Hebrews 11:1 NKJV.

134   Federalist Papers, 226–446.

135   Ibid.

136   Winthrop, "City Upon a Hill." The Politics of the Sacred in America. The role of civil religion in Political Practice (New York: Springer), 62–63.

137   "The Lincoln-Douglas Debates," Ushistory.org, Independence Hall Association, www.ushistory.org/us/32b.asp.

138   Proverbs 22:28 NKJV.

139   Patterson, *Eagle and The Shield*, 6–35.

140   Ibid.

141   Ibid.

142   Ibid.

143   Ibid.

144   Ibid.

145   Ibid.

146   Ibid.

147   Ibid.

148   Ibid.

149   Ibid., 6–35, 74–76.

150   Ibid.

151   Michael E. Eidenmuller, Online Speech Bank: Franklin's Prayer Speech at the Constitutional Convention of 1787, www.american-rhetoric.com/speeches/benfranklin.htm.

152   Founders Online: From Franklin to Sarah Bache, 26 January 1784, founders.archives.gov/documents/Franklin/01-41-02-0327.

153   From the First Great Seal Committee to the modern Great Seal of the United States is a tale of the despiritualization of historic symbols. As a nation, we moved from a spiritualized to a despiritualized society. It also reflects a major shift from the foundation of federal court interpretation as to the Founders' original intent.

154   Federalist Papers, 226–446.

155   "Constitutional Convention," *Franklin Historical Society*, www.benjamin-franklin-history.org/constitutional-convention/#:~:-text=Thus%20I%20consent%2C%20Sir%2C%20to,and%20here%20they%20shall%20die.

156   Stan Klos, "Abolition of Slavery," Abolition of Slavery (BenjaminFranklin.org, 2013), https://www.benjaminfranklin.org/p/in-his-later-years-benjaminfranklin.html.

157   "Franklin Address to the Public," PBS, www.pbs.org/benfranklin/pop_address.html. Signed by order of the society. B. Franklin, President, Philadelphia, November, 9, 1789.

158   Thomas Jefferson, *Notes on the State of Virginia* (Boston: Lilly and Wait, 1832). https://www.loc.gov/item/03004902/, 144–47.

159   Federalist Papers, 226–446.

160   Alexander Hamilton, Letter to Mr. Childs. October 17, 1787, *Daily Advertiser*, Caesar II, One- month anniversary of the signing of the Constitution, http://www.leaderu.org/orgs/cdf/onug/hamilton.

161   Jefferson Bible, 11.

162   Matthew 6:9-13 KJV.

163   Luke 11:1-4 KJV.

164   "Founders Online: A New Version of the Lord's Prayer, [Late 1768?]." National Archives and Records Administration. National Archives and Records Administration. Accessed October 2, 2021. https://founders.archives.gov/documents/Franklin/01-15-02-0170.

165   MacArthur, John D. "Charles Thomson- Principal Designer of the Great Seal." GreatSeal.com. John, 1998. https://www.greatseal.com/committees/finaldesign/thomson.html.

166   Charles Thomson, A Synopsis of The Four Evangelists: or, A Regular History of the Conception, Birth, Doctrine, Miracles, Death, Resurrection, and Ascension of Jesus Christ, in The Words

of the Evangelists. (Philadelphia, PA: Wm. M'Culloch, Printer, 1815).

167

168 Thomas Jefferson, The Jefferson Bible: The Life and Morals of Jesus of Nazareth Extracted Textually from the Gospels in Greek, Latin, French & English (Washington D.C., DC: Smithsonian Books, 2011), 39.

169 Eidenmuller, Online Speech Bank; John Adams, "A Defence of the Constitutions of Government of the United States of America against the Attack of M. Turgot in His Letter to Dr. Price, Dated the Twenty-Second Day of March 1778" (Lawbook Exchange, 2001).

170 "Constitutional Convention." *Franklin Historical Society*, www.benjamin-franklin-history.org/constitutional-convention/.

171 Ralph Louis Ketcham, The Anti-Federalist Papers; The Constitutional Convention Debates (Signet, 2003), 130.

172 Ibid., 402.

173 Commander of the army and repriever pardoner® is a wordmark registered with the USPTO. It describes an individual who is trained in Quantum Linear Theology, a Method and System of Teaching Quantum Linear Theology and Method of Measuring National and Presidential Spirit Energy Using Computer and Application Based Timelines filed with the USPTO 16/350,317.

174 Ibid.

175 Ibid.

176 Federalist Papers, 446.

177 Article II Section 2: Constitution Annotated: Congress.gov: Library of Congress, accessed April 4, 2021, https://constitution.congress.gov/browse/article-2/section-2/.

178 Federalist Papers, 446.

179 From August 6, 1787, until the final act on September 17, 1787, the architects hid the finger of God with a firm reliance on providence that it would be revealed in a future they would not live to see.

180 "America Dedicated to God," Alliance For Religious Freedom, accessed May 21, 2021, https://allianceforreligiousfreedom.com/educate-yourself/america-dedicated-to-god/#:~:text=America%20Dedicated%20to%20God%20On%20April%2030%20th,the%20Inauguration%20of%20our%20first%20president%2C%20George%20Washington.

181 "June 28, 1787: Franklin's Proposal for Prayer (U.S. National Park Service)," National Parks Service, US Department of the

Interior, accessed May 21, 2en021, https://www.nps.gov/articles/constitutionalconvention-june28.htm?back=https%3A%2F%2F-www.google.com%2Fsearch%3Fclient%3Dsafari%26as_qdr%3Dall%26as_occt%3Dany%26safe%3Dactive%26as_q%3DBenjamin%2BFranklin%2Bprayer%2Bdelivered%2B-Thursday%2C%2BJune%2B28%2C%2B1787%26channel%3Daplab%26source%3Da-app1%26hl%3Den.

182 John 14:12 KJV.

183 Brian Auten et al., "H. G. Wells on the Historicity of Jesus," *Apologetics* 315 (June 2, 2013), https://apologetics315.com/2013/06/h-g-wells-on-the-historicity-of-jesus/.

184 John Quincy Adams, "The Historical Magazine and Notes and Queries Concerning the Antiquities, History and Biography of America," Internet Archive (Morrisania, NY: Henry B. Dawson), January 1, 1970, https://archive.org/details/historicalmaga-ziv4morr/page/194/mode/1up?view=theater; letter to an autograph collector (identified: "Washington, 27th April, 1837"), published in *The Historical Magazine* 4:7 (July 1860), 193–94; this became slightly misquoted by John Wingate Thornton in *The Pulpit of The American Revolution* (1860): "The highest glory of the American Revolution, said John Quincy Adams, was this: *it connected, in one indissoluble bond, the principles of civil government with the principles of Christianity.*"

185 Federalist Paper 74, "The People Who Mean To Be Their ..." n.d., https://thefederalistpapers.org/.

186 Citizens United v. Federal Election Commission, 558 U.S. 310 (2010).

187 James Madison, "Memorial and Remonstrance against Religious Assessments," ca. June 20, 1785, https://founders.archives.gov/documents/Madison/01-08-02-0163.

188 Marco Virtruvious Pollio, *Kitap Projesi & Cheapest Books* (Istanbul: Kitap Projesi & Cheapest Books, 1960). p. 14, 79.

189 "The African American Vitruvian," iStock, Chris Gorgio.

190 "U.S. Constitution—Ninth Amendment: Resources: Constitution Annotated," Library of Congress, accessed May 21, 2021, https://constitution.congress.gov/constitution/amendment-9/#amendment-9.

191 Federalist Paper 74 by Alexander Hamilton describing the pardon power after the Constitution in 1787 and written in 1788 before the Bill of Rights of 1791 reads in pertinent part,

Humanity and good public policy conspire to dictate that the benign prerogative of pardoning should be as little as possible fettered or embarrassed. The criminal code of every country partakes so much of necessary severity that without an easy access to exceptions in favor of unfortunate guilt, justice would wear a countenance to sanguinary and cruel. As the sense of responsibility is always strongest in proportion as it is undivided, it may be inferred that a single man would be most ready to attend to the force of those motives which might plead for a mitigation of the rigor of the law, and lease apt to yield to considerations which were calculated to shelter a fit object of its vengeance. The reflection of the fate of a fellow-creature depended on his sole fiat would naturally inspire scrupulousness and caution; the dread of being accused of weakness or connivance would beget equal circumspection, though of a different kind. On the other hand, as men generally derive confidence from their numbers, they might often encourage each other in an act of obduracy and might be less sensible to the apprehension of suspicion or censure for an injudicious or affected clemency. On these accounts, one man appears to be a more eligible dispenser of the mercy of the government than a body of men.

192 "U.S. Constitution—Second Amendment: Resources: Constitution Annotated," Library of Congress, accessed April 17, 2021, https://constitution.congress.gov/constitution/amendment-2/.

193 "Founders Online: From Thomas Jefferson to William Stephens Smith, 13 November 1 ...," National Archives and Records Administration (National Archives and Records Administration), accessed September 12, 2021, https://founders.archives.gov/documents/Jefferson/01-12-02-0348.

194 "Article II Section 2: Constitution Annotated," Library of Congress, accessed April 17, 2021, https://constitution.congress.gov/browse/article-2/section-2/.

195 *Ex-Parte Garland* 71 *U.S. 333* (1866) according to Jeffrey Crouch in *The Presidential Pardon Power* (University of Kansas Press, 2009), 31–32. In 1866, the *ex parte Garland* Court described the extremely flexible clemency power. Here, the majority opinion by Justice Steven Feld noted that the pardon power granted by the Constitution,

> thus conferred is unlimited, with the [impeachment] exceptions stated. It extends to every offence known to the law, and may be exercised at any time after its commission, either before legal proceedings are taken, or during their pendency, or after conviction and judgment. This power of the president is not subject to legislative control. Congress can neither limit the effect of his pardon, nor exclude from its exercise any class of offenders. The benign prerogative of mercy reposed in him cannot be fettered by any legislative restrictions.

Crouch said, according to Garland, that the pardon power may be used at any time after a crime is committed, whether before, during, or after legal proceedings, conviction, and judgment. The timing of a presidential pardon mentioned in *Garland* has been reaffirmed in subsequent cases. Crouch mentioned another, more-controversial passage from *ex parte Garland* that suggested an extraordinarily wide-ranging effect.

> A pardon reaches both the punishment prescribed for the offence and the guilt of the offender; and when the pardon is full, it releases the punishment and blots out of existence the guilt, so that in the eye of the law the offender is as innocent as if he had never committed the offence. If granted before conviction, it prevents any of the penalties and disabilities consequent upon conviction from attaching; if granted after conviction, it removes the penalties and disabilities, and restores him to all his civil rights; it makes him, as it were, a new man, and gives him a new credit and capacity. There is only this limitation to its operation: it

does not restore offices forfeited, or property or interests vested in others in consequence of the conviction and judgement.

196   To sin is to live one's life outside the agreed-upon rules and regulations of society, the common law of the people. The highest glory of the American Revolution was that it connected in an indissoluble bond the principles of civil government with the principles of Christianity.

> From the day of the Declaration ... they (the American people) were bound by the laws of God, which they all, and by the laws of The Gospel, which they nearly all, acknowledge as the rules of their conduct. —John Adams

> The law given from Sinai was a civil and municipal as well as a moral and religious code; it contained many statutes . . . of universal application—laws essential to the existence of men in society, and most of which have been enacted by every nation which ever professed any code of laws. —John Adams

197   Ex parte Garland, 1866.

198   Charles Spurgeon Kruppa and Patricia Stallings, "The Life & Times of Charles H. Spurgeon," *Christian History*, January 1, 1991, www.christianitytoday.com/history/issues/issue-29/life-times-of-charles-h-spurgeon.html.

199   "Christ—Our Substitute," The Spurgeon Center, April 15, 1860, https://www.spurgeon.org/resource-library/sermons/christ-our-substitute/#flipbook/.

200   Matthew 25:40–45 KJV.

201   Ibid.

202   Luke 12:48 KJV.

203   Isaiah 2:4 KJV.

204   Citizens United v. Federal Election Commission, 558 U.S. 310 (2010).

205   The Vitruvian empathic Black man properly placed in the Founders' constitutional framework and structure.

206 Michael Lipka, "Half of Americans Say Bible Should Influence U.S. Laws, including 28% Who Favor It over the Will of the People," Pew Research Center, August 18, 2020, https://www.pewresearch.org/fact-tank/2020/04/13/half-of-americans-say-bible-should-influence-u-s-laws-including-28-who-favor-it-over-the-will-of-the-people/.

207 Founders Online: John Adams to Thomas Jefferson, 25 December 1813, founders.archives.gov/documents/Jefferson/03-07-02-0040.

208 Founders Online: From John Adams to Massachusetts Militia, 11 October 1798, founders.archives.gov/documents/Adams/99-02-02-3102.

209 Founders Online: John Adams to Thomas Jefferson, 4 November 1816, founders.archives.gov/documents/Jefferson/03-10-02-0378#:~:text=The%20Ten%20Commandments%20and%20The,the%20Jesuits%2C%20is%20in%204.

210 Founders Online: From Thomas Jefferson to John Adams, 11 April 1823, founders.archives.gov/documents/Jefferson/98-01-02-3446#:~:text=and%20the%20day%20will%20come,in%20the%20brain%20of%20Jupiter.

211 Founders Online: From Thomas Jefferson to Waterhouse, 26 June 1822, founders.archives.gov/documents/Jefferson/98-01-02-2905.

212 Howard Thurman, "Whole," in *Jesus and the Disinherited* (Boston: Beacon Press, 1996).

213 Jesse Jackson Jr., AZQuotes.com, Wind and Fly, 2021. https://www.azquotes.com/quote/1442790, accessed April 7, 2021, "Jesse Jackson Jr. going to prison; says he 'manned up,'" by Dan Merica, Larry Lazo, and Leslie Bentz, www.cnn.com. August 14, 2013.

214 Ibid., https://www.azquotes.com/quote/1442789, accessed April 7, 2021.

215 https://www.rollcall.com/2013/08/14/jesse-jackson-jr-and-wife-sentenced-to-jail-time/; https://www.cnn.com/2013/08/14/justice/jesse-jackson-jr-sentencing/index.html.

216 "Jesse Jackson Jr. to Serve Two and a Half Years in Prison," MSNBC, April 20, 2014, www.msnbc.com/now-with-alex-wagner/watch/jesse-jackson-jr-to-serve-two-and-a-half-years-in-prison-42294851618.

217 Viktor Frankl, *Man's Search for Meaning* (Beacon Press, 2006).

218 A conversation with my father, Rev. Jesse Jackson Sr., FPC Butner North Carolina, ca. 2013.

219 Introduction to MMUF and Dr. E. Mays, Special Academic Programs (Mellon Mays Undergraduate Fund), accessed April 7, 2021, https://osap.williams.edu/fellowships/mmuf-intro/.

220 Howard Thurman, Footprints of a Dream: the Story of the Church for the Fellowship of All Peoples (Eugene, OR: Wipf & Stock, 2009), 7.

221 "This Theologian Helped MLK See the Value of Nonviolence," Smithsonian Institution, January 12, 2018, http://www.smithsonianmag.com/history/this-theologian-helped-mlk-see-value-nonviolence-180967821/.

222 Adam Martin, "Jesse Jackson Jr. Pleads Guilty to Squandering Campaign Cash on Elk Heads," *Intelligencer*, February 21, 2013, https://nymag.com/intelligencer/2013/02/jesse-jackson-jr-pleads-guilty-to-fraud.html.

223 A conversation with my father, Rev. Jesse Jackson.

224 Frankl, Man's Search.

225 Rick Warren, *The Purpose Driven Life* (MI: Zondervan, 2002), 17–26.

226 Ibid.

227 Mike Flannery conversation on November 28, 1995, Cannon House Office Building.

228 Frankl, Man's Search.

229 ABC News, accessed April 7, 2021, https://abcnews.go.com/Blotter/ConductUnbecoming/story?id=6431739&page=1.

230 Henry Wadsworth Longfellow, *The Complete Poetical Works of Henry Wadsworth Longfellow* (Lexington, KY: Windham Press Classic Reprints, 2014).

231 Ibid.

232 John 8:11 KJV.

233 Dr. Nassir Ghaemi, In a First-Rate Madness: Uncovering the Links between Leadership and Mental Illness (New York: Penguin, 2012), 114–47.

234 Frankl, Man's Search.

235 John Adams, Bruce Braden, and Thomas Jefferson, "Ye Will Say I Am No Christian": The Thomas JEFFERSON/JOHN Adams Correspondence on Religion, Morals, and Values (Amherst, NY: Prometheus Books, 2006).p.53-54

236 Elijah Mays, "The Eulogy for Martin Luther King Jr." *The Atlantic*, January 29, 2021, https://www.theatlantic.com/magazine/archive/2018/02/benjamin-mays-mlk-eulogy/552545/.

237 Warren, *Purpose Driven Life*, 17–26.

238 Matthew 22:36–40 KJV.

239 Thomas Jefferson, *Declaration of Independence* (Jackson, MS: Applewood Books).

240 Matthew 22:36–40 KJV.

241 Ibid.

242 A quote from a conversation with my cellmate Abrahaman Muhammad.

243 Viktor E. Frankl et al., *Man's Search for Meaning* (Boston, MA: Beacon Press, 2015). p. ix-x

244 Ibid, xv-xvi

245 Fannie Lou Hamer, "I'm Sick and Tired of Being Sick and Tired—Dec. 20, 1964," Archives of Women's Political Communication (Iowa State University), accessed April 10, 2021, https://awpc.cattcenter.iastate.edu/2019/08/09/im-sick-and-tired-of-being-sick-and-tired-dec-20-1964/.

246 A conversation in prison with my father, Rev. Jesse Jackson.

247 A conversation in prison with my father, Rev. Jesse Jackson.

248 Amanda Arnold, "Inmates Across the Nation Are Striking Against 'Modern-Day Slavery' in Prison," *The Cut*, August 29, 2018, https://www.thecut.com/2018/08/prison-strike-dates-support.html.

249 Matthew 15:34 KJV.

250 During the fiftieth anniversary commemoration of the Selma to Montgomery march, more than a dozen former colleagues boarded a bus from the event and spent the afternoon with me. The warden remarked that he had never seen anything like it. Warden Stamper was a listener! He met with my colleagues before they visited with me, and he met with them after our visit. Later, he told me that he had not heard from a single member that I had a single complaint about the prison or my treatment. He said he was listening for it. Prison taught me to listen and become a better listener because listening is revealing.

251 Sister Claudette Muhammed sent me *Final Call* newspapers every week for three years. It is published by a Muslim organization founded by Elijah Muhammad now led by Louis Farrakhan.

252 Howard Thurman, "Whole," in *Jesus and the Disinherited* (Boston: Beacon Press, 1996), 11.

253 Founders Online: From Thomas Jefferson to William Short, 13 April 1820, https://www.founders.archives.gov/documents/Jefferson/98-01-02-1218.

254 "The Real Story Behind Apple's 'Think Different' Campaign," *Forbes* magazine, July 9, 2020, https://www.forbes.com/sites/onmarketing/2011/12/14/the-real-story-behind-apples-think-different-campaign/.

255 Neel Burton, "Depressive Realism," *Psychology Today*, June 5, 2012, https://www.psychologytoday.com/us/blog/hide-and-seek/201206/depressive-realism.

256 Dr. Ghaemi, *First-Rate Madness*, 114–47.

257 Ibid.

258 *A Few Good Men* is a 1992 American legal drama film based on Aaron Sorkins's 1989 play of the same name.

259 King, Strength to Love, 1–2.

260 Thomas Jefferson, *The Jeffersonian Cyclopedia*, 726, no. 7015.

261 King, Strength to Love.

262 Chester Hartman, Housing Policy Debate, volume 9, number 2, 1998.

263 Matthew 18:21-22.

264 Thomas Jefferson and John P. Foley, The Jeffersonian Cyclopedia: A Comprehensive Collection of the Views of Thomas Jefferson Classified and Arranged in ALPHABETICAL ORDER.. (New York, NY: Funk & Wagnell, 1967). p. 726

265 Karl Barth, *The Word of God and the Word of Man* (New York: Harper, 1957), 63–64.

266 Federal jurists are a function of progressive ideology over time. Expanding human rights to all would overcome the inherent separate and unequal system that has plagued the nation since its inception.

267 L. Kermit Hall, *The Oxford Companion to the Supreme Court* (New York: Oxford University Press, 1992), 590.

268 "Founders Online: From Benjamin Franklin to Richard Price, 9 October 1780," National Archives and Records Administration (National Archives and Records Administration), accessed September 14, 2021, https://founders.archives.gov/documents/Franklin/01-33-02-0330.

269 William O. Douglas, *The Bible and the Schools* (New York, NY: Little, Brown, 1966). p.58

270 https://guides.loc.gov/federalist-papers/text-51-60#:~:text=If%20men%20were%20angels%2C%20no%20government%20would%20be%20necessary.&text=In%20framing%20a%20government%20which,oblige%20it%20to%20control%20itself.

271 Cornel West, "'Justice Is What Love Looks like in Public,'" Pride Foundation, March 6, 2019, https://pridefoundation. org/2017/02/justice-is-what-love-looks-like-in-public/#:~:-text=Cornel%20West%20famously%20said%2C%20 %E2%80%9CJustice,the%20only%20true%20path%20forward.

272 Martin Luther King and Coretta Scott King, "Strength to Love," in *Strength to Love* (Philadelphia, PA: Fortress, 2010), p.127.

273 King, Martin Luther, and Coretta Scott King. Essay. In *Strength to Love*, 1–2. Philadelphia, PA: Fortress, 2010. p.130

274 Jackson and Watkins, *A More Perfect Union*, 494.

275 Ibid.

276 Samuel D. Proctor, The Substance of Things Hoped for: A Memoir of African-American Faith (New York: G. P. Putnam's Sons, 1996), xx.

277 Ibid.

278 Joel Kovel, History and Spirit: An Inquiry into the Philosophy of Liberation (Beacon Press, 1991), 54–58.

279 Elton Trueblood, *The Conjunct Life* (Prinit Press, 1985).

280 Normal distribution is a function that represents the distribution of many random variables as a symmetrical, bell-shaped curve.

281 The sum of the generations of DPE from Abraham (one) to Jesus (forty-two) times the integral of human spirit energy, times the time constant, equals infinity.

282 The lineage of David is a subset of the lineage of Abraham; it has twenty-eight generations between David and Jesus and is best represented by the equation the sum of the generations of DPE from David (fourteen) to Jesus (forty-two) times the integral of human spirit energy, times the time constant, equals infinity.

283 *f(x)* is a function of the unknown.

284 Founders Online: Memorial and Remonstrance against Religious Assessments, founders.archives.gov/documents/ Madison/01-08-02-0163.

285 Matthew 22:36–40 KJV.

286 COTAARP™ takes the first letter of the words *commander of the army and repriever pardoner*® to create a single idea in theology. The COTAARP™ is a person and an action verb—a function. The COTAARP™ is the constant in the Constitution. By election, we change the person but not the function.

287 The function of the lineage of David equals the function of the sum of the DPSE between David (fourteen) and Jesus (forty-two) times

the integral of human spirit energy times constant, which equals COTAARP,™ which equals infinity.

288   A noun and a verb of action organized and placed in the Constitution on September 17, 1787.

ABOUT THE AUTHOR

Former Congressman Jesse L. Jackson, Jr. began service in the U.S. House of Representatives on December 12, 1995, and served for 17 years. He has co-authored several books with his father Reverend Jesse Jackson, Sr.; Legal Lynching: Racism, Injustice and the Death Penalty. Jesse Jackson, Jr. resides in the Second Congressional District of Illinois, Chicago.

Printed in the United States
by Baker & Taylor Publisher Services